𝒞

*THE SOVIET MODEL
AND UNDERDEVELOPED COUNTRIES*

"... do not, I beg, remain on
*this shore.* . . . Better to perish
with the revolution than to seek
refuge in the almshouse of reaction."

ALEXANDER HERZEN, *From the Other Shore*

# THE SOVIET MODEL
# AND UNDERDEVELOPED COUNTRIES

*by Charles K. Wilber*

*THE UNIVERSITY OF NORTH CAROLINA PRESS*
*CHAPEL HILL*

*To my beloved wife*
*Mary Ellen*
*I dedicate this book*
*which owes all to her*
*love and encouragement*

This book is about economic development, that is, it specifically analyzes the strategy of development followed by the Soviet Union. It is hoped that the Soviet experience will provide some useful lessons, both negative and positive, for policy-makers in underdeveloped countries.

Continued underdevelopment is bringing untold suffering to millions of people. Unfortunately, both capitalist and Soviet development generated new sufferings in the process of eliminating the old. Neither the Soviet Union nor the United States has created a truly human society. The United States has been so interested in money-making and the Soviet Union in catching up to the United States that human values have been relegated to a secondary position in both countries.

Perhaps the leaders in underdeveloped countries, while eliminating the sufferings of underdevelopment as rapidly as possible, will draw upon the best from capitalist and Soviet experience and combine it with their own uniqueness to produce a new and humanistic civilization. To this end my book is offered.

Every writer is deeply indebted to those who have helped him. Some of my greatest debts are to those whom I know only through their writings—Emmanual Mounier, Karl Polanyi, R. H. Tawney, and Pierre Teilhard de Chardin. Their example of scholarship and social commitment has been a guide and inspiration. I was fortunate to study under Professor Dudley Dillard who helped me see that economics was an exciting field concerned with human beings, not just a branch of applied mathematics.

It is a pleasure to acknowledge my great indebtedness to Professor Norton T. Dodge for his helpful and critical advice at each successive stage of this book. Professors Robert L. Bennett and Robert E. L. Knight critically reviewed the entire manuscript at an early stage and made many helpful suggestions. I am also indebted to the late Professor Paul Baran, to Mr. Victor Perlo, and to Professor Jeremy Anderson, who read sections of an earlier draft and made numerous valuable suggestions. I am especially grateful to Professors James Blackman and Holland Hunter who critically reviewed the final draft and gave me their warm encouragement. Needless to say, none of these persons is responsible for the content of this work or for any errors that remain.

I am further indebted to my friend and colleague, Professor W. Michael Bailey, for our many conversations on the material of this book and for his insights into the philosophic, historical, and moral problems involved. I want to thank Miss Maurie Goldberg for her invaluable help in editing and proofreading. I also want to thank Mrs. Ann Ferguson, Mrs. Julia Simon, Mrs. Lois Walk, and Miss Shirley Warren for their typing skills. My greatest debt, however, is to my wife, Mary Ellen, and our seven children: Kenneth, Teresa, Matthew, Alice, Mary, Angela, and Louis. They have been patient with and understanding of the frequently absent husband and father during the five-year gestation period of this book.

# CONTENTS

# LIST OF TABLES

*Part One*

*THE MODEL*

# I. INTRODUCTION

The economic development of underdeveloped countries is the "paramount practical problem"[1] confronting economists in the second half of the twentieth century. This is not a new problem; underdeveloped countries have always existed. But it is only in the last twenty years that economic development has captured the attention of economists and statesmen alike. Simon Kuznets gives three reasons for this recent emphasis. First is the realization that international division of labor has not brought the benefits expected by nineteenth-century economic theory. Second, the pressure for economic development exerted by the newly independent countries suggests that lack of freedom from want in underdeveloped countries may well mean lack of freedom from fear in developed countries. The third and probably most important reason "is the emergence of a different social organization which claims greater efficiency in handling long-term economic problems"[2]—the socialist economy of the Soviet type.

To the extent that one can estimate the historical significance of any recent development, the U.S.S.R. seems to have opened a new chapter in world economic history—the era of forced economic growth in agriculturally overpopulated countries. The U.S.S.R. produced the world's first example of rapid economic development centrally planned and directed; and this example—that is, both Soviet strategy and planning procedure—excercises today a deep influence on the underdeveloped countries. Nicolas Spulber has cogently explained why the Soviet experience has captured the imagination of a great part of the new Asian, African, and Latin American intelligentsia.

1. Leo Rogin, *The Meaning and Validity of Economic Theory: A Historical Approach* (New York: Harper & Brothers, 1956), p. 4.
2. Simon Kuznets, *Economic Growth and Structure* (New York: W. W. Norton & Co., Inc., 1965), p. 3.

3

The crucial importance within these countries of the relationship between a small industrial and an overwhelming agricultural sector; the decisive importance of massive investments for developing certain new domestic industries, and the possible advantages accruing from the adoption of the most advanced technology in at least some key processes; the possibility of automatically fulfilling "realistic" capital formation targets by planning in physical terms, in countries with defective statistical information and unresponsive price mechanisms—all these render the Soviet planning model . . . extremely adaptable to backward countries. The antipathy to private enterprise, often identified with colonialism; the currently wide acceptance of the idea that the government necessarily assumes an important role in the consumption, allocation, and management of the country's resources; and finally, the almost charismatic character of the newly independent states render the early Soviet-type planning theory and methods attractive for even noncommunist underdeveloped countries.[3]

There are, of course, factors restraining underdeveloped countries from adopting a program of forced industrialization along Soviet lines. Some of these are ". . . the fears of the upper and middle classes faced with a revolutionary upheaval; the dislike of totalitarian methods felt by part of the . . . intelligentsia educated in the West; and above all the pressure of Western creditors."[4]

Economic growth in the Soviet Union has been very great. Indices of industrial production and agricultural production will be presented in the following chapters. At this point only statistics on gross national product will be used to illustrate the success of the Soviet model of economic development.

Table I-1 clearly brings out the tempo of Soviet economic development. Growth rates of this magnitude have had a profound effect upon the leaders of underdeveloped countries.

Since the specifics of Soviet industrial development were more the product of improvisation in the face of various pressing imperatives than of deliberate design, we must look to Soviet reality rather than to the writings of Marx, Lenin, or Stalin to find the causes of this growth. Therefore, the present study attempts to construct the model of economic development implicit in the historical experience of the U.S.S.R. and to evaluate it in that context. No attempt is made to prove that alternative models are inadequate or that the

3. Nicolas Spulber, *Soviet Strategy for Economic Growth* (Bloomington: Indiana University Press, 1964), pp. 127-28.

4. S. Swianiewicz, *Forced Labour and Economic Development: An Enquiry into the Experience of Soviet Industrialization* (London: Oxford University Press, 1965), p. 271.

TABLE I-1

*Average Annual Growth Rates of Gross National
Product in Selected Countries*

|  | % Total | % Per Capita |
|---|---|---|
| U.S.S.R.: | | |
| 1928-1963: | | |
| Ruble factor cost of 1937 | 4.9 | 3.7 |
| Composite, 1937 base | 6.5 | 5.2 |
| 1928-1940 and 1948-1963 | | |
| (Effective years)[a] | | |
| Ruble factor cost of 1937 | 6.4 | 4.9 |
| Composite, 1937 base | 8.5 | 6.9 |
| U.S.A.: | | |
| 1840-1880 | 4.0 | 1.3 |
| 1880-1920 | 3.5 | 1.6 |
| GREAT BRITAIN: | | |
| 1765/85-1785/1805 | 1.5 | 0.6 |
| 1801/11-1831/41 | 2.9 | 1.5 |
| GERMANY: | | |
| 1871/75-1913 | 3.1 | 1.9 |
| FRANCE: | | |
| 1841/50-1861/70 | 2.2 | 1.8 |
| 1871/80-1901/10 | 2.0 | 1.8 |
| SWEDEN: | | |
| 1861/65-1881/85 | 2.9 | 2.1 |
| 1881/85-1921/25 | 2.7 | 2.0 |
| JAPAN: | | |
| 1878/82-1918/22 | 4.1 | 3.0 |
| MEXICO: | | |
| 1940-1960 | 6.1 | 3.2 |

Sources:

The index for the U.S.S.R. was spliced together from three sources. For 1928-55, Abram Bergson, *The Real National Income of Soviet Russia Since 1928* (Cambridge: Harvard University Press, 1961), p. 217. The separate weighting systems apply only through 1955. For 1955-60, U.S. Congress, Joint Economic Committee, *Dimensions of Soviet Economic Power*, 87th Cong., 2nd Sess., 1962, p. 75. For 1960-63, U.S. Congress, Joint Economic Committee, *Current Economic Indicators for the U.S.S.R.*, 89th Cong., 1st Sess., 1965, p. 13. For the other countries: Simon Kuznets, *Economic Growth and Structure* (New York: W. W. Norton & Co., Inc., 1965), pp. 305-7; Phyllis Deane and W. A. Cole, *British Economic Growth: 1688-1959* (Cambridge: Cambridge University Press, 1964), pp. 80, 170, 172; Robert L. Bennett, *The Financial Sector and Economic Development* (Baltimore: The Johns Hopkins Press, 1965), p. 187.

[a] Omitting the war and reconstruction years of 1940-48.

Soviet model is a sufficient *and necessary* condition of rapid economic growth. Rather, the less ambitious attempt is made to demonstrate that the Soviet model can provide some useful lessons for underdeveloped countries.

### THE PROBLEM OF METHOD

As the word is used here, "Soviet" means primarily the Soviet Union. The experience of the other Soviet-type economies is used only to provide modifications of the basic model. The term "model" does not mean a detailing of every strategy, correct and incorrect, that was used by the Soviet Union. Rather it is an abstraction of the essentials from the Soviet experience modified by the later experience of the various socialist countries. Except for the excellent article by John Montias[5] this concept of the "Soviet Model" has not been followed on the subject.[6]

It is possible, and indeed necessary, to abstract from the secondary attributes of the individual cases and to concentrate on their essential common characteristics. This approach has always been the primary tool of all analytical effort—whether it be Marx's "pure capitalism," Marshall's "representative firm," or Weber's "ideal type." That the resulting "model" does not take into account every peculiarity of the given case does not invalidate its usefulness. Its value lies in the establishment of a framework which gives interpretation and meaning to the facts and descriptions assembled by quantitative research.

There is no question, therefore, that a theoretical approach must

5. John M. Montias, "The Soviet Economic Model and the Underdeveloped Countries," in *Study of the Soviet Economy*, ed. Nicolas Spulber, Russian and Eastern European Series, Vol. 25 (Bloomington: Indiana University, 1961), pp. 57-82.

6. See, for instance: W. Donald Bowles, "Soviet Russia As a Model for Underdeveloped Areas," *World Politics*, Vol. XIV, No. 3 (April, 1962), pp. 483-504; Oleg Hoeffding, "The Soviet Union: Model for Asia—State Planning and Forced Industrialization," *Problems of Communism*, Vol. VIII, No. 6 (November-December, 1959), pp. 38-46; Alex Inkeles, "The Soviet Union: Model for Asia?—The Social System," *ibid.*, pp. 30-38; Alec Nove, "The Soviet Model and Underdeveloped Countries," *International Affairs*, Vol. XXXVII, No. 1 (January, 1961), pp. 29-38; Francis Seton, "Planning and Economic Growth: Asia, Africa and the Soviet Model," *Soviet Survey*, XXXI (January-March, 1960), 38-40; Spulber, *Soviet Strategy for Economic Growth;* Swianiewicz, *Forced Labour and Economic Development*; and Alfred Zauberman, "Soviet and Chinese Strategy for Economic Growth," *International Affairs*, Vol. XXXVIII, No. 3 (July, 1962), pp. 339-52.

be used in analyzing the process of economic development. Rather the important question to be answered is what theory should be used. "Theory is in the first and last place a logical file of our factual knowledge pertaining to a certain phenomenological domain. . . . To each theory, therefore, there must correspond a specific domain of the reality."[7] In determining the proper domain of a theory the question arises whether an economic theory which successfully describes one economic system, say capitalism, can be used to successfully explain another economic system, say feudalism or socialism. This problem seldom bothers the physical sciences for no evidence exists that the behavior of matter varies with time or social system. In contrast, human societies vary widely, with both time and locality. Some would argue that these variations are only different instances of a unique archetype and that consequently all social phenomena can be encompassed by a single theory. It is sufficient to point out that when ". . . the theories constructed by these attempts do not fail in other respects, they are nothing but a collection of generalities of no operational value whatever. . . . For an economic theory to be operational at all, i.e. to be capable of serving as a guide for policy, it must concern itself with a specific type of economy, not with several types at the same time."[8]

Every theory is a model of a particular economic system because it must assume certain institutional and cultural traits. Thus, orthodox theory (neoclassical and Keynesian) assumes that individuals act hedonistically, that entrepreneurs seek to maximize cash profits, and commodities can be exchanged on the market at uniform prices and none exchanged otherwise. When it is realized that for economic theory an economic system is characterized exclusively by institutional traits, it becomes obvious that orthodox theory is not valid as a whole for the analysis of a noncapitalist economy. A particular proposition of the theory may be valid for a noncapitalist economy, but its validity must be established anew, either by empirical evidence or by logical derivation from the new model. Even the analytical tools developed by orthodox theory cannot be used indiscriminately in the analysis of other economies. Most analytical tools are hard to transplant from one economic theory to another. This is not to say, however, that orthodox theory does not provide

7. Nicholas Georgescu-Roegen, "Economic Theory and Agrarian Economics," *Oxford Economic Papers*, Vol. 12 (February, 1960), p. 2.
8. *Ibid.*

useful patterns for asking the right kind of questions and for seeking the relevant constituents of any economic reality.[9]

Further problems arise in attempting to use orthodox economic theory to analyze the process of economic development. Great strides have been made in the study of economic growth in the last few years. But a distinction should be made between economic growth, analyzed in terms of changes in the value of economic parameters in given institutional conditions, and economic development, when changes in the value of economic parameters are accompanied or even preceded by institutional changes. Orthodox theory is a more efficient instrument for analysis of the quantifiable short-run determinants of income than of the process of economic development. In income analysis or even growth theory, long-run factors of a socio-political nature may be held constant, regarded as given. Economic development, however, is a process which affects not only purely economic relations but the entire social, political, and cultural fabric of society. In the dynamic world of economic development, the data usually impounded in *ceteris paribus* are in constant motion as factors making for change.

Because the very essence of economic development is rapid and discontinuous change in institutions and the value of economic parameters, it is impossible to construct a rigorous and determinate model of the process. An economist must be willing to settle for less. Henry Bruton expresses the problem well when he says that "elegance and rigor are important attributes of effective economics, but they must take second place to relevance and applicability. The student or teacher who likes his economics in the form of neat theorems is alerted that few have been found in the field of technology, education, population growth, and a dozen other aspects of development."[10] Stuart Bruchey goes further and argues that the more rigorous the model, the higher its degree of technical success may be, but the greater its inability to explain economic development.[11]

9. Professor Dudley Dillard has argued that there is no reason why a concept developed within the context of one system of theory, such as the Marxian labor theory of value, cannot be used in another system of theory, as in the case of Keynes. Dudley Dillard, "The Status of the Labor Theory of Value," *Southern Economic Journal*, Vol. 11 (April, 1945), p. 347.

10. Henry J. Bruton, *Principles of Development Economics* (Englewood Cliffs: Prentice-Hall, Inc., 1965), p. iv.

11. Stuart Bruchey, *The Roots of American Economic Growth, 1607-1861: An Essay in Social Causation* (New York: Harper & Row, Inc., 1965), pp. 8-11. Also, "the generalization may be made—to which there are honorable

Such a model necessarily omits too many of the most significant variables in economic development. It follows that an inquiry into the causal origins of economic development ought not to commence with a highly generalized, highly abstract model to frame the analysis. If a rigorous and determinate model is not utilized to study the process of economic development, a less rigorous but more richly textured model which accounts for the most important socioeconomic variables must be constructed. To this writer the use of economic history, together with theoretical logic, holds out the greatest prospect for success.

*Economic History and Economic Development.* It has been said that scholars ". . . come to Economic History either as historians in search of a soul, or as economists in search of a body."[12] Many economic theorists are too fond of clever abstractions and too dependent on arbitrary concepts and models which are empty of empirical content and possess little, if any, relationship to the mutability of historical reality. Many historians allow their aversion to orthodox theory to prejudice their research and writing to the point where they become mere "fact grubbers" and "story tellers." The problem lies in a confusion between a "theoretical approach" and particular theories and concepts. A particular theory can be useful or useless, depending on the problem addressed. A "theoretical approach" is an essential step toward comprehension of historical reality. This theoretical approach or framework, of course, should not be a procrustean bed in which historical reality is forced to fit. If the economic historian is dissatisfied with the tools and theories that economic theorists have developed, then he must adapt them or seek others—if necessary, he must construct his own.[13] However, it is unlikely that the economic historian can ignore all the many fruitful analytical tools already available.

---

exceptions—that the elegance moves in direct proportion with irrelevance to economic problems." Douglas Dowd, *Thorstein Veblen* (New York: Washington Square Press, Inc., 1964), p. 71.

12. Sidney Pollard, "Economic History—A Science of Society?" *Past and Present,* No. 30 (April, 1965), p. 3.

13. "That the library of models constructed by theorists may fail to contain constructs suitable to the specific phenomenon an historian wants to explain does not relieve him of the burden of having to employ hypothetico-deductive methods. It merely means that the historian must assume a task that would otherwise have been fulfilled by the economic theorist." Robert William Fogel, *Railroads and American Economic Growth: Essays in Econometric History* (Baltimore: The Johns Hopkins Press, 1964), p. 247.

*The Method Adopted.* What is a historical-theoretical approach to economic development? First of all, it involves a study of the historical experience of economic development in various countries to discern their differences and similarities, and, secondly, it involves the use of theoretical tools and concepts to order and analyze the historical and empirical evidence.

Alexander Gerschenkron is probably the most successful practitioner of this general approach. From his study[14] of the economic development of European countries in the nineteenth century he is able to derive a number of historical-theoretical propositions. His concept of "relative backwardness" is useful in explaining differences in development among European countries in the nineteenth century. This concept, coupled with his other concept of substitution, highlights the fact that while it is necessary to perform similar *functions* in economic development, *institutional implementation* of these functions will vary greatly depending on the historical circumstances. For example, while accumulation of capital is a necessary function, its financing may be undertaken by firms as in England, by banks as in Germany, or by the state as in Russia. Or, again, some binding force must be utilized to keep the social fabric from being destroyed by the stresses and strains of development. This binding force has taken the form of puritanism, nationalism, and communism. Gerschenkron also shows that the more backward the country on the eve of its industrialization drive the more pronounced was the coerciveness and comprehensiveness of the institutional implementation. The concepts of relative backwardness and substitution will be used to relate Soviet development experience with past European development and with the problems facing underdeveloped countries today .

14. Alexander Gerschenkron, *Economic Backwardness in Historical Perspective* (New York: Frederick A. Praeger, Inc., 1965). Better known, but less successful, at least in this writer's view, is W. W. Rostow. See, for instance, W. W. Rostow, *The Stages of Economic Growth: A Non-Communist Manifesto* (New York: Cambridge University Press, 1960). All of Karl Marx's work, of course, used this approach. See also W. W. Rostow (ed.), *The Economics of Take-off into Sustained Growth*, Proceedings of a Conference held by the International Economic Association (New York: St. Martin's Press, Inc., 1963); Thomas C. Cochran, "An Historical Approach to Economic Development," *Contributions-Communications*, First International Conference of Economic History (Paris: Moulton & Co., 1960); and W. E. G. Salter, "Productivity Growth and Accumulation As Historical Processes," in *Problems in Economic Development*, ed. E. A. G. Robinson, Proceedings of a Conference held by the International Economic Association (London: Macmillan & Co., Ltd., 1965).

The tools of analysis utilized are of two types. The first is the rather crude but highly useful concept of the "social surplus." The second is the usual marginal analysis familiar to economic theorists. These tools complement each other well in the context of the development model constructed in this book.

The concept of the "social surplus" was widely used by the classical writers. Adam Smith labeled it the "surplus part of the produce" and David Ricardo as the "net produce." John Stuart Mill defined it as the "surplus of the produce of labour . . . the fund from which the enjoyments, as distinguished from the necessaries, of the producers are provided . . . from which all are subsisted, who are not themselves engaged in production, and from which all additions are made to capital."[15] In view of the value connotation associated with Karl Marx's use of the concept "surplus value" and the attendant concept of "rate of exploitation," later economists discarded it completely. The social product was viewed in terms of "cost of factors," savings being no longer conceived as the result of an existing social surplus but as the result of an act of "abstinence" or "waiting." But as a contemporary developmental economist points out, "from the point of view of the theory of development, in which the accumulation process acquires great importance, there is some convenience in coming back to the classic concept of the surplus, leaving aside . . . any intimation of moral values."[16]

The concept of the social surplus has been used as an analytical tool by a number of modern writers. V. Gordon Childe uses it to analyze the development of early societies. He defines it as "a regular and reliable supply of food over and above what is consumed by the actual productive members of a group, together of course, with infants and a very few people too old to get their own food."[17] In

15. Adam Smith, *The Wealth of Nations* (New York: The Modern Library, 1937), p. 17; David Ricardo, *On the Principles of Political Economy and Taxation*, Vol. I of *The Works and Correspondence of David Ricardo*, ed. Piero Sraffa (10 vols.; Cambridge: Cambridge University Press, 1951), p. 391; and John Stuart Mill, *Principles of Political Economy*, ed. Sir W. J. Ashley (London: Longmans, Green and Co., 1929), pp. 163-64.

16. Celso Furtado, *Development and Underdevelopment* (Berkeley: University of California Press, 1964), p. 79.

17. V. Gordon Childe, "Early Forms of Society," in *A History of Technology*, ed. Charles Singer *et al.* (5 vols.; Oxford: Oxford University Press, 1954), I, 41-42. See also Melville J. Herskovits, *Economic Anthropology: The Economic Life of Primitive Peoples* (New York: W. W. Norton & Co., Inc., 1965), chap. 18.

addition to Celso Furtado, it has been used to analyze the process of economic development by Paul Baran.[18]

The social surplus may be viewed as a residual factor—that which remains from total output after necessary consumption has been subtracted. In every organization of society, past or present, the total annual production of goods and services may be divided into two separate parts—the necessary subsistence of the population and a surplus which may be either consumed or saved in the form of additions to the country's stock of capital. Of course, the level of necessary consumption may be expected to vary from country to country and from time to time. For the purposes of the present study this should cause no serious difficulties.

To make it more useful it is possible to differentiate two variants of the concept of social surplus. The first is the *actual social surplus* —the difference between a country's *actual* current production and its *actual* current consumption. The second is the *potential social surplus*—the difference between the output that *could* be produced in a given natural and technological environment and what might be regarded as *necessary* consumption.

It should be obvious that the main features of economic development have to do with the size and distribution of the social surplus. Thus it is that a model of development must be examined in terms of its impact on the size and utilization of the surplus. In every society minority groups have arisen, which, in one way or another have managed to appropriate the permanent or occasional social surplus of the economy. Appropriation not only makes accumulation easier but also facilitates the transformation of the surplus into productive capacity. This in turn, of course, increases total output and the size of the social surplus for the next period. The emphasis in this study will be on the role of central planning and agricultural collectivization in increasing and utilizing the social surplus. The methods used in socialist industrialization will be compared and contrasted with those used in the capitalist development of the West.

The tools of marginal analysis will be used to test the logic of the historically derived methods and strategies of development in the Soviet model. Empirical data will likewise be used to test the efficacy of these methods and strategies.

18. Paul A. Baran, "Economic Progress and Economic Surplus," *Science and Society*, Vol. XVII, No. 4 (Fall, 1953), pp. 289-317. See also his *The Political Economy of Growth* (New York: Monthly Review Press, 1957), pp. 22-43.

No pretense is made of constructing a complete theory of a socialist economy. Rather, the aim is much more limited. This study is concerned only with the development process and within this process only with those variables which seem to be crucial to an understanding of the process. This approach is necessary for any causal analysis. In Rogin's words, "the paramount issue thus largely dictates the scope and direction of the selective appeal to fact and indicates the permissible degree of violence which may be done the selected facts for the purpose of incorporating them into the premises of the theory."[19]

## THE MODEL OUTLINED

The Soviet model, as historically derived from socialist development experience, can be subdivided into three aspects: the preconditions of the model, the institutions characteristic of the model, and the strategy of development in the model.

The preconditions of the model include severance of any existing colonial bond with capitalist countries, elimination of economic domination by foreign capitalists, and redistribution of political and economic power. In sum this will usually mean a social revolution which, at least nominally, redistributes political and economic power to the workers and peasants.

The institutions characteristic of the model include collectivized agriculture, publicly owned enterprises, comprehensive central planning, centralized distribution of essential materials and capital goods, and a system of administrative controls and pressures on enterprises, in addition to incentives, to ensure compliance with the plan.

The strategy of development in the model encompasses high rates of capital formation; priority of basic capital goods industries; bias in favor of modern, capital-intensive technologies in key processes combined with labor-intensive techniques in auxiliary operations; an import-substitution policy in international trade; utilization of underemployed agricultural labor for capital formation; and heavy investment in human capital.

## RELEVANCE OF THE MODEL FOR UNDERDEVELOPED COUNTRIES

Some broad limitations on the applicability of the Soviet model should be noted. For small, resource-poor countries, such as Costa

19. Rogin, *The Meaning and Validity of Economic Theory*, p. 3.

Rica, Surinam, or Yemen, the Soviet model can be of little use. Soviet-style development is possible only in countries having natural and human resources and the required market potential necessary for the development of large-scale, capital goods industries. Among countries possibly possessing these prerequisites are India, Indonesia, Pakistan, the Philippines, Turkey, the Congo, Ghana, Nigeria, Argentina, Brazil, Colombia, Mexico, and Venezuela. The combined population of these countries is more than 900 million and represents a substantial portion of the population of the noncommunist, underdeveloped world. For this substantial group of low income countries, the Soviet model of development can provide some possible alternatives to capitalist methods offered by the West.

A number of writers have argued that the Soviet Union in 1913 was more developed than underdeveloped countries today and have thus concluded that the Soviet Union's experience is irrelevant. Due to the lack of adequate national income statistics a nonmonetary index has been constructed in Chapter VII to measure the level of development in Soviet Central Asia (1926-28) relative to selected underdeveloped countries today.[20] If the Soviet Union is included and the results converted to a set of scores where the most developed country is 100, the outcome would be that shown in Table I-2. Since the Soviet Union was more developed than many underdeveloped countries, a case study of Soviet Central Asia also is included in this book to test the application of the Soviet model to an area of extreme underdevelopment. Moreover, the level of development of the Soviet Union in 1913 was probably below that of most South American countries today.

Oleg Hoeffding[21] stresses that the collectivization of Soviet agriculture contributed to industrialization only because a "surplus" could be extracted and in many Asian countries little or no such "surplus" exists. This argument is considered in Chapter III. For now it is enough to say that if there is almost no agricultural "surplus," development by any means will be almost impossible.

A final point on the relevance of the Soviet model of development needs to be made. No model is transferable complete and in detail and the Soviet model is no exception. Each country must take into account its own resource base, factor proportions, and historical and cultural traditions when evaluating development strat-

20. A detailed description of this index will be found on pp. 147-55 of chap. VII.
21. Hoeffding, "The Soviet Union: Model for Asia," pp. 38-46.

TABLE I-2

*Relative Levels of Economic Development*

| Country | Year | Score |
|---------|------|-------|
| Colombia | 1960-62 | 100 |
| Turkey | 1960-62 | 75 |
| U.S.S.R. | 1913 | 66 |
| India | 1960-62 | 52 |
| Iran | 1960-62 | 48 |
| Pakistan | 1960-62 | 39 |
| Soviet Central Asia | 1926-28 | 37 |

Source: See sources of Table VII-1

egies and how to adapt them. In a very few cases this will mean only minor modifications of some basic model. More often it will mean a major overhauling of the model to adapt it to local conditions. For instance, Poland has not collectivized agriculture and Cuba does not stress heavy industry.

The basic concern of this study is to develop the model that emerges from Soviet experience and to evaluate it in that context. To determine in what degree the model is relevant for Brazil, Turkey, or any other country would require a separate analysis for each one.

Chapter II will analyze the role of social change; Chapter III, the role of collectivized agriculture; Chapter IV, the role of central planning; Chapter V, the strategy of development, involving investment and technology, human capital, and international trade; and Chapter VI, will attempt to analyze the social cost of economic development under the Soviet model. All of Part II analyzes an actual application of the model to an underdeveloped area. For this purpose a case study of Soviet Central Asia (the republics of Kazakhstan, Uzbekistan, Kirgizia, Tadjikistan, and Turkmenistan) is presented. Part III presents a summary of the findings and conclusions.

## II. SOCIAL CHANGE IN THE SOVIET MODEL
## OF DEVELOPMENT

---

The preconditions of the Soviet model include national liberation if this has not already been attained, elimination of economic domination by foreign capital, and redistribution of political and economic power. The expropriation of foreign capital and domestic industry is treated in Chapter IV and the collectivization of agricultural property in Chapter III. This chapter is concerned with the social change generated by the redistribution of political and economic power. More specifically, the focus of the chapter will be on those policies designed to generate in people the willing acceptance of sacrifice and on those policies that lead to human capital formation.

### SOCIAL CHANGE AND CAPITALIST DEVELOPMENT IN THE WEST[1]

The development of capitalism in the West was faced with the need for change in the social structure so that the change-oriented middle class could become the leaders of society. This often involved a more or less violent struggle for supremacy between the old social order and the emerging new one. The English Revolution of 1640, ending with the Supremacy of Parliament in 1688, replaced the feudal lords with the landed gentry and urban middle class as the dominant classes in England, thus preparing the way for later economic progress. The French Revolution of 1789 replaced the old aristocracy with the new middle class. The lack of such social change was a major factor in the economic stagnation of Spain after the seventeenth century.

This change in social structure enabled the social surplus to be productively used. As Professor Dudley Dillard has pointed out: "Productive use of the 'social surplus' was the special virtue that

1. See Dudley Dillard, *Economic Development of the North Atlantic Community* (New York: Prentice-Hall Inc., 1967) and David S. Landes (ed.), *The Rise of Capitalism* (New York: The Macmillan Co., 1967).

16

enabled capitalism to outstrip all prior economic systems. Instead of building pyramids and cathedrals, those in command of the social surplus chose to invest in ships, warehouses, raw materials, finished goods and other material forms of wealth. The social surplus was thus converted into enlarged productive capacity."[2]

Before this productive investment could have taken place the social surplus had to be channeled into the hands of the new progressive class of society. In England, the profit inflation (the rise of money prices faster than money wages and/or rents) of 1540-1640 and 1795-1815 redistributed income in the first instance from landlords with fixed money rents to the rising gentry and merchants, and in the second from wage earners to profits on capitalist enterprise. Also the lag of real wages behind increases of productivity in the eighteenth and nineteenth centuries further increased profits from which new investment was made. This accumulation of capital enabled new technology to be utilized and this, in turn, by reducing costs, enabled more capital to be accumulated.

Such a period of development is always characterized by discontent and unrest because of the great changes taking place. This required, in the case of the development of the capitalist countries, actions on the part of a powerful national state to facilitate the social changes and accumulation of capital, and suppression of any attempted interference with the process.

The appearance of a new "spirit" not only facilitated social change in the capitalist countries but also promoted capital accumulation and economic development. The Protestant ethic encouraged thrift and reinvestment of savings by the middle classes, and hard work and obedience by the working classes.

The sum of these historical events was a social revolution that destroyed the old feudal social order and brought to the fore a new class that was change-oriented, and into whose hands the social surplus was channeled for productive use. This, coupled with the rationalization of agriculture that took place, enabled capital to accumulate and economic development to proceed.

THE IMPORTANCE OF SOCIAL CHANGE IN UNDERDEVELOPED AREAS

It is widely recognized that radical change in the existing social structure is necessary for economic development in most underdeveloped countries.

2. Dudley Dillard, "Capitalism," *Encyclopedia Britannica* (1963 edition, reprint), p. 2.

At the end of the middle ages western Europe stood about where many underdeveloped economies stand in the 20th century. . . . Achieving . . . sustained growth requires virtually a social revolution.

Power must be transferred from reactionary to progressive classes; new energies must be released, often by uprooting the old order; the prevailing religious outlook may constitute a barrier to material advancement. A new social and political framework must be created within which cumulative economic change can take place.[3]

Capitalism has entered most underdeveloped countries the "Prussian way"—not through the growth of small, competitive enterprise but through the transfer from abroad of advanced large-scale business. Thus, capitalist development in these countries has not been accompanied by the rise of a strong property owning middle class and by the overthrow of landlord domination of society. Rather an accomodation has taken place between the newly arrived business class and the socially and politically entrenched agrarian aristocracy.[4]

Therefore, there is neither vigorous competition between enterprises striving for increased output and rationalized production, nor accumulation of the social surplus in the hands of entrepreneurs forced by the competitive system and the spirit of a middle class society to reinvest as much as possible in the continuous expansion and modernization of their business. The result is that production is well below the potential level, with agriculture still being operated on a semi-feudal basis, and with waste and irrationality in industry protected by monopoly, high tariffs, and other devices.[5]

For these and other reasons the actual social surplus is much lower than the potential social surplus. A large share of the potential social surplus is used by aristocratic landlords on excess consump-

3. *Ibid.* pp. 2-3. Also, see Edward Mason, *Economic Planning in Under-developed Areas* (New York: Fordham University Press, 1958), p. 27; Zbigniew Brzezinski, "The Politics of Underdevelopment," *World Politics*, IX (October, 1956), 55-75; Laura Randall (ed.), *Economic Development: Evolution or Revolution?* (Boston: D. C. Heath & Co., 1964); and W. W. Rostow, *The Stages of Economic Growth: A Non-Communist Manifesto* (Cambridge University Press, 1960), pp. 26-31.

4. See Paul A. Baran, "On the Political Economy of Backwardness," in *The Economics of Underdevelopment*, eds. A. N. Agarwala and S. P. Singh (Oxford: Oxford University Press, 1958), pp. 75-92. Celso Furtado, *Diagnosis of the Brazilian Crisis* (Berkeley: University of California Press, 1965), pp. 20-21, 115-18.

5. While the infant industry argument for tariffs can be good economic policy, too often it is used in underdeveloped countries to protect inefficient monopolistic business from a foreign competition that might force modernization. See Furtado, *Diagnosis of the Brazilian Crisis*, pp. 96-124.

tion and the maintenance of unproductive laborers. In addition, a large share of the actual social surplus is taken by businessmen for commercial operations promising large and quick profits, or for the accumulation of investments or bank accounts abroad as a hedge against domestic social and political hazards. Furthermore, in order to obtain social status and the benefits and privileges necessary for the operation of a business, they must emulate the dominant aristocracy in its mode of living. The potential social surplus is further reduced by the substantial quantity of resources used to maintain elaborate and inefficient bureaucratic and military establishments.

Although other factors undoubtedly have much to do with the inadequacy of the amount and composition of investment, the waste of a large portion of the social surplus due to the prevailing social structure is probably one of the major causes of economic stagnation.

In addition the prevailing social and economic structure breeds a system of social relations, habits, customs, and culture that retard social and economic development. "Existing social relationships, income distribution, individual values, and human motivations are so inhibiting to economic development of any sort . . . that it is hard to see how the elementary preconditions of development can be established short of political revolution."[6]

Certainly the agricultural structures of large feudal estates and small peasant holdings must be changed, but this will be reserved for Chapter III. The preindustrial attitudes of peasants and workers operate against change but even more important is the attitude of the ruling classes[7] and the state which they usually dominate. These ruling classes know that if social and economic development comes, their power, status, and way of life will be threatened. Therefore, they continuously and actively oppose all kinds of social change. ". . . modernization undermines the traditional society on which the power of the aristocracy rests. The aristocracy and its allies . . . have almost everywhere fought a rear guard action against modern Western dress and customs, against the type of education and out-

6. Mason, *Economic Planning in Underdeveloped Areas*, p. 27.

7. "The capitalist virtues of saving and investment are alien to the aristocracy and appear contemptible to it. As a class living by exploitation of the peasantry and the soil, investing no part of their product in the expansion or improvement of the process of production, the aristocracy is inclined not to save but to waste freely and spend generously, not toward investment but toward conspicuous consumption. It regards generosity and waste, rather than accumulation and investment of wealth, as symbols of prestige." John H. Kautsky (ed.), *Political Change in Underdeveloped Countries: Nationalism and Communism* (New York: John Wiley & Sons, 1962), p. 99.

look on life characteristic of industrial societies—just as they did in Europe for some centuries."[8]

George Dalton points out that in Liberia ". . . only those changes in economic and social structure are allowed that do not threaten the political control of the Americo-Liberians, and these changes alone are simply insufficient to transform the economy."[9]

The governments of these countries are poor agencies for enforcing the necessary changes, even though they claim to desire to do so, because often they are controlled or at least heavily influenced by these same wealthy classes. For example, Dalton points out that "the governing authorities of Liberia have no intention of developing the national economy and the Liberian people."[10] Governments which have attempted basic alterations in the social and economic structure have usually fallen victims of a *coup d'état*.[11] Alexander Eckstein has clearly explained the incapacity of the state in underdeveloped countries.

Historically . . . particularly in the underdeveloped countries, the state—and the social structure on which it was based—was one of the very agencies hampering economic development. The same conditions that create the need for massive state intervention . . . also tend to breed a type of state which is singularly unequipped to intervene effectively on behalf of economic development. . . . Thus in China, for instance, the state . . . played a passive to actively negative role *vis-à-vis* the economy. The very concept of economic change and economic dynamism was alien to such a society. . . . The function of the economy was a largely static one, being charged with the primary task of supporting the ruling elite. . . .[12]

Many of these governments fear the prospects of development, for, better than we, their ruling classes realize the revolutionary potential which is contained in social change. They realize that even an attempt at peaceful, evolutionary development could quickly gain

8. *Ibid.*, p. 42.
9. George Dalton, "History, Politics and Economic Development in Liberia," *Journal of Economic History*, Vol. XXV, No. 4 (December, 1965), pp. 581-82.
10. *Ibid.*, p. 591.
11. The countries that have undergone this fate are legion—Arbenz's Guatemala, Bosch's Dominican Republic, Goulart's Brazil, Frondizi's Peru, Mossadegh's Iran.
12. Alexander Eckstein, "The Role of the State in Economic Growth," *Capitalism, Market Socialism, and Central Planning*, ed. Jesse W. Markham (Boston: Houghton Mifflin Co., 1963), pp. 311-12.

momentum and proceed to a situation where whole social classes are destroyed and basic institutions remolded. "The opposite to resisting industrialization would be for an aristocracy to embrace it so wholeheartedly as to liquidate itself. This, too, is a possible but not very probable reaction. It would, of course, mean suicide by the aristocracy as a class. . . ."[13] This they do not want.

UNDERDEVELOPMENT AND SOVIET METHODS OF SOCIAL CHANGE

It is conceivable that the ruling classes in an underdeveloped country will voluntarily give up their vested interests in the *status quo* in order to promote social and economic development. The Alliance for Progress seems to be based on this belief. It is possible that Albert Hirschman's policy of sequential reforms will succeed. But even he is careful to qualify his position by pointing out that ". . . many situations have existed and still exist in Latin America as elsewhere in which power is so concentrated, opposition to change so fierce, and the social and political structure so rigid that any nonrevolutionary change is, short of a miracle, impossible, *besides* being inconceivable."[14]

It seems more likely that social change will not come about by completely peaceful, evolutionary means, but rather by a social revolution which will destroy the power of the old ruling classes.

Without the discontent and the desire for change that set off revolution, these societies remain far from the threshold of the industrial revolution. Neither the appropriate ideology and dynamism, nor the leadership of social and economic development have emerged or operated in any underdeveloped country in the past few decades without a revolution. Revolution—it remains to be said—need not be one of iron and blood; but even if it is one of ideas, it has to involve a radical shift in the pattern of power to enable the leadership groups to come to the center of authority.[15]

This is what happened in the English Revolution of 1640, the French Revolution of 1789, the Mexican Revolution of 1910, the Russian Revolution of 1917, the Chinese Revolution of 1949, and the Cuban Revolution of 1959. And Japan ". . . as a consequence

13. Kautsky, *Political Change in Underdeveloped Countries*, p. 99.
14. Albert O. Hirschman, "Revolution by Stealth: The Case for Sequential Reforms," in *Economic Development: Evolution or Revolution?* ed. Laura Randall, p. 86.
15. Yusif Sayigh, "Nationalism and Economic Development," in *ibid.* p. 11.

of political and social revolutions in the 1860's . . . was able to break through the insular crust of tradition. . . ."[16]

Economic development is not a smooth evolutionary process of change; ". . . the happy picture of a quiet industrial revolution proceeding without undue stir and thrust has been . . . seldom reproduced in historical reality."[17] Rather it is a:

> . . . painful process, which involves breaking up established ways of life, hurting many strongly-entrenched vested interests. . . . To make the sweeping social changes which modernization involves, one needs determined men who believe in what they are doing, can in the last resort overcome resistance, and possess organization and ideology to mobilize people to carry out difficult tasks. The Communist Party, whatever its other defects, is adapted to this. It is an unfortunate fact that dominant Western political-social philosophies are not.[18]

The Soviet approach of eliminating the excess consumption of the former ruling class, transferring numerous unproductive workers to socially productive occupations, rationalizing the agricultural and industrial structure, capturing economies of scale, and eliminating capital flight has greatly expanded the actual social surplus available for economic development. But this has meant a complete destruction of the old order, its values and institutions, and their replacement with a new ethic based on a belief in the efficacy of science and the possibility of building a new and better world.

Some, such as Alex Inkeles, would stress the cost of this destruction of the old social order, ". . . the Soviet model of change . . . promises to entail a virtually absolute destruction of traditional values and institutions that would be extremely harsh in its impact."[19] And yet it is recognized that it may be a case of maintaining the old social institutions and stagnation, or development and destruction of the existing social order. "What ever their intrinsic worth in terms of

16. Barry E. Supple (ed.), *The Experience of Economic Growth* (New York: Random House, 1963), p. 41.

17. Alexander Gerschenkron, *Economic Backwardness in Historical Perspective* (New York: Frederick A. Praeger, Inc., 1965), p. 213.

18. Alec Nove, "The Soviet Model and Under-Developed Countries," *International Affairs*, Vol. 37, No. 1 (January, 1961), pp. 31-32. Professor Gerschenkron adds that ". . . in a backward country a very strong ideological medicine is needed to overcome the barriers of stagnation and routine and to elicit popular support. . . ." Gerschenkron, *Economic Backwardness in Historical Perspective*, p. 191.

19. Alex Inkeles, "The Soviet Union: Model for Asia?—The Social System," *Problems of Communism*, Vol. VIII, No. 6 (November-December, 1959), p. 35.

human, nonmaterial values, it is recognized . . . that the institutions must be seriously modified, if not eliminated, if the fruits of modern technology are to be shared by . . . [the] people."[20] Despite his antipathy towards the Soviet system, Inkeles admits: "If Asian leaders are looking for a system designed to permit total mobilization of the population for economic objectives; if they seek means of extracting surpluses for capital accumulation. . . ; if they must have agencies and methods for breaking the resistance of traditional ways to desired changes—then, certainly, the Soviet model can show them the way. It is, however, a grim road to travel."[21]

This "grim road" or social cost of the Soviet model of development will be considered in Chapter VI. For now it is enough to say that in the past every country's economic development has been a "grim road."

THE ROLE OF SOCIAL CHANGE IN SOVIET EXPERIENCE

In the transition from feudalism to capitalism in the West, serf labor was replaced by free labor, status of birth by status of wealth, handicraft production by factory production, the temporal power of the church by the state, and the old Catholic ethic by the new Protestant ethic. The feudal landlords were replaced by the "new men"—the entrepreneurs—as the dominant and guiding force of society.

In the Soviet Union the new institutions revolved around the Communist party, which fulfilled the traditional role of the entrepreneur, providing the ruthless energy, organizing ability and leadership without which rapid economic development would have been impossible. The social surplus was channeled into the hands of the Communist party and Marxism was substituted for the Protestant ethic in motivating this new ruling class and in providing ideological cohesion for society.

The major impact of Soviet policy on the country's social structure was the destruction of the power of the old ruling classes via expropriation of private property in landed estates and industrial enterprises. Those elements of the old order which still attempted to obstruct the social and economic changes were rendered ineffective in their opposition by the use of several different methods. If they

20. W. Donald Bowles, "Soviet Russia as a Model for Underdeveloped Areas," *World Politics,* Vol. XIV, No. 3 (April, 1962), p. 501.
21. Inkeles, "The Soviet Union: Model for Asia?" p. 37.

actively resisted they were driven into exile,[22] sent to "corrective labor" camps, or even shot as counterrevolutionaries. Those who were passive were allowed to take a regular place in society—landlords became peasants, and factory owners, managers—or were "pensioned off." This process, however, caused a temporary breakdown in the economy.

China, learning from the Russian experience, avoided most of the dislocations stemming from such a radical transformation because "the transformation of private business, like the similar change in the field of agriculture, was apparently brought about, not mainly by physical coercion or outright expropriation, but by the application of the strongest possible political pressure short of compulsion, coupled with almost unchallengeable financial inducements and penalties."[23] The Soviets also uprooted all of the other features of the old social structure which impeded rapid development—such as the extended family system with its patriarchical domination, superstition, and religious domination of education.

After destroying the inhibiting elements of the old social structure, new institutions were introduced that were conducive to development.[24] To replace the old order the Soviets strove for universal literacy and education, equality of races and sexes, economic rewards for individual effort, and attempted to instill hope for the future and enthusiasm for change and development.

Investment in physical assets is a key factor in economic development, but possibly more important is investment in human capital. And this is the most impressive achievement of the Soviet program of social change.

*Education.* In the Soviet Union great stress was placed on education to create a skilled work force, the necessary scientific and technical personnel, and managerial cadres. Not only was there a

22. It is more likely that they voluntarily went into exile rather than live under what they considered intolerable conditions. This phenomenon has been characteristic of all major social transformations. For example, at the conclusion of the American Revolution more than a hundred thousand "loyalists" fled to Canada, the Bahamas, and Great Britain. Their property was confiscated by indivdual states and the land was sold or given to revolutionaries.

23. T. J. Hughes and D. E. T. Luard, *The Economic Development of Communist China: 1949-1960* (2nd ed.; London: Oxford University Press, 1961), p. 101.

24. The major institutions of collective agriculture and public ownership and central planning of industry will be discussed in chap. III and IV.

lack of skilled workers and technicians, but even of persons able to read or write.

The great increase in literacy—from 28.4 per cent in 1897 to 56.6 per cent in 1926, 87.4 per cent in 1939, and 98.5 per cent in 1959[25]—has been due to the strongly developed compulsory school system and to the mass campaigns launched against adult illiteracy.

Total outlays on education (in 1937 prices) were 3.9 billion rubles in 1928, 19.9 billion in 1940, and 28.1 billion in 1955.[26] The results of these expenditures are summarized in Table II-1. Further data can be found in Tables V-2 and VIII-3.

*TABLE II-1*

*Educational Statistics for the U.S.S.R.: Selected Years,
1914 to 1962*

| Year | Total number of students in all levels | | Students in higher educational establishments | |
|---|---|---|---|---|
| | Number in 1,000's | Per cent of population | Number in 1,000's | Per cent of population |
| 1914-15 | 8,044 | 5.75 | 112 | 0.08 |
| 1927-28 | 11,996 | 8.11 | 168 | 0.11 |
| 1940-41 | 35,552 | 18.52 | 812 | 0.42 |
| 1961-62 | 39,086 | 17.93 | 2,640 | 1.21 |

Sources:

TsSU, *Kulturnoye stroityelstvo SSSR: statisticheskiy sbornik* (Moscow: Gosudarstvyennoye Statisticheskoye Izadatyelstvo, 1956), p. 6. TsSU, *Narodnoye khozyaystvo SSSR v 1961 godu: statisticheskiy* (Moscow: Gosstatizdat, 1962), pp. 685, 691.

Massive efforts were made to train both skilled workers and technico-engineering personnel. Numerous schools known as F. Z. U. (factory and worker apprentices' schools) were opened at enterprises to train apprentices for skilled trades, as well as evening courses for adult workers. During the First Five-Year Plan period, the F. Z. U. schools trained over 450 thousand skilled workers.[27] Students in

25. TsSU, *Itogi vsyesoyuznoi pyeryepisi nasyelyeniya 1959 goda, SSSR* (Moscow: Gosstatizdat, 1962), p. 88.
26. Abram Bergson, *The Real National Income of Soviet Russia Since 1928* (Cambridge: Harvard University Press, 1961), p. 355.
27. U.S. Department of Education, *Education in the U.S.S.R.* Bulletin

receipt of scholarships and maintenance grants at universities and higher technical schools and at technical and other secondary schools for the training of cadres increased rapidly after 1928 and by 1939 the great majority of students were on stipends of some sort.

This great expansion in the availability of education at all levels, even to the very poorest, was a major factor fostering the development of new attitudes and habits conducive to industrialization.

*Medical and Social Services.* Great emphasis was placed on health and social services. Free medical care, community social halls, vacation resorts, and sickness benefits were provided early in the development program. These measures were taken to provide for a healthy work force and to create loyalty to and enthusiasm for the regime. The support of the populace, at least in the beginning, made the imposition of sacrifices for development easier.

In the Soviet Union, a social insurance system was established by the Labor Code of 1922 and amended in 1927 and 1937. The system is composed of three parts. The first, the provision of actual medical facilities, applies both to wage earners and their families and includes the service of specialists and the provision of medicines and appliances and hospital treatment as well as the advice of a general practitioner. The second consists of old-age pensions and pensions to the totally disabled. Old-age pensions vary between 50 and 100 per cent of the normal wage according to industry and level of earnings. They are 100 per cent of the lowest earnings and 50 per cent of the highest. Total disablement benefits, payable for accident or illness reasons, amount to between 60 and 100 per cent of the normal wage. The third part consists of a combined insurance covering disablement and maternity benefit, funeral allowances, children's aid, the provision of rest homes and sanatoria, and assistance to travel. The social insurance system is a noncontributory scheme in the sense that contributions to the fund come entirely from general tax revenues.

Total outlays on health care (in 1937 prices) increased from 2.1 billion rubles in 1928 to 9.5 billion in 1940 and 15.8 billion in 1961.[28] The number of physicians increased from 23.2 thousand in 1913 to 63.2 thousand in 1928, 141.7 thousand in 1940, and 425.7 thousand in 1961. The number of available hospital beds

---

1957, No. 14, 1957, p. 130. On-the-job training is discussed further in chap. V.

28. Bergson, *The Real National Income of Soviet Russia Since 1928*, p. 347.

increased from 207.6 thousand in 1913 to 246.5 thousand in 1928, 790.9 thousand in 1940, and 1,845.4 thousand in 1961.[29]

This investment in medical care has increased the health of the population as evidenced by the decline in mortality rates. Crude death rates declined from 30.2 per thousand in 1913 to 18.1 in 1940 and 7.2 in 1961. Infant mortality rates declined from 273 per thousand in 1913 to 184 in 1940 and 32 in 1961.[30]

CONCLUSION

The Soviet policies of social change discussed so far have had beneficial effects on the development process. On the other hand, some Soviet practices have negated some of these gains. A number of these will be discussed in the following chapters but some need to be mentioned at this point. There are many examples—collectivization of livestock, attempts at too rapid a pace of collectivization where the vast majority of peasants were not ready for it, and the destruction of handicrafts. These have thrown away much good will and alienated large groups of the population. Most of these can be counted as mistakes due to misjudgment, overzealousness, dogmatism, or pressure of circumstances. But other Soviet practices seem to be followed from principle, such as intolerance of dissent and persecution of religion as religion instead of as an institution with vested interests in the *status quo* (with the honorable exception of Cuba). There will always be opposition to radical change but these Soviet practices tend to increase this opposition and thus to lessen the beneficial effects of the changes.[31]

Soviet methods were successful in establishing institutions conducive to social change and economic development. By eliminating the excess consumption of the previous ruling classes and channeling it into productive investment the difference between the actual and potential social surplus was narrowed and the actual surplus productively used. The increase of educational, medical, and cultural expenditures increased labor productivity which in turn increased

29. TsSU, *Forty Years of Soviet Power: In Facts and Figures* (Moscow: Foreign Languages Publishing House, 1958), pp. 309, 314. TsSU, *Narkhoz, 1961*, pp. 743, 746.

30. TsSU, *Narkhoz, 1961*, p. 28.

31. It will be argued in the final chapter of this study that the greatest drawback to the Soviet model is its operation by a Communist party. It is possible that a halfway democratic-socialist regime, unencumbered by Communist dogmatism, could operate the basic model more efficiently.

the actual social surplus and thus made further productive investment possible. These policies, in addition, have helped the populace to become oriented toward change and modernization. A relatively educated and healthy people have emerged; they are now utilizing their increased energies and talents to further transform and develop their society.

# III. AGRICULTURE AND ECONOMIC DEVELOPMENT: SOVIET AGRICULTURAL INSTITUTIONS AND POLICY

---

## THE AGRARIAN REVOLUTION

One of the major consequences of the social revolution in the Soviet model is the dispossession of the feudal-minded landlord class. This agrarian revolution is not a matter of mere "land reform" but rather is an integral part of the change in social structure generated by the social revolution.

There is little disagreement that feudal and semi-feudal agrarian structures must be radically transformed if development is not to be seriously impeded. But this transformation is not easy to carry out for it involves fundamental social and economic change. Professor Robert Alexander has argued that in Latin America "agrarian reform is the fundamental revolutionary act. . . . It represents the definitive destruction of the power and position of the traditional oligarchy which has ruled Latin America since the conquest of the area by Spain and Portugal. It involves dispossessing the oligarchy of the land which for four and a half centuries has been the basis of its dominant position and the granting of their property to someone else."[1]

The traditional agrarian system gives rise to large incomes which are not reinvested in production. It gives rise also to social attitudes inimical to investment. Landowners spend conspicuously, virtually as a badge of aristocracy; buy more land; or invest in urban housing; or lend at usurious rates of interest to peasants for nonproductive purposes. In addition, most of the peasant population is kept out of the market and a large part of the arable land is kept out of cultivation since the large landholders have little incentive to use it.[2]

1. Robert J. Alexander, "Nature and Progress of Agrarian Reform in Latin America," *Journal of Economic History*, Vol. XXIII, No. 4 (December, 1963), p. 559.
2. For an elaboration of these arguments, see *ibid.*, pp. 559-63, and Doreen

Some type of change in agrarian structure is necessary to utilize modern scientific agricultural methods, to provide the increased food to feed the growing industrial labor force and the raw materials for the factories, and to provide a supply of labor for the expanding industrial sector of the economy. While there is little dispute over the need for change, there are large differences of opinion over what form the new agrarian structure should take. In the Soviet model, collective forms of agriculture were adopted to replace the old agrarian structures.

THE ROLE OF SOCIALIST AGRICULTURE IN THE SOVIET MODEL

Contrary to the popular belief that agriculture hindered Soviet development, it can be shown that agriculture has successfully contributed to the economic development of the Soviet Union. The agricultural sector contributed both labor and capital to the development effort. It provided the food and raw materials (two forms of capital) necessary for an expanding industrial sector and the exports required to pay for imports of scarce capital goods. In addition, agriculture provided a large share of the industrial labor force.

Johnston and Mellor have listed five important ways in which agriculture can contribute to economic development. First, economic development expands the demand for food which, if unfulfilled, would impede further development. Second, exports of agricultural products can increase badly needed foreign exchange earnings. Third, agriculture must supply a significant part of the expanding labor needs of the industrial sector. Fourth, agriculture, as the dominant sector in a peasant economy, must provide capital for industry and social overhead investment; and fifth, rising cash incomes in agriculture can be an important source of demand.[3]

In the Soviet model, however, the first requirement loses some of its urgency because of the large number of controls available in a socialist economy. The fifth requirement is relatively unimportant in a planned economy, since the plan determines the size and composition of demand. Thus, there remain essentially two major roles

Warriner, "Land Reform and Economic Development," in *Agriculture in Economic Development*, eds. Carl Eicher and Lawrence Witt (New York: McGraw-Hill Book Co., 1964), pp. 283-90.

3. Bruce F. Johnston and John W. Mellor, "The Role of Agriculture in Economic Development," *American Economic Review*, Vol. LI, No. 4 (September, 1961), pp. 571-72.

for the agricultural sector: the provision of capital in the form of food and raw materials for industry and for export, and the freeing of large numbers of rural workers to join the urban labor force. The key to these requirements is twofold: a growing marketed surplus of agricultural products and a freeing and utilization of surplus labor through structural reorganization, and increasing agricultural productivity per man. The collective farm system in the Soviet Union was designed to provide these solutions.

Soviet agriculture has gone through two stages since industrialization began. The first stage, during the Stalin period, lasted from 1928 to 1953. During this stage agricultural investment was held to the minimum necessary to provide industry with sufficient food, raw materials, and labor. Thus many agricultural problems, that did not immediately affect industry, were allowed to accumulate. By 1953, these accumulated problems had brought the economy to a crisis. Possibly a major achievement of this period was the successful deferral of these problems until the economy was better able to handle them. Beginning in 1954, the regime began a program of agricultural reform to alleviate these problems. Agricultural investment was increased, the new lands program was started, procurement prices were increased, etc. However, these reforms did not change the basic structure of Soviet agriculture.

In this chapter, agricultural growth will be measured for the two stages discussed above. Statistics for the period from 1928 to 1940 will be used for the first stage. This is done because more data are available for 1940 and because the war and reconstruction period of 1940-48 causes serious distortions. Agriculture was slow to recover from the effects of the war. In 1953, the 1940 output level had been barely regained.

Soviet agriculture is organized on the basis of state and collective farms. Because workers on state farms receive regular wages and collective farmers are only residual claimants to their output, the collective farm system was a more effective system to mobilize the agricultural surplus during the early period of industrialization. Because of its predominance during the industrialization period (90 per cent of output during the first stage and 70 per cent after the new lands program) only the collective farm system will be examined in detail.

There were several characteristics of the collective farm system that made it fit into the Soviet strategy of economic development.[4] Collective farms were formed as co-operative associations, established on government owned land given to the farms on indefinite tenure. The farms were required to sell a major part of their output to the state at prices set well below the free market level.

The goal set for the collective farms was maximization of the marketed agricultural output. In addition, special emphasis was placed on the maximization of a particular product-mix of the marketed output. This goal was to be achieved by emphasizing increased output per man instead of increased yields per acre. At the same time this would release needed labor for industry.

The distribution of the collective farm output was regulated by a set of general priorities established by the collective farm charter. In descending order of priority these were: (1) deliveries of the share of output purchased by the state, (2) payment of direct taxes in kind to the state, (3) reimbursement for cost of seed and outside production costs such as services of the machine tractor stations, and (4) distribution of the residual (the wage fund) among collective farm members in accordance with their contribution of labor to production.

The collective farm members were required to render labor services for which they were paid in two forms. First was the assignment of a small plot of land for private use. The output could either be consumed by the collective farm family or sold on the free market. The second form of payment consisted of an unspecified volume of agricultural products in kind and an unspecified money payment out of the total wage fund, which reflected the member's relative share of each farm's total labor time expended in production.

The major decisions of the collective farms were subject to the administrative direction of the state and the actual execution of the decisions was under state control. The state constantly intervened in the internal affairs of the collective farms in order to assure compliance with its policy objectives.

*Collection of the Agricultural Surplus.* In providing a marketed surplus, agriculture was a source of savings and in the Soviet economy, where saving and investment decisions coincide, it was a source of capital accumulation. This put the Soviet agricultural problem

4. See Arcadius Kahan, "The Collective Farm System in Russia: Some Aspects of Its Contribution to Soviet Economic Development," in *Agriculture in Economic Development*, eds. Eicher and Witt, pp. 252-55.

back in the world of classical economics where capital accumulation is limited by the wages fund (conceived as a stock of food). It should be noted that this agricultural surplus was a function not only of surplus manpower, but also of increased total output, increased yields per man, and the level of the peasants' consumption.

The crux of economic development is the capture of this potential agricultural surplus. Ragnar Nurkse points out that "this crucial problem of collecting the food seems to be solved in Soviet Russia by the system of collective farms. The word 'collective' has here a double meaning. The collective farm is not only a form of collective organization; it is above all an instrument of collection."[5]

The collection of the marketable agricultural surplus was facilitated in two ways. First, the state, not the market, determined industrial and agricultural prices. The collective farm had to accept both the amount and the prices of the marketed output set by the state. Therefore, the planners could increase the amount of agricultural products needed to exchange for manufactured goods. This shift in the rural-urban "terms-of-trade" in effect forced the agricultural sector to "save."

Second, the collective farm organization enabled the marketed share of output to be determined independently of the size of total agricultural output. Any short-fall in total production was absorbed by a reduction in the residual received by peasant households. Thus, 25 million tons of grain were delivered to the state in 1937 and 24 million tons were delivered in 1939 out of a harvest 20 million tons smaller.[6] There were, of course, constraints in the form of minimum peasant health and morale (constraints that during 1932-34 Stalin either miscalulated or ignored).

The success of the collective farm system in capturing the marketable agricultural surplus can be seen from the following figures. The percentage of total agricultural output marketed was 20.3 per cent in 1913 and, during the crucial period of industrialization, it was 28.8 per cent in 1937, and 36.2 per cent in 1939.[7] The marketed output of grain averaged 18.2 million tons per year over the period 1928-32, 27.5 million tons over 1933-37, 32.1 million tons over

5. Ragnar Nurkse, *Problems of Capital Formation in Underdeveloped Countries* (Oxford: Basil Blackwell, 1958), pp. 38-39.
6. Kahan, "The Collective Farm System in Russia," in *Agriculture in Economic Development*, eds. Eicher and Witt, p. 259.
7. *Ibid.*

1938-40, and 43.5 million tons over the period 1954-58.[8] Marketings of all agricultural products were 65 per cent greater in 1940 and 300 per cent greater in 1961 than in 1913.[9]

Limiting the size of the collective farm's wage fund facilitated Soviet economic growth in another way. The resulting low incomes of the peasants, coupled with high prices of manufactured consumer goods, repressed the effective demand for these goods. Thus, the Soviets were able to restrict investment in consumer goods industries and concentrate most of the investment in capital goods industries, which increased the growth rate of the strategic sectors of industry. It can be concluded therefore, that ". . . the socialization drive in agriculture achieved to a large extent its major economic purpose of serving as a basis for the industrialization drive."[10]

Agricultural marketings not only provided a source of capital by feeding the rapidly expanding industrial labor force, but also by providing exportable products. The large imports of capital equipment in the 1930's were paid for with foreign exchange earned by food and raw material exports. The effectiveness of agricultural exports, however, was severely restricted by the decline of primary product prices on the world market in the 1930's. In addition, agriculture played an important role in a policy of import substitution. Industrial crops such as cotton and sugar beets were rapidly expanded to replace imports of these goods and thus free foreign exchange for the importation of capital goods.

*The Release and Utilization of Agricultural Labor.* Rapid industrialization ordinarily requires a large increase in the nonagricultural labor force. This demand for labor can be fulfilled either by utilizing available urban labor resources or by freeing a part of the labor force employed in agriculture. The urban labor sources, however, are usually small and quickly used up. Thus, agriculture must carry the main burden of providing the nonagricultural labor force.

In the Soviet Union, where the agricultural structure consisted of individual ownership with the land worked in small plots, potentially surplus labor existed mainly as seasonal unemployment or

8. TsSU, *Narodnoye khozyaystvo SSSR v 1961 godu: statisticheskiy yezhegodnik* (Moscow: Gosstatizdat, 1962), p. 341. (Hereinafter, *Narkhoz*).
9. *Ibid.*, p. 296.
10. Naum Jasny, *The Socialized Agriculture of the U.S.S.R.: Plans and Performance*, Grain Economic Series No. 5 (Stanford: Stanford University Press, 1949), p. 33.

underemployment of self-employed farmers, tenants, and hired agricultural workers. Year-round disguised unemployment was probably less important because, given the existing technique (the essence of which was individual, small-scale cultivation), a significant proportion of agricultural labor could not be transferred without causing a fall in total farm output. There was little possibility of freeing labor for year-long, off-the-farm work or for seasonal work on capital formation projects without structural reorganization and mechanization. Both were important in the agricultural strategy adopted in the Soviet Union.

To release surplus labor for capital formation projects, seasonal underemployment had to be transformed into seasonal unemployment. Collectivization facilitated this process by converting agriculture from a small-scale unorganized operation into a large-scale planned activity. In the off seasons, farm operations were handled by just part of the farmers, each continuing to work full time, instead of all the farmers working a few hours each. The labor of the released farmers was then utilized in capital formation. The average number of days worked per year was greatly increased by this method. Thus in the Soviet Union the work-year per person at work in agriculture was lengthened from around 120 days to approximately 185 days.[11]

The Soviet collective farm system also served as a convenient organizational framework for the mobilization of this seasonal unemployment for capital formation. The Fergana irrigation canal was dug by 165 thousand collective farm members from Uzbekistan and Tadjikstan. The Uralo-Kushumskii canal in Kazakhstan and the Samur-Divichinskii canal in Azerbaidjan were each constructed by tens of thousands of collective farmers. In addition, the collective farms supervised the implementation of the statutory obligation of peasants to work six days a year on road construction. Since the collective farms supplied almost all of the labor and some of the equipment they made substantial contributions to capital formation. All together the collective farms contributed labor equal to an annual average of about one million yearly workers.[12] Since this labor was rendered during the off season and without compensation by the state (the greater number of workdays earned divided into the un-

11. U.S. Congress, Joint Economic Committee, *Comparisons of the United States and Soviet Economies*, 86th Cong., 1st Sess., 1960, p. 213.
12. Kahan, "The Collective Farm System in Russia," in *Agriculture in Economic Development*, eds. Eicher and Witt, p. 258.

changed total income would give each workday a lower value), there was a net gain for the economy. The Soviets did not, however, make use of all the available possibilities. For example, in October, 1938, a decree was issued discouraging industrial activity unconnected with agriculture on the farm.[13]

Off-season employment of agricultural labor in construction, transportation, forestry, road and railroad construction, and even in mining and manufacturing existed under the traditional agrarian structures of Tsarist Russia and the Soviet New Economic Policy of the 1920's. The collective farm system, however, did more. It enabled the Soviets to organize and control the flow of temporary off-the-farm labor. The Soviet Union established *Organizovannyi Nabor* (organized recruitment) among the collective farms which, in turn, assigned certain members to work off the farms for various time periods. The total number recruited between 1931 and 1940 was 28.7 million workers. The average time worked off the farm per person was five to six months during 1933 to 1935 and eight to nine months in 1940.[14] The demand for this type of seasonal labor declined over the period, however, for several reasons. There was a decrease in demand for unskilled labor in general, an increase in labor recruitment through vocational schools, and an increasing demand for permanent rather than seasonal labor in nonagricultural work.

While the organized use of seasonal farm labor on agricultural capital formation projects and temporary urban work was important, even more important was the release of agricultural labor for permanent relocation in the urban areas. This required that output per *man* be increased so that at least the same output could be produced with a smaller agricultural work force. Both reorganization of the agrarian structure and mechanization contributed to this needed increase in productivity per man.

13. Alec Nove, "Collectivization of Agriculture in Russia and China," in *Symposium on Economic Problems of the Far East*, ed. E. F. Szczpanik (Hong Kong: Hong Kong University Press, 1962), p. 24.

14. Kahan, "The Collective Farm System in Russia," in *Agriculture in Economic Development*, eds. Eicher and Witt, pp. 255-56. An interesting question concerning the use of surplus agricultural labor was the transportation cost incurred in getting labor to the job site. The Soviets minimized this cost by full utilization of existing transportation facilities. Railroad passenger cars designed to hold one hundred riders were loaded with maybe double that number. The real cost was absorbed, therefore, by the reduced comfort of the riders.

Reorganization through consolidation of small peasant holdings increased the division of labor and the degree of specialization, thus raising productivity per man. Instead of each peasant performing all of the farm tasks, some specialized in plowing, some in weeding, some in animal husbandry, and so on. In addition, labor was saved through the consolidation of farm buildings, equipment, and the like. The labor required, for example, to maintain one set of farm buildings was less than that required to maintain fifty smaller but separate ones. Also idle machine time was reduced on pre-existing farm equipment, even small-scale hand tools, rakes, hammers, and the like. Instead of each farmer requiring a full set of tools with much duplication, gains were made by computing needs on an economic, not a legal, foundation.

More important, consolidation of land holdings made possible the widespread use of tractors, sheaf-binders, threshing machines, cultivators, seed selection apparatus, combine-harvesting machines, and other agricultural equipment, which improved cultivation of the soil, saved labor, and prevented harvesting losses. This mechanization, by increasing labor productivity, also released labor for permanent nonagricultural work.

Nonagricultural employment in the Soviet Union increased very rapidly after 1928. The number of workers employed outside of agriculture increased from 9.0 million in 1929 to 19.6 million in 1932, 28.2 million in 1940, and 61.8 million in 1963.[15] The same trend is evident when data reflecting the transfer of the rural population to urban areas are examined. Between 1926 and 1939, 18.7 million people moved from rural to urban areas and between 1939 and 1959 another 24.6 million moved, for a total of 43.3 million as compared to a net increase in the urban population of 73 million between 1926 and 1959.[16]

The success of reorganization and mechanization in increasing productivity per man and thus freeing labor for industry is summarized in Table III-1. It must be emphasized that this productivity increase is *per man*, not *per man-hour*. If the lengthened work-year is taken into account there was little, if any, increase in output per man-hour before 1940. The success of the collective farm system

15. U.S. Congress, Joint Economic Committee, *Current Economic Indicators for the U.S.S.R.*, 89th Cong., 1st Sess., 1965, p. 71.
16. Kahan, "The Collective Farm System in Russia," in *Agriculture in Economic Development*, eds. Eicher and Witt, p. 256.

TABLE III-1

_Labor Productivity in U.S.S.R. Agriculture:_
_1928-1959_

|  | 1928 | 1940 | 1959 |
|---|---|---|---|
| Agricultural labor force (millions) | 70.6 | 60.0 | 52.8 |
| Index of gross agricultural output | 100.0 | 120.3 | 190.0 |
| Index of output per man | 100.0 | 144.4 | 253.4 |
| Average annual percentage increase in output per man: |  |  |  |
| 1928 to: |  | 3.1 | 3.1 |
| 1928 to (effective years):[a] |  | 3.1 | 4.1 |
| 1940 to: |  |  | 3.0 |
| 1940 to (effective years):[a] |  |  | 5.2 |

Sources:
Kahan, "The Collective Farm System in Russia," in _Agriculture in Economic Development_, eds. Eicher and Witt, p. 268. U.S. Congress, Joint Economic Committee, _Comparisons of the United States and Soviet Economies_, 86th Cong., 1st Sess., 1960, p. 204. Abram Bergson and Simon Kuznets (eds.), _Economic Trends in the Soviet Union_ (Cambridge: Harvard University Press, 1963), p. 77.

[a] The eight year period of war and reconstruction, 1941-48, is excluded.

can be summed up by saying it was an excellent mobilizer of productive inputs.[17]

Table III-2 presents data on mechanization and electrification in the Soviet Union's agricultural sector from 1928 to 1963. The mechanization of agriculture was specifically designed to replace animal draft power and expedite the transfer of labor from agriculture to industry. Mechanization was biased in favor of plowing and grain harvesting so that a large decrease in peak seasonal employment could be obtained. Ploughing of spring crops by tractor-drawn ploughs increased from 1 per cent of the total in 1928 to 62 per cent in 1940 and 92 per cent in 1953. Harvesting of grain crops by combines increased from 0.2 per cent in 1928 to 46 per cent in 1940 and 79 per cent in 1953.[18]

17. It is worth noting that in their new study, Moorsteen and Powell find that the "dominant source of Soviet growth has been the increase in the quantity of productive resources employed." See Richard Moorsteen and Raymond P. Powell, _The Soviet Capital Stock, 1928-1962_ (Homewood, Illinois: Richard D. Irwin, Inc., 1966), p. 292.

18. TsSU, _Narkhoz, 1959_, p. 421.

*TABLE III-2*

Mechanization and Electrification
of Soviet Agriculture

|                                                      | 1928       | 1932 | 1937 | 1940 | 1963   |
|------------------------------------------------------|------------|------|------|------|--------|
| Number of tractors in use (1000's)                   | 27         | 72   | 454  | 531  | 1,442  |
| Number of combines in use (1000's)                   | (2 units)  | 15   | 129  | 182  | 517    |
| Number of trucks in use (1000's)                     | 0.7        | n.a. | n.a. | 228  | 922    |
| Electric power consumed in agriculture (million kwh) | 35         | 86   | 330  | 538  | 16,130 |

Sources:
TsSU, *Narkhoz, 1961,* p. 414. TsSU, *Narkhoz, 1963,* pp. 332, 337.

PERFORMANCE AND PROBLEMS OF AGRICULTURE
IN THE SOVIET MODEL

The above discussion has shown that Soviet agriculture has succeeded in fulfilling its two major functions of providing a growing marketed surplus of agricultural products and of freeing and utilizing surplus agricultural labor.

The collective organization of agriculture was the key to this success. Increases in output per man and in man days worked were effected through land reorganization and mechanization. These increases enlarged the potential marketable surplus, which was then taken by the state for investment in industry, and freed the labor necessary for the expanding industrial sector. However, most Western scholars would argue that Soviet agriculture has been a handicap, not an aid, to development. This judgment is usually based, however, on an inappropriate comparison. Present day Soviet yields are compared with those in Western Europe or the United States. This ignores geographic and cultural differences, relative capital endowments, the element of time, and differential development strategies.

Better evidence on the relative success or failure of Soviet agriculture can be obtained from a comparison of Soviet agricultural *growth* with other countries. Table III-3 compares the growth of total agricultural production in the Soviet Union with selected other countries. Since the concern here is with the role of agriculture during economic development, wherever possible, time periods have been chosen to cover the years of industrialization in the respective countries. Because of the inadequacy and unreliability of official Soviet statistics most of the data used in this study are taken from computations made by Western scholars. In comparison with other countries, the growth of total and per capita agricultural output in the Soviet Union has been respectable. Only Mexico and the United States had higher average annual growth rates. In the Mexican case the result probably is somewhat distorted by the exclusion of the thirty-year period following the revolution of 1910. In the United

*TABLE III-3*

*Average Annual Growth Rates of Agricultural Production*
*in Selected Countries*

| Countries | Total | Per capita |
|---|---|---|
| 1. U.S.S.R.: | | |
|     1928-1964/65 | 2.3 | 1.1 |
|     1928-1940 and 1948-1964/65 | | |
|     (Effective years) | 3.0 | 1.5 |
| 2. U.S.A.: | | |
|     1870-1900 | 3.3 | 1.2 |
|     1910-1940 | 1.0 | −0.2 |
|     1928-1959 | 1.6 | 0.3 |
| 3. GREAT BRITAIN: | | |
|     1760-1790 | 0.6 | −0.3 |
|     1801/11-1831/41 | 1.2 | −0.5 |
| 4. GERMANY: | | |
|     1882-1909/13 | 1.8 | 0.6 |
| 5. FRANCE: | | |
|     1830/34-1860/64 | 1.6 | 0.8 |
|     1860/64-1895/99 | 0.4 | 0.2 |
| 6. SWEDEN: | | |
|     1861/65-1891/95 | 1.7 | 1.0 |
|     1896/1900-1926/30 | 1.0 | 0.4 |
| 7. JAPAN: | | |
|     1878/82-1913/17 | 2.0 | 0.8 |
| 8. MEXICO: | | |
|     1940-1960 | 5.1 | 2.2 |

Sources:
(1) Table III-1 and U.S. Department of Agriculture, *The U.S.S.R. and Eastern Europe Agricultural Situation* (Washington: Government

Printing Office, 1966), p. 2. The Department of Agriculture's Index for 1957/59-1964/65 was spliced to Kahan's index for 1928-1959. The effect was to raise the average growth rate by 0.1 to 0.2 per cent. (2) U.S. Bureau of the Census, *Historical Statistics of the United States: Colonial Times to 1957* (Washington: Government Printing Office, 1960), pp. 7, 288; U.S. Bureau of the Census, *Historical Statistics of the United States; Continuation to 1962 and Revisions* (Washington: Government Printing Office, 1965), pp. 1, 44. (3) B. R. Mitchell and Phyllis Deane, *Abstract of British Historical Statistics* (Cambridge: Cambridge University Press, 1962), pp. 3, 8; Phyllis Deane and W. A. Cole, *British Economic Growth: 1688-1959* (Cambridge: Cambridge University Press, 1964), pp. 78, 170. (4) Colin Clark, *The Conditions of Economic Progress* (3rd ed.; London: Macmillan & Co., Ltd., 1957), p. 263; D. V. Glass and E. Grebenik, "World Population, 1800-1950," *The Cambridge Economic History of Europe,* eds. M. M. Postan and H. J. Habakkuk (Cambridge: Cambridge University Press, 1965), VI, 61-62. (5) Clark, p. 262; Glass and Grebenik, pp. 61-62. (6) Clark, p. 268; Glass and Grebenik, pp. 61-62. (7) W. W. Lockwood, *The Economic Development of Japan: Growth and Structural Change, 1868-1938* (Princeton: Princeton University Press, 1954), p. 86. Ohkawa and Rosovsky, "The Role of Agriculture in Modern Japanese Economic Development," in *Agriculture in Economic Development,* ed. Eicher, p. 47. (8) Howard F. Cline, *Mexico: Revolution to Evolution, 1940-1960* (New York: Oxford University Press, 1963), p. 336. Robert L. Bennett, *The Financial Sector and Economic Development: The Mexican Case* (Baltimore: The Johns Hopkins Press, 1965), p. 187.

States, and the Soviet Union, the growth of total, but not per capita, agricultural output is biased upwards by the large influx of immigrants and the acquisition of the Baltic States respectively.

Table III-4 compares total and per capita agricultural production growth rates over the period 1952/53-1954/55 to 1964/65 for the Soviet Union, the Communist countries of eastern Europe, and the rest of the world by regions. The comparison loses some of its value because the same period is used for all countries and regions. On the one hand, the Soviet Union's growth rate is probably biased upward relative to the other regions because this is the period when the "new lands" were opened. On the other hand, the last few years have seen the Soviet growth rate slowing. Between 1952/53-1954/55 and 1961/62, Soviet agricultural growth was 4.1 per cent per year. Between 1961/62 and 1964/65 it was 0.6 per cent.[19] Also, regions like the United States and Canada were attempting to de-

19. U.S. Department of Agriculture, *The U.S.S.R. and Eastern Europe Agricultural Situation* (Washington: Government Printing Office, 1966), p. 2.

*TABLE III-4*

Average Annual Growth of World Agricultural Production
by Regions: 1952/53–1954/55 to 1964/65

| Countries and regions | Total | Per capita |
|---|---|---|
| U.S.S.R. | 3.3 | 1.8 |
| Eastern Europe | 2.3 | 1.4 |
| Western Europe | 2.1 | 1.3 |
| U.S. | 1.7 | 0.0 |
| Canada | 2.0 | —0.4 |
| Latin America | 2.6 | —0.2 |
| Far East[a] | 3.0 | 0.9 |
| Western Asia | 2.9 | 0.2 |
| Africa | 2.8 | 0.6 |
| Australia-New Zealand | 3.3 | 1.2 |

Sources:
   U.S. Department of Agriculture, *The 1965 World Agricultural Situation* (Washington: Government Printing Office, 1964), p. 4.
   [a] Excluding Communist Asia.

crease production, not expand it. However, taken in conjunction with other evidence, the comparison does support the position that Soviet agriculture has grown at a respectable rate.

Another measure of the "success" or "failure" of Soviet agriculture is the increase in output per man over time. Table III-5 summarizes data on changes in labor productivity for a number of selected countries. Here again the Soviet Union has a respectable performance. Only the United States in the period 1928 to 1959 exceeds it.

Another indicator of performance is increase in agricultural output per unit of land. Table III-6 summarizes the available data for the Soviet Union, the United States, and Japan. Land area used is not available for the remaining countries listed in Table III-5. The Soviet Union did less well on this indicator than on increases in total output or output per man. This result is to be expected, of course, given the strategy of emphasizing output per man that was discussed above.

The data used in constructing Table III-5 and III-6 and even III-2 are rough in most cases and the degree of accuracy varies widely. However, the sum total of the data does reveal a pattern that is probably reasonably accurate. The picture that emerges does not

*TABLE III-5*

### Average Annual Growth Rates of Agricultural
### Output per Man in Selected Countries

| Countries and Years | % Growth Rate |
|---|---|
| U.S.S.R.: | |
| 1928-1959 | 3.1 |
| 1928-1940 and 1948-1959 (Effective Years) | 4.1 |
| U.S.A.: | |
| 1910-1940 | 1.7 |
| 1928-1959 | 3.4 |
| GREAT BRITAIN: | |
| 1801/11-1831/41 | 0.2 |
| GERMANY: | |
| 1882-1909/13 | 0.6 |
| FRANCE: | |
| 1830/34-1860/64 | 2.1 |
| 1860/64-1895/99 | 0.9 |
| SWEDEN: | |
| 1861/65-1891/95 | 1.6 |
| 1896/1900-1926/30 | 0.8 |
| JAPAN: | |
| 1878/82-1913/17 | 2.1 |

Sources:
See Table III-3; U.S. Bureau of the Census, *Historical Statistics*, pp. 42, 280; Mitchell and Deane, *Abstract of British Historical Statistics*, p. 143. For Germany, France, and Sweden, the only agricultural labor force statistics available are for male workers. The growth of output per man was obtained by dividing the index of agricultural output by the index of agricultural work force.

support the contention that Soviet agriculture has been a "failure." Rather, in the context of its role as a development aid, it has been reasonably "successful." However, as noted earlier, growth was purchased by "successfully" deferring some agricultural problems to the future. These are now coming home to roost. Fortunately for the Soviet Union they are easier to solve at this stage of development.

Individual product statistics add to this general pattern. Net production of milk increased from 907 kilograms per cow in 1928 to 1,406 kilograms in 1957.[20] Net wool production increased from 1.80 kilograms per sheep in 1928 to 2.56 kilograms in 1957.

20. U.S. Congress, *Comparisons of the United States and Soviet Economies*, p. 237.

*TABLE III-6*

*Average Annual Growth Rates of Agricultural*
*Output per Unit of Land in Use in*
*Selected Countries*

| Countries and Years | % Growth Rate |
|---|---|
| U.S.S.R.: | |
| 1928-1964/65 | 0.5 |
| 1928-1940 and 1948-1964/65 (Effective Years) | 0.7 |
| Grains, potatoes, vegetables, and industrial crops: | |
| 1928-1959 | 0.9 |
| 1928-1940 and 1948-1959 (Effective Years) | 1.2 |
| U.S.A.: | |
| 1910-1940 | 0.7 |
| 1928-1959 | 1.1 |
| JAPAN: | |
| 1878/82-1913/17 | 1.2 |

Sources:

See Table III-3; TsSU, *Narkhoz, 1964*, p. 267; U.S. Bureau of the Census, *Historical Statistics*, p. 281; U.S. Bureau of the Census, *Historical Statistics Continuation to 1962*, p. 42; D. Gale Johnson, "Agricultural Production," in *Economic Trends in the Soviet Union*, eds. Bergson and Kuznets, pp. 220, 227. The index for grains, potatoes, vegetables, and industrial crops was constructed by Johnson, p. 227. For the United States, the figures are for crop production per harvested acre. Thus, the U.S. figures are closer in concept to the Johnson index.

Average crop yields between 1925-29 and 1955-58 increased from 7.91 centners (100 kilograms) per hectare to 9.49 centners for grain, from 8.32 centners to 20.24 centners for cotton, from 132.0 centners to 185.6 centners for sugar beets, from 6.24 centners to 9.31 centners for sunflower, from 79.3 centners to 90.9 centners for potatoes, and from 2.08 centners to 2.53 centners for flax fiber.[21]

The few statistics available on labor productivity for individual crops reflect the same pattern. The labor used per hectare of land per year by peasant farms in 1925-26 and by collective farms in 1956-57 decreased from 20.8 man-days to 8.6 man-days for grain, from 61.3 man-days to 58.0 man-days for potatoes, and from 117.2 man-days to 108.0 man-days for cotton. The labor used per centner of output by peasant farms in 1925-26 and by collective farms in 1956-57 decreased from 21.0 man-hours to 7.3 man-hours for grain,

21. *Ibid.*, p. 211.

from 6.3 man-hours to 5.1 man-hours for potatoes, and from 106.5 man-hours to 42.8 man-hours for cotton.[22]

The respectable performance of Soviet agriculture since 1928 does not, of course, imply that it is highly productive. The usual type of comparison made between the Soviet Union and the United States proves how relatively backward is Soviet agriculture. Table III-7 sets forth some of these comparisons.

*TABLE III-7*

*Crop Yields per Hectare and per Man-Hour in the U.S.A. and U.S.S.R.: 1956-1957*

| Crops | Centners per hectare | | Man-hours per centner U.S.S.R. | | |
|---|---|---|---|---|---|
| | U.S.A. | U.S.S.R. | U.S.A. | State farms | Collective farms |
| Grain | 21.0 | 9.7 | 1.0 | 1.8 | 7.3 |
| Cotton | 14.6 | 20.2 | 18.8 | 29.8 | 42.8 |
| Sugar beets | 387.0 | 180.6 | 0.5 | 2.1 | 3.1 |
| Potatoes | 193.7 | 91.0 | 1.0 | 4.2 | 5.1 |

Sources:

U.S. Congress, Joint Economic Committee, *Comparisons of the United States and Soviet Economies*, p. 215. Johnson, "Agricultural Production," in *Economic Trends in the Soviet Union*, eds. Bergson and Kuznets, pp. 223-24.

There are several reasons, however, why Soviet agriculture makes such a poor showing in this type of comparison in spite of its relatively rapid growth since 1928. The most important concern (*a*) the head start other countries possessed, (*b*) soil and climatic conditions, (*c*) excesses of the collectivization drive, (*d*) incentives, and (*e*) differential development strategies.

*The Headstart of Other Countries.* As was seen above, the growth of Soviet agriculture has been as rapid as that of most developed countries, whether the measure is total output, output per man, or output per unit of land. However, countries such as the United States, Great Britain, and even Japan have been developing for a much longer period. Great Britain began industrializing in the eigh-

22. *Ibid.*, pp. 214-15.

teenth century, the United States around 1840, and Japan after 1868. The Soviet Union, while there were some abortive spurts under the Tsars, began a systematic effort only after 1928. As a result these countries have had more time to accumulate capital in agriculture, to diffuse technical knowledge, and to implement modern techniques. With less sown land than in the U.S.S.R., the United States had 4.6 million tractors, 2.9 million motor trucks, and 1.0 million grain combines on farms in 1964, while the Soviet Union only had 1.4 million tractors, 0.9 million motor trucks, and 0.5 million grain combines. Agricultural consumption of electricity in 1962 was 28 billion kilowatt-hours in the U.S., while it was 14.1 billion in the Soviet Union. Commercial fertilizer consumption in 1963 was 62 pounds per acre in the United States and 15 pounds in the Soviet Union.[23] While Soviet emphasis on industry accounts for part of the disparity, time is still the most important factor. Thus, even though Soviet agriculture is progressing, it still has a long headstart to overcome.

*Soil and Climatic Conditions.* While mechanical equipment and fertilizer can do wonders for agriculture, geography is still the most important single determinant of relative productivity between countries. The richest Soviet land, the Ukraine, lies along the same parallel that divides Montana and North Dakota from the Prairie Provinces of Canada. In a pamphlet on Soviet agriculture, the United States Department of Agriculture stated that "although the Soviet Union is one of the leading agricultural countries of the world, much of its land is not suitable for farming. Agriculture is confined largely to a heartland represented by a so-called 'fertile triangle.' . . . But even in the fertile triangle there are important climatic limitations on agriculture. Much of the triangle is characterized by a continental semiarid climate similar to that of the spring wheat region of the Prairie Provinces of Canada and the Dakotas of the United States."[24]

Johnson makes the point that "in themselves, differences in national average yields of various crops or trends in national yields, do

23. U.S. Congress, *Current Economic Indicators for the U.S.S.R.,* p. 56.
24. U.S. Department of Agriculture, *Soviet Agriculture Today: Report of 1963 Agriculture Exchange Delegation,* Foreign Agricultural Report No. 13 (Washington: Government Printing Office, December, 1963), p. 2. Exactly the same point is made by Naum Jasny in discussing "the legend of the vast Russian land resources" when he argues that "very limited natural resources in relation to population constitute one of the major reasons for the small progress made by Soviet agriculture since World War I." Jasny, *The Socialized Agriculture of the U.S.S.R.,* pp. 103, 132.

not indicate either comparative performances of the two agricultures or the potentialities for yield increases of the lower yielding areas. Climatic and soil conditions are dramatically different in certain instances, especially for grains, and cotton and sugar beets are grown under quite different conditions in the two countries."[25]

Because of the importance of grain in both countries, it is pertinent to compare yields in the Soviet Union with geographically similar areas in the United States. North Dakota, South Dakota, Nebraska, Montana, and Wyoming in the United States and the Prairie Provinces of Canada are the most climatically comparable areas.[26] In one respect these areas are not comparable with the Soviet Union. Since these low yielding areas are not the only source of grain supply for Canada and the United States, a large portion of the land can be left fallow in any one year. This cannot be done in the Soviet Union. This, in itself, will favor higher yields in these U.S. and Canadian areas.

Three of these states (North Dakota, South Dakota, and Nebraska) compare climatically quite closely with about half of the total Soviet grain area. The major difference is that in the eastern parts of Nebraska and South Dakota corn can be grown reasonably well, and corn land makes up about 30 per cent of the area sown to grain. Table III-8 presents a comparison between the U.S.S.R. and the relevant U.S. and Canadian areas.

The comparison in Table III-8 of yields in the five states and the prairie provinces with yields in the Soviet Union indicates ". . . that grain yields in that country are at reasonable levels."[27] Given these geographical and climatic limitations Soviet agriculture seems to have performed reasonably well.

*Excesses of the Collectivization Drive.* Collectivization did have one major negative effect on Soviet agriculture. The attempt to go too far too fast led to resistance by the Russian peasant, particularly by the livestock owning kulaks, and resulted in a massive slaughter of livestock (not to mention people). Between 1928 and 1933 the

25. D. Gale Johnson, "Agricultural Production," in *Economic Trends in the Soviet Union*, eds. Bergson and Kuznets, p. 225.

26. *Ibid.*, pp. 225-27. Also, D. Gale Johnson, *Climatic and Crop Analogies for the Soviet Union: A Study of the Possibilities of Increasing Grain Yields*, Research Paper No. 5716 (University of Chicago Office of Agricultural Economics, December 16, 1957).

27. Johnson, "Agricultural Production," in *Economic Trends in the Soviet Union*, eds. Bergson and Kuznets, p. 226.

*TABLE III-8*

Grain Yields of the U.S.A. and Canada, 1945-1954 Compared
with the U.S.S.R., 1954-1959

|  | Grain yields (centners per hectare) | U.S.S.R. as a per cent of U.S. |
|---|---|---|
| U.S.A. AND CANADA: | | |
| Five states and prairie provinces: | | |
| Wheat, oats, and barley | 11.2 | 86.6 |
| PRAIRIE PROVINCES: | | |
| Wheat, oats, and barley | 12.7 | 76.4 |
| Wheat, oats, and barley including summer fallow | 8.4 | 115.5 |
| NORTH DAKOTA, SOUTH DAKOTA, AND NEBRASKA: | | |
| Wheat, oats, and barley | 9.8 | 99.0 |
| U.S.S.R., all grains | 9.7 | — |

Source:

Johnson, "Agricultural Production," in *Economic Trends in the Soviet Union*, eds. Bergson and Kuznets, pp. 223, 226.

number of horses fell from 33.4 to 14.9 million, of cattle from 70.4 to 33.7 million, and of sheep and goats from 145.9 to 41.8 million.[28] Collectivization was carried out by urban activists who were ignorant of rural life and unsympathetic to the peasants. The process was a crude improvisation. Even the organizational pattern of a collective farm was unclear. The decision to collectivize all livestock, soon reversed, led to the mass slaughter of animals by the peasants. The decision to collectivize all livestock was a costly mistake—a mistake, needless to say, that need not be repeated. As Alec Nove has remarked:

Chinese collectivization was altogether smoother and encountered much less resistance possibly because the peasants were 'softened up' by earlier measures of loose cooperation, or because of more effective Party organization, or because the peasant attitude to the Communists was less unfavourable; and also because the principal domestic animal, the pig, was left in private hands at this stage. The Chinese were able to avoid mass slaughter of livestock and famine in carrying through full-

28. Jasny, *The Socialized Agriculture of the U.S.S.R.*, p. 324.

scale collectivization in 1955-56. In fact, there appears to have been no appreciable effect on production.[29]

Thus, there is nothing inherent in collectivization that requires a repetition of the originally disastrous results that occurred in the Soviet Union. A country that looks to Soviet agricultural strategy as a model need not repeat all of the mistakes made by the Soviet Union. However, agriculture in the Soviet Union was adversely affected. The slaughter of livestock meant that much of the mechanization of the 1930's merely went to replace work animals. As a result *net* investment in agriculture was sharply lowered compared to *gross* investment. In addition the loss of livestock led to a large reduction of fertilizer available for crops. Also the bungling and brutality of collectivization probably had severe disincentive effects.[30]

*Incentives.* The question of incentives must be considered in any analysis of the collective farm system. This is a difficult subject because there is so little factual information available. Usually a number of arguments are mixed together when incentives are discussed. The first argument centers on the role of monetary incentives. As long as wage differentials (in collective farming, different numbers of workdays earned for different tasks) exist, then monetary incentives exist. Monetary incentives for industrial workers do not seem to have been any less efficient in the Soviet countries than in capitalist ones.

In agriculture, however, prices paid by the state for the required deliveries of the collective farms have been far below equilibrium prices, and often even have been below the cost of production. The crops were then sold in state retail stores at much higher prices. This price difference was one of the major sources of capital accumulation in the Soviet Union. The price structure, however, has had a disincentive effect on the collective farm workers, particularly since they could sell the produce (or at least a part of it) from their private plots at free market prices. Hence, there was an incentive to

29. Nove, "Collectivization of Agriculture in Russia and China," in *Symposium on Economic Problems of the Far East*, p. 19. When the eastern European countries encountered resistance against collectivization, they did not force it through the way the Russians did. They would halt for a while and then start again later. Poland and Yugoslavia still have not collectivized a majority of the farms.

30. A halfway democratic socialist regime, unencumbered by Communist dogmatism, could probably avoid these actions more easily. The tragic destruction of human life that occurred in collectivization will be discussed in chap. VI.

minimize effort on the collective farm lands and to maximize effort on the private plots. Higher prices for the required deliveries would have reduced this disincentive effect. While this would have reduced the original capital contribution of agriculture to development, over a longer period a larger annual agricultural production might have been obtained.

The second argument relating to incentives concerns the role of private property. It is sometimes argued that it is because the individual plots are privately owned that collective farm workers expend more effort on them. There is no evidence to sustain this view, while there is evidence to support the importance of price differentials between sales to the state and in the collective farm market. This is the view implied, for instance, by Arcadius Kahan when he states that "the collective farm system by itself is mostly 'neutral' with regard to incentive policies."[31]

The problem with analyzing the importance of private property is the impossibility of separating out other factors. Comparisons between capitalist and socialist countries are possible if conditions are the same. Usually they are not. Thus, differences in capital endowments, fertility of soil, cultural receptiveness to change, and general level of development make it almost impossible to measure the efficiency of private property relative to the collective farm system.

There are enough bits and pieces of evidence to cast reasonable doubt upon the importance of private property. What accounts for the fact that, in 1962, milk yields per cow were 10,320 pounds in California, 5,990 pounds in Montana, and 3,780 pounds in Mississippi?[32] Dairy farms in California are typically large scale "factories in the fields" while in Mississippi individual farm ownership is more important. Differences in capital endowments and technology probably account for most of the difference. Or, again, why were the average wheat yields per acre, in 1955-59, 22.3 bushels in the United States, 58.8 bushels in Denmark, 43.4 bushels in East Germany, 30.0 bushels in Czechoslovakia, and 16.2 bushels in Rumania?[33] Differences in climate, soils, capital equipment, and technology must be the major causes. In the Soviet Union, in 1959, milk yield per cow was 2,315 kilograms on state farms, 2,004 kilograms on col-

31. Kahan, "The Collective Farm System in Russia," in *Agriculture in Economic Development,* eds. Eicher and Witt, p. 254.

32. U.S. Department of Agriculture, *Agriculture Statistics: 1964* (Washington: Government Printing Office, 1964), p. 380.

33. *Ibid.,* pp. 5-6.

lective farms, and 1,600 kilograms for privately owned cows.[34] In Yugoslavia, the average yield of corn per hectare on private farms in 1959 was 23 quintals and on socialist farms it was 50 quintals. In 1961, the wheat yield on private farms was 12.9 quintals per hectare and 30.5 quintals on socialist farms.[35] However, the socialist farms in Yugoslavia occupy a large share of the more productive land area of the country.

There seems to be no evidence that the collective farm system itself has disincentive effects. Particular policies, such as low delivery prices, probably are the major causes of existing disincentives.

*Differential Development Strategies.* The Soviet strategy of using agriculture primarily to aid industrial development meant that agricultural development per se was given low priority. This is another major reason for Soviet agriculture's relative backwardness.

The main reasons for the relative backwardness of Soviet agriculture in comparison with the United States can be summed up by the statement of Alec Nove: "Soviet soil is, on average, less naturally fertile; the climate is very much less favorable, the risk of drought and frost damage much greater; there is a much greater density of rural population in relation to the area of cultivatable land, and it was scarcely possible to shift peasants into non-agricultural employment faster than was in fact done. One might also take the human situation into account; the Russian peasant is not an American farmer, and a large proportion of the Soviet labour force consists of women."[36]

In addition, Naum Jasny points out a strong sociological limitation: "Serfdom in Russia ceased to exist in 1861, two years before the emancipation of the slaves was proclaimed in the United States. . . . Where would the agriculture of the U.S. be now, had it depended entirely for its advancement on the South? . . . The situation in Russia was more unfavorable."[37]

34. Johnson, "Agricultural Production," in *Economic Trends in the Soviet Union*, eds. Bergson and Kuznets, p. 232.

35. Earl R. Long, "Agronomic Problems of Southeastern Europe," *Soviet Agriculture and Peasant Affairs*, ed. Roy D. Laird (Lawrence: University of Kansas Press, 1963), pp. 196-97.

36. Alec Nove, *The Soviet Economy* (New York: Frederick A. Praeger, Inc., 1961), pp. 297-98. The reason for the disproportionate share of women in the agricultural labor force is because of the large number of male peasants killed in World War II.

37. Jasny, *The Socialized Agriculture of the U.S.S.R.*, p. 133.

CONCLUSION

In spite of the many difficulties noted above, Soviet agricultural strategy succeeded in fulfilling its role in the development process and facilitated the construction of a modern industrial economy. Collectivization increased output per man, thus releasing labor for industry and rural capital formation projects. Collectivization also facilitated the collection of the agricultural surplus and its allocation to the industrial and export sectors. In this way, Soviet agriculture has been a success when evaluated in terms of its assigned development goals. Of course, as the Soviet economy approached maturity in the 1950's, this agricultural strategy became less and less appropriate.

# IV. INDUSTRIAL INSTITUTIONS AND POLICY

The institutions characteristic of the Soviet model include collectivized agriculture, publicly owned enterprises, comprehensive central planning, centralized distribution of essential materials and capital goods, and a system of administrative controls and pressures on enterprises, in addition to incentives, to ensure compliance with the plan. Collectivization was treated in the previous chapter. This chapter will concentrate on industrial institutions.

## THE ROLE OF PUBLIC OWNERSHIP

Following the 1917 Revolution most productive property in industry, trade, finance, and transportation was nationalized on a piece-meal basis during the period of War Communism (1917-21). During the period of the New Economic Policy (1921-28) most retail and wholesale trade and small business firms were returned to private control. With the adoption of the First Five-Year Plan in 1928, public ownership and control were reasserted.

Expropriation, with or without compensation, is not a feature peculiar to the Soviet model. Extra-legal transfer of productive property has been used in most countries at one time or another. Private property in land was established in England by the enclosure movement. In the United States after the American Revolution, the property of "loyalists" was expropriated and sold. The tribal lands of the American Indians were consistently expropriated throughout the eighteenth and nineteenth century. The somewhat peculiar feature of the Soviet model is the expropriation from individuals for public ownership and use.

In the Soviet Union a large share of the income earned by the previous owners on the nationalized property had not been productively reinvested. Rather it had been used for luxury consumption and investment abroad. After nationalization the Soviets used the net income from the property largely for developmental investment.

Thus, nationalization increased the size of the actual social surplus. In addition, it stopped the outflow of profits being repatriated by foreign companies on their investments in Russia. As a consequence, it was possible to increase the rate of investment. Many underdeveloped countries with large property incomes and low investment rates could possibly learn a lesson from the Soviet experience.[1]

Bronfenbrenner points out one major problem of expropriation.[2] Damage to property during a revolutionary upheaval (if there is one), exodus of trained technicians and managers, and lack of allocative machinery in a socialized economy may make public ownership less efficient than private. There is no denying the first two parts of the problem. However, this writer agrees with Bronfenbrenner that over any reasonable period of time, the increased investment rate possible after expropriation will more than cover these losses. In regard to the possible loss in allocative efficiency, both the present chapter and Chapter V consider this problem in detail.

There are a number of other problems connected with the expropriation and nationalization of productive property. The Soviets did not, but should compensation be paid for expropriated property? If so, how much? If compensation is paid at the owner's estimated market value, the state's gain from expropriation will be considerably reduced.[3] If nothing or a nominal compensation is paid, there is the

1. An indication of the amount of national income which would be affected by expropriation is given by the following United Nations' figures. In Brazil (1960), property income accounted for 52 per cent of the total national income, in Ceylon (1962), 47 per cent, in Colombia (1961), 54 per cent, in Jordan (1959), 58 per cent, in South Korea (1962), 58 per cent, in Peru (1960), 55 per cent, and in the Philippines (1962), 55 per cent. The top 5 per cent of the income receivers received 30.7 per cent of the personal income in Venezuela (1957), 31.0 per cent in Ceylon (1952-53), 65.3 per cent in Rhodesia (1946), and 50.9 per cent in Kenya (1949). That part of these incomes not used for necessary consumption or productive investment would be made available for developmental investment by nationalization. United Nations, Department of Economic and Social Affairs, *Statistical Yearbook, 1963* (New York: United Nations, 1964), pp. 530-33; United Nations, *Economic Development of Latin America in the Post-War Period* (New York: United Nations, 1964), p. 73; and Simon Kuznets, "Quantitative Aspects of the Economic Growth of Nations: Distribution of Income by Size," *Economic Development and Cultural Change*, Vol. XI, No. 2, Part II (January, 1963), p. 13.

2. M. Bronfenbrenner, "The Appeal of Confiscation in Economic Development," *Economic Development and Cultural Change*, Vol. III, No. 3 (April, 1955), pp. 201-18.

3. The American occupation authorities partially expropriated land in the Japanese agrarian reform by paying 1939 market prices in greatly inflated postwar currency.

danger that expropriation will greatly increase domestic and international hostility. This is particularly true if the expropriated property is foreign owned. Therefore, the gains discussed above must be weighed against the losses of future foreign investment and foreign aid, and against the possibility of political, economic, and military sanctions.

The loss of foreign aid and foreign investment may not, however, outweigh the gains of nationalization. To date foreign aid has been insufficient to materially aid more than a few countries.

The efficacy of foreign investment is measured by the net inflow of capital it generates and the resultant "spread" or "backwash" effects. Between 1950 and 1964 the inflow of direct foreign investment from the United States amounted to $20.5 billion. The outflow of repatriated profits transferred to the United States during the same period amounted to $33.1 billion. Thus, there was an actual net outflow from the countries invested in to the United States of $12.6 billion. Table IV-1 breaks down the same data for underdeveloped and developed countries as a whole.[4] For the period 1950-64, there was a net outflow from the underdeveloped countries to the United States of $15.4 billion.

In straight quantitative terms, therefore, the loss of foreign investment may not be of major significance. In fact it might be a net gain. However, there are still the "spread" and "backwash" effects to be considered. If foreign investment "spread" its effects throughout the underdeveloped country's domestic economy, there would definitely be a net gain. Economists such as Hans Singer and Gunnar Myrdal have argued that this has not happened, instead backwash effects have predominated.[5] As Table IV-2 shows, most direct foreign investment in underdeveloped areas is in export oriented industries,[6] and these industries have never become a part of the internal eco-

4. Included in the developed country category are the United States, Canada, Europe, Oceania, Japan, and the Union of South Africa. All other areas are counted as underdeveloped.

5. H. W. Singer, "The Distribution of Gains Between Investing and Borrowing Countries," *American Economic Review*, Vol. XL, No. 2 (May, 1950), pp. 473-85; and Gunnar Myrdal, *Economic Theory and Underdeveloped Regions* (London: Gerald Duckworth & Co., Ltd., 1957).

6. A regional breakdown shows that 53 per cent of all U.S. direct investment in Latin America is in mining and petroleum. For Africa, it is 72 per cent and for Asia, 73 per cent. Other investments, such as those in plantation agriculture, are also export biased. See U.S. Bureau of the Census, *Statistical Abstract of the United States, 1963* (Washington: Government Printing Office, 1965), p. 856.

nomic structure except in the purely geographical and physical sense. Economically speaking, they have been really an extension of the economies of the more developed investing countries. The major secondary multiplier effects have taken place not in the underdeveloped country where the investment is physically located but in the developed countries from which the investment has come. In this sense foreign investment in export oriented industries should be considered as a form of "domestic" investment by the developed countries.

Because of its concentration in export industries, foreign investment has not significantly contributed to "widening the market" in underdeveloped areas. Because extractive industries often have a high capital/labor ratio there has been little impact on factor markets. The investing companies bring in their own skilled labor and technicians and thus have little impact on the domestic labor market.

*TABLE IV-1*

*U.S. Direct Investments and Income Receipts from Direct Investments: 1950-1964 (Millions of Dollars)*

| Area | Total U.S. direct investment in area (1964) | Inflow of capital to area (1950-1964) | Outflow of income transferred to United States (1950-1964) | Net inflow (+) or outflow (−) to/ from the area (1950-1964) |
|---|---|---|---|---|
| Underdeveloped countries | $13,951 | $ 6,132 | $21,506 | −$15,374 |
| Developed countries | 30,392 | 14,325 | 11,596 | + 2,729 |
| Total | $44,343 | $20,457 | $33,102 | −$12,645 |

Sources:

U.S. Department of Commerce, Bureau of Business Economics, *Balance of Payments Statistical Supplement: A Supplement to the Survey of Current Business* (Rev. ed.; Washington: Government Printing Office, 1963), pp. 176-77, 184-87. Samuel Pizer and Frederick Cutler, "U.S. International Investments," *Survey of Current Business*, Vol. 43, No. 8 (August, 1963), pp. 18-19. Samuel Pizer and Frederick Cutler, "Foreign Investment in 1963-64," *Survey of Current Business*, Vol. 44, No. 8 (August, 1964), pp. 10-11. Samuel Pizer and Frederick Cutler, "Foreign Investment, 1964-65," *Survey of Current Business*, Vol. 45, No. 9 (September, 1965), pp. 24-25.

TABLE IV-2

The Distribution of United States Private Direct
Foreign Investments: 1962 (Millions of Dollars)

| Item and area | Total | Mining and smelting | Petroleum | Manu-facturing | Other |
|---|---|---|---|---|---|
| Invested Capital: (Book value on 12/31/62) | | | | | |
| Underdeveloped | $12,547 | $ 1,551 | $ 6,032 | $ 2,183 | $ 2,781 |
| Developed | 24,598 | 1,632 | 6,629 | 11,029 | 5,308 |
| Earnings: | | | | | |
| Underdeveloped | 2,219 | 252 | 1,476 | 212 | 279 |
| Developed | 2,026 | 115 | 240 | 1,098 | 573 |
| Income repatriated: | | | | | |
| Underdeveloped | 1,883 | 241 | 1,405 | 100 | 137 |
| Developed | 1,167 | 73 | 173 | 641 | 280 |
| Profit rate: | | | | | |
| Underdeveloped | 17.8 | 16.3 | 23.3 | 9.6 | 10.0 |
| Developed | 8.2 | 7.2 | 3.6 | 10.0 | 10.8 |

Source:
See Table IV-1.

In Venezuela, petroleum accounts for over 90 per cent of exports but the oil industry employs only 2 per cent of the labor force.[7] In the Middle East, less than 5 per cent of the oil revenue is paid out in wages.[8] Quite often the foreign companies maintain stores for their workers that are largely stocked from abroad.[9] Commenting on the Anglo-Iranian Company's investment policy, Eugene Staley reported that ". . . in its years of operation in Iran it had little impact on the day to day economic life of the bulk of the Iranian people, who continued to eke out a scanty subsistence by a primitive agriculture under a system of near serfdom." And he added: "The Arabian-American Oil Company in Saudi Arabia is another instance."[10]

7. Ragnar Nurkse, *Problems of Capital Formation in Underdeveloped Countries* (Oxford: Basil Blackwell, 1958), p. 23.
8. C. E. Rollins, "Mineral Development and Economic Growth," *Social Research*, XXIII (October, 1956), 253-80.
9. *Ibid.*
10. Eugene Staley, *The Future of Underdeveloped Countries: Political*

All of this does not mean that foreign investment can never be a great aid for economic development. However, to date it has not, except where people accompanied the capital in opening new lands, as in Canada, Australia, and the United States. Singer takes the position that "all we can say is that the process of traditional investment taken by itself seems to have been insufficient to initiate domestic development, unless it appeared in the form of migration of persons."[11]

The major problem of utilizing foreign investment as a development aid is that the import of private capital requires the creation of what is known as a "favorable investment climate." This is one in which foreign capital would be relatively free of taxes, where there would be unrestricted repatriation of profits and government guarantees against nationalization, and the possibility of obtaining profits greater than in the investing country. These conditions, however, might conflict with planned economic development.

The above discussion in no way implies that the Soviet example should be slavishly imitated. Indeed, the Soviets made many mistakes. The Soviet Union seems to have been led by a dogmatic theory of socialism to seize all property—even in handicraft industry and petty trade. The state was in no position to take over and operate these activities. Thus, in the Soviet Union, the decline in production of private handicrafts resulted in a net loss to the economy.[12] An underdeveloped country today should carefully investigate the degree of nationalization that best suits its particular conditions. It is doubtful that an a priori determination can be made of the optimum extent of nationalization.

One key factor in determining the extent of public ownership is the requirement of central planning. In the Soviet Union, public ownership enabled productive resources to be concentrated on key development goals. As long as ownership of the bulk of productive property is in the hands of private individuals or corporations, governmental policy can be obstructed and frustrated by private decision

---

*Implications of Economic Development* (New York: Harper and Brothers, 1954), p. 288.

11. Singer, "The Distribution of Gains Between Investing and Borrowing Countries," p. 477.

12. "There are certain typically Communist irrationalities. One is the virtual suppression of individual small handicrafts, which can be a valuable source of national wealth." Alec Nove, "The Soviet Model and Under-Developed Countries," *International Affairs*, Vol. 37, No. 1 (January, 1961), p. 35.

making. This is particularly a problem when public development policy does not coincide with short-run profit maximizing decisions of private individuals. Public ownership to the extent existing in the Soviet Union is unnecessary to gain the full benefits of central planning.[13]

CENTRAL PLANNING

For several reasons, the process of industrialization and economic development was facilitated in the Soviet Union by the centralized disposal of economic resources. All of the country's resources were concentrated on certain objectives and their dissipation on other objectives, not conducive to rapid industrialization, was avoided. The lack and weakness of industrial cadres made it desirable to concentrate the available talent on high priority objectives. Thus, in the Soviet Union, planning in the early stages of development was characterized by administrative management and administrative allocation of resources on the basis of priorities centrally established. The Soviet model in the early stages of the development process can be best described as a *"sui generis* war economy."[14]

During World War I and even more so during World War II, capitalist countries used war economy methods. Resources were concentrated towards the one basic objective of producing war materials. Resources were centrally allocated to prevent leakages to production not connected with the prosecution of the war. Essential consumer goods were rationed. The production of consumer durables such as automobiles and refrigerators was prohibited. The average work week was lengthened. Patriotic appeals were used to maintain labor productivity and discipline. The share of consumption in gross national product in the United States declined from 75.4 per cent in 1940 to 53.9 per cent in 1944.[15]

These same features characterized the Soviet economy during its war on economic underdevelopment. It is somewhat strange that

13. The late Oskar Lange argued that central planning ". . . is made possible by the existence in the economy of a large socialist sector which controls . . . the 'commanding heights' of economic life. This is the minimum requirement of establishing a planned economy." Oskar Lange, "Role of Planning in Socialist Economy," in *Problems of Political Economy of Socialism*, ed. Oskar Lange (New Delhi: Peoples Publishing House, 1962), p. 16.

14. *Ibid.*, p. 18.

15. U.S. Congress, Joint Economic Committee, *Soviet Economic Growth: A Comparison with the United States*, 85th Cong., 1st Sess., 1957, p. 127.

Western economists who applauded war economy methods in World War II do not understand their analogous use in the Soviet Union's industrialization and by extension in underdeveloped countries today.

A major advantage of public ownership and central planning in the Soviet Union was its ability to overcome Nurkse's famous "vicious circle of poverty."

On the supply side, there is the small capacity to save, resulting from the low level of real income. The low level of real income is a reflection of low productivity, which in its turn is due largely to the lack of capital. The lack of capital is a result of the small capacity to save, and so the circle is complete.

On the demand side, the inducement to invest may be low because of the small buying power of the people, which is due to their small real income, which again is due to low productivity. The low level of productivity, however, is a result of the small amount of capital used in production, which in its turn may be caused at least partly by the small inducement to invest.[16]

The Soviet Union was able to break the circle on the supply side (i.e., raise the savings rate) because of its ability to collect the economic surplus from the agricultural sector and its control over the division between consumption and investment in the industrial sector.[17] Public ownership allowed the former luxury consumption from property income to be converted into savings for investment purposes. The ability of central planning to concentrate on the one goal of development permitted the Soviet Union to channel savings and thus resources into the most productive purposes and to reduce the proportion of savings going into (from the point of view of rapid growth) unproductive investment.

The demand side of the problem was also controlled by central planning in the Soviet Union. Since long-range development, not short-run profits, was the goal, finding buyers for what was produced did not exist. The state, through central planning, created the necessary demand by its decision to produce. In making decisions about the allocation of resources between the production of capital goods or consumer goods, the state made *ipso facto* a savings decision. In real terms both investment and savings must refer to the difference

16. Nurkse, *Problems of Capital Formation in Underdeveloped Countries,* pp. 4-5.

17. A planned economy is, of course, still limited in raising the savings rate by the minimum standard of living necessary to maintain the efficiency and morale of the agricultural and industrial work force.

between total production and consumer goods production. Thus, there is an identity of savings decisions and investment decisions.[18]

*External Economies.* A closely related problem is that of external economies.[19] If an economy is far from equilibrium, current market prices and profit maximization are poor signals for investment decisions. In neo-classical terms, equilibrium occurs when firms (and the industry) are at the bottom of their long-run cost curves, that is, where there are constant or decreasing returns to scale. In addition, *ex ante* co-ordination of investment decisions is excluded. In underdeveloped countries such as the Soviet Union in the 1930's, firms (and industries) are likely to be on an increasing returns section of the cost curve. And since they are far from the technological frontier, the cost curves will shift downward over time. The presence of potential external economies makes preplanned co-ordination among development projects highly desirable. Moreover, in many development schemes, there exists such a high degree of physical interdependence among different projects that the productivity of any one cannot be maximized in isolation. Multipurpose river basin planning, hydroelectricity generation, organization of an iron and steel industry, and the development of chemicals are examples of this nature. The individual project within such a scheme can seldom be examined by itself and in estimating its operational efficiency it has to be jointly considered with its related units.

In underdeveloped countries, private marginal productivity of

18. The mechanisms necessary to ensure this result will be discussed in a later section of this chapter. There are certain problems. The amount of real investment is susceptible to market influence if enterprise managers have discretion as to the size of inventories they hold, and even under the most centralized planning they are bound to have considerable *de facto* discretion. See Maurice Dobb, *Soviet Economic Development Since 1917* (London: Routledge & Kegan Paul Ltd., 1960), pp. 356, 382; and R. W. Davies, *The Development of the Soviet Budgetary System* (Cambridge: Cambridge University Press, 1958), pp. 158, 231.

19. At this point, external economies can be considered the divergence between private profit and public benefit. See Tibor Scitovsky, "Two Concepts of External Economies," *The Economics of Underdevelopment*, eds. A. N. Agarwala and S. P. Singh (Oxford: Oxford University Press, 1958), pp. 295-308; P. N. Rosenstein-Rodan, "Problems of Industrialization of Eastern and South-Eastern Europe," *The Economics of Underdevelopment*, pp. 245-56; Maurice Dobb, *An Essay on Economic Growth and Planning* (London: Routledge & Kegan Paul, Ltd., 1960), pp. 5-13; and Hla Myint, *The Economics of the Developing Countries* (New York: Frederick A. Praeger, Inc., 1964), pp. 118-25.

capital frequently falls short of its social marginal productivity.[20] In developed economies, external economies of various industries support each other and thus help to bridge the gap between private and social productivity. Lack of basic industrial structures and of social overhead capital does not permit the capture of potential external economies in underdeveloped countries. The net productivity of capital, therefore, does not attain a sufficiently high level to stimulate productive private investment. Thus, since a modern industrial structure is highly interdependent, any particular investment project, by itself, frequently appears uneconomic, unless viewed in the perspective of interrelated growth of other firms and industries. Since "the lifetime of equipment is long . . . the investor's foresight is likely to be more imperfect than that of the buyer and seller or of the producer. The individual investor's risk may be higher than that confronting an over-all investment program."[21] The volume and cost of production have to be computed on the basis of the anticipated future and since each project has to be so viewed, the plans for any one project cannot be finished until the plans for all the others are known. The price system fails in these computations because the external economies of individual projects get interrelated and the supply prices depend upon the levels of outputs, which in turn are related to the over-all input requirements of the entire development scheme. It is important to remember that when the economy is far from equilibrium, present prices are poor indicators of future prices, and there is no guarantee that the *sequence* of investment dictated by the market will maximize the rate of growth toward equilibrium. To promote co-ordinated industrial expansion, therefore, the perspective of growth must be known well in advance. This is what the state, through central planning, provided in the Soviet Union.

The most important question is where most of the external economies are to be found. In the present context, external economies can be classified into two types—horizontal external economies of demand and vertical externalities of forward and backward linkage. These two types of external economies lie at the heart of both the debate over balanced growth versus unbalanced growth and the

20. See Alfred E. Kahn, "Investment Criteria in Development Programs," *Quarterly Journal of Economics*, LXV (February, 1951), 38-61; and Hollis B. Chenery, "The Application of Investment Criteria," *Quarterly Journal of Economics*, LXVII (February, 1953), 76-96.

21. P. N. Rosenstein-Rodan, "The Flaw in the Mechanism of Market Forces," *Leading Issues in Development Economics*, ed. Gerald M. Meier (New York: Oxford University Press, 1964), p. 417.

question of investment criteria. As such they will be considered in detail in Chapter V when the strategy of development in the Soviet model is discussed. For now it is enough to say that because of interdependence of demand and of industries a system of central planning more easily provides for the realization of potential external economies.[22] Individual investors will be less motivated to do so because the benefits of external economies accrue to society as a whole, or at least to some members of it, without bringing a direct return to the investor that can be anticipated by using profit maximization and current prices as criteria.

PLANNING PROCEDURES AND MECHANISMS IN THE SOVIET UNION

The details of Soviet planning are of little concern in the context of this study, and thus only the basic principles and their significance for economic development will be considered here.[23] Variations and changes of a minor nature in recent years are not taken into consideration, nor are the most recent reforms. Soviet planning utilizes a combination of administrative and market mechanisms. All levels of the Soviet hierarchy, from Gosplan down to the firm, participate in drawing up the plan. The Council of Ministers, under instructions of the party, draws up very general goals, such as the target increase in industrial production and agricultural production, the level of investment expenditures, and the volume of consumer goods sales. Through a trial and error balancing process Gosplan works out the implications for each major sector of the economy. The highly aggregative requirements for output, labor force, materials, investment, and productivity increases are then channeled down the proper units

22. ". . . complete integration of all industries would be necessary to eliminate all divergence between private profit and public benefit." Scitovsky, "Two Concepts of External Economies," p. 305. And, it is necessary that the ". . . whole of the industry to be created is to be treated and planned like one huge firm or trust." Rosenstein-Rodan, "Problems of Industrialization of Eastern and South-Eastern Europe," p. 248.

23. This section draws upon the following sources: Herbert A. Levine, "The Centralized Planning of Supply in Soviet Industry," *Comparisons of the United States and Soviet Economies*, U.S. Congress, Joint Economic Committee, 86th Cong., 1st Sess., 1960, pp. 151-76; Paul A. Baran, "National Economic Planning: The Soviet Experience," in *The Soviet Economy: A Book of Readings*, eds. Morris Bornstein and Daniel Fusfeld (Homewood, Illinois: Richard D. Irwin, Inc., 1962). pp. 69-83; and Franklyn D. Holzman, "Financing Soviet Economic Development," in *The Soviet Economy*, eds. Bornstein and Fusfeld, pp. 145-60.

of the administrative hierarchy, where an increasing amount of detail is added.

In the process of formulating the plan, the central planners concentrate on certain key commodities and sectors. For about 1,500 crucial commodities the planners spell out in the plan their output and disposition in physical terms. The method of "material balances" is used to reconcile the supply and demand for these commodities.[24] This is the heart of the plan. Major commodities and industries such as steel, nonferrous metals, and machine building are handled this way. Other materials and commodities are handled at lower levels, with little interference from above.

The planning process involves constant interaction among the various levels of the administrative hierarchy. Each level passes down limits and directives in regard to the plan to the next lower level, with each lower level further disaggregating these limits and directives and allocating them among its constituent units. Finally, each operating enterprise receives limits and directives for such items as total output, labor force, materials, and investment. There is a great deal of conflict in the process. An enterprise may feel its assignment in the plan is unreasonable unless its output targets are lowered or its input supply increased. In this case it complains to the next higher level, which may in turn complain to the level above it, and so on. Once these conflicts are settled the final version of the aggregative plan is prepared and accepted and the final limits and directives are again passed down the line until each enterprise has its individual plan.

Flexibility is built into this physical plan in two ways. The higher levels of the planning hierarchy can hold in reserve some of the inputs allocated to them, to meet emergencies wherever they arise in their subordinate units. This is akin to the strategic reserves than an army commander holds in readiness. Second is the system of priorities built into the system. If during the plan period the actual increases in labor force, productivity, and supply materials fall short of the planned amounts and the entire plan cannot be fulfilled, then the error is corrected *ex post* by diverting resources from low priority (usually the consumer goods sector) to high priority objectives.

One outcome of this planning procedure is that the division of national income between consumption and investment is determined

24. See John M. Montias, "Planning with Material Balances in Soviet Type Economies," *American Economic Review*, Vol. XLIX, No. 5 (December, 1959), pp. 963-85.

by the allocations in the physical plan. The choice of investment projects is also determined primarily by these physical allocations. The rationale of these determinations will be examined in Chapter V when development strategy is discussed.

The physical allocation of resources is reinforced by a system of financial controls designed to ensure financial equilibrium. A system known as "control by the ruble" is used to prevent the individual enterprise from purchasing more than its allocated share of resources. Each enterprise must pay for its supply of resources by bookkeeping transfers from its account with the state bank. The bank, therefore, is able to keep a day-by-day and transaction-by-transaction control over the enterprise. In aggregate terms the role of the financial system is to establish an equilibrium between the value of consumer goods produced and the volume of purchasing power received by households. The planned wholesale price is designed to leave the producer only a small profit above costs. In the wholesale distribution system, however, a heavy excise tax, called the turnover tax, is placed on consumer goods, which raises their retail price well above the wholesale price. By varying the amount of the turnover tax the planners can equate the retail cost of consumer goods production with household purchasing power. The turnover tax and a portion of producer's profits are transferred to the state budget to finance new investment and general government functions.

In attempting to achieve plan fulfillment, administrative pressures are used on enterprises in addition to monetary incentives. Bonuses are paid to enterprises that fulfill or overfulfill their plan. The major problem is what type of indicators should be used to measure success. At an early stage of development this is less important than after a degree of sophistication has been achieved in the economy.[25] Administrative pressures and controls are extensively used to supplement monetary incentives. Gosplan, Gosbank, and the Communist party all have auditors who continually check on the enterprise operations. In addition, the manager of an enterprise faces the possibility of losing his job or even being charged with criminal negligence if he fails to fulfill his planned targets. "Thus it can be said

25. See Alec Nove, "The Problem of 'Success Indicators' in Soviet Industry," *Economica*, Vol. XXV, No. 97 (February, 1958), pp. 1-13; Joseph S. Berliner, *Factory and Manager in the U.S.S.R.* (Cambridge: Harvard University Press, 1967); and Robert W. Campbell, *Soviet Economic Power* (Boston: Houghton Mifflin Co., 1960), pp. 114-44.

without cavil that Soviet managers are highly motivated to try and fulfill the plans which are handed down to them."[26]

While this planning system sounds cumbersome and complex, it was feasible for a relatively simple economy such as the Soviet Union in the 1930's. Because of the very low consumption levels, planning the production of consumer goods was fairly easy. It was the basic necessities that were needed. And since there was a seller's market, the problems of style and variety could be ignored. Also, capital goods were standardized and thus more susceptible to planning. In this context, Robert Campbell has pointed out that ". . . these features of the Soviet economy are shared by any underdeveloped country embarking on a program of industrialization. As a result, the difficulties of coordination which might make economic planning inappropriate for an economy with high levels of consumption such as ours are less important for the Russians or, by extension, for those underdeveloped countries that might be tempted to choose the Soviet planning approach to industrialization."[27]

None of the above is meant to imply that the implementation of central planning in an underdeveloped country is easy. The economic development literature is filled with reasons why planning is difficult and with examples of poor planning.[28] The paucity of statistical data and the absence of trained personnel to draft and implement a plan are most often cited. In some countries this might make central planning impossible. But in many countries a less ambitious planning system than the Soviets adopted might not be any more difficult or less successful than relying on a private enterprise approach. Also, further study might show that it is the political, eco-

26. Campbell, *Soviet Economic Power*, p. 122.

27. *Ibid.*, p. 98. Professor Spulber points out that although "Soviet policy makers . . . are departing from some of the planning theories and methods of the 1920's . . . other Communist leaders, those of backward China for instance, continue to stick to the old methods of planning, apparently both by conviction and convenience. Perhaps the crude methods of the 1920's are after all better suited to a lower level of development." Nicolas Spulber, *Soviet Strategy for Economic Growth* (Bloomington: Indiana University Press, 1964), p. 129.

28. See W. Arthur Lewis, *Development Planning* (New York: Harper & Row, 1966); Richard L. Meier, *Developmental Planning* (New York: Mc-Graw-Hill Co., 1965); Gerald Sirkin, *The Visible Hand: The Fundamentals of Economic Planning* (New York: McGraw-Hill Co., 1968); W. F. Stolper, *Planning Without Facts: Lessons in Resource Allocation from Nigeria's Development* (Cambridge: Harvard University Press, 1966); and Albert Waterson, *Development Planning* (Baltimore: The Johns Hopkins University Press, 1965).

nomic, and social structure that makes planning so difficult in these nonsocialist underdeveloped countries.

Because the Soviet planning system was developed for use in a backward economy it must be altered as the economy develops and becomes more complex. The Russian economy today seems to have reached such a level of sophistication that these old planning techniques are no longer appropriate. However, since the focus of this study is on the appropriateness of the techniques for the simple economies of underdeveloped countries this is of no concern here.

RESOURCE ALLOCATION AND CENTRAL PLANNING

A persistent criticism levied against the Soviet system of central planning by Western economists is that it leads to a misallocation of resources. It is argued that since there is no market for intermediate goods, no interest charge on capital, and subsidies and taxes are used to arrive at final prices, Soviet prices do not reflect relative scarcities and thus distort resource allocation.

It is true that there are many examples of miscalculation and misallocation in the Soviet Union. However, similar examples of misallocation can be found in every economy, including the United States. No country does a perfect job of allocating resources. The important question is in what country do the fewest misallocations occur. While this writer feels an advanced market economy (not, however, an underdeveloped one) probably allocates resources better than a Soviet-type economy, there is insufficient empirical evidence to give a conclusive answer.

Since empirical proof is not available, Western economists have turned to economic theory to prove the inefficiency of the Soviet system. However, recent advances in welfare economics and particularly the theory of second best have also invalidated this approach. Maximum efficiency is attained when available resources are allocated in such a way as to maximize the particular output mix determined by consumers' perferences (in a market economy) or planners' preferences (in a Soviet-type economy). To achieve this allocation the first order welfare conditions of price equals marginal cost must be fulfilled in *all* markets (there are other conditions but these need not detain us). Further, there is no logical way of determining whether an economy with only one sector failing to attain the price equals marginal cost condition is more efficient in resource allocation than an economy with no sector fulfilling the first order conditions.[29] That is, if any one price does not reflect relative scarcities (i.e., price equals marginal cost) there is no way of theoretically saying that one set of prices is more rational than another. The conclusion from this is that ". . . it is impossible to demonstrate the irrationality —or rationality—of centrally planned economies on the basis of standard welfare economics."[30]

All of the above is concerned with a static welfare analysis of resource allocation. If the problem of resource allocation is placed in the dynamic context of economic development, then an entirely different approach to evaluation is required. In a dynamic setting the questions of external economies and changing resource scarcities become of prime importance.

The Soviet approach to the specific resource allocation problems of investment allocation and choice of production techniques (including factor proportions) will be thoroughly analyzed in Chapter V. For now it is enough to say that their approach centered on the capture of external economies and economizing the obviously scarce factors—capital and skilled labor.

In addition, recognition of constantly changing resource scarcities led to the use of a pricing system that deviated markedly from current resource scarcities. It is worthwhile at this point to analyze the Soviet price system in some detail.

To repeat, almost every Western specialist on Soviet-type economies has argued that the Soviet pricing system is irrational, in the sense that it does not reflect the relative scarcities of resources derived from the structure of planners' preferences. Two important points are made. First, it is argued that Soviet prices do not include an interest rate on capital.[31] While an appropriate interest rate is theoretically determinable, practically it is very difficult. The Soviet use of the "coefficient of relative effectiveness" has been a rough

29. There may not be a satisfactory second-best solution at all or a third-best, fourth-best, or nth-best; and, if there is, the rules for achieving it may be almost impossible to implement.

30. Alastair N. D. McAuley, "Rationality and Central Planning," *Soviet Studies*, Vol. 18, No. 3 (January, 1967), p. 353. For a thorough treatment of resource allocation see E. J. Mishan's "A Survey of Welfare Economics, 1939-1959," and "A Reappraisal of the Principles of Resource Allocation," both in E. J. Mishan, *Welfare Economics* (New York: Random House, 1964), pp. 3-97, 155-83.

31. Soviet adherence to the Marxian labor theory of value did lead them astray in computing costs. A noncommunist regime using the Soviet model would not have to contend with this particular dogma.

substitute.[32] Second, it is argued that Soviet subsidization of some capital goods and taxation of consumer goods distorts present relative scarcities, and, more importantly, the low price of capital relative to the price of labor does so also. However, as seen above, these arguments are not logically valid. Furthermore, in the context of economic development this pricing system might even make good sense.

A planned economy such as the Soviet Union's attempts to secure a co-ordinated set of investment decisions *ex ante*, that is, in advance of any commitment of resources. In a market economy the allocation of investment is the result of the estimates and expectations of independent entrepreneurs, revised in the long-run by *ex post* movements of market prices. The differences between the planned and market approach are important. Current investment changes both productive capacity and employment and thus exercises an important influence upon market prices by changing relative scarcities. Accordingly, the present structure of market prices cannot be used as a sure measure of the future structure of prices or, therefore, of what will be the return on any particular investment project. Kenneth Boulding argues that "there is not the slightest reason . . . to suppose that the equilibrium price set, in the sense of classical or neoclassical equilibrium theory, is the price set which will go with the maximum rate of economic development."[33]

The appropriate price structure will depend on a number of con-

32. The "coefficient of relative effectiveness" (CRE) is given by the formula $e = \dfrac{V^1 - V^2}{K^2 - K^1}$, where $V^1$ and $V^2$ represent the annual operating costs (including depreciation) of two alternative projects producing the same output, and $K^1$ and $K^2$ represent the corresponding capital outlays. Since capital outlays usually vary inversely with operating expenses, $e$ represents the savings in operating expense realized per ruble of additional capital outlay. The choice between two projects depends on whether $e \gtrless E$, where $E$ is some CRE taken as a standard. Thus $K^1V^1$ is chosen if $e < E$; $K^2V^2$ if $e > E$; and the two projects are equally desirable if $e = E$. Another procedure for project selection that has been used involves reformulating the CRE criterion as $\sum_{n=0}^{n} (V_n + K_n)(1 + E)^{-n} = \text{minimum}$. Thus the project chosen must be the one for which total costs are a minimum, and where total costs are the sum of the present values of operating expenses and capital outlays, with $E$ utilized as the rate of discount. See Abram Bergson, *The Economics of Soviet Planning* (New Haven: Yale University Press, 1964), pp. 250-65.

33. Kenneth E. Boulding and Pritam Singh, "The Role of the Price Structure in Economic Development," *American Economic Review*, Vol. LII, No. 2 (May, 1962), pp. 29, 30. See also Jan Tinbergen, *The Design of Development* (Baltimore: The Johns Hopkins Press, 1958), pp. 39-42; and Dobb, *An Essay on Economic Growth and Planning*, pp. 5-8.

siderations. Where there is a divergence between the private and social returns on investment in a particular area due to external economies:

> . . . there is a strong argument for distorting the price structure away from what would be a market equilibrium by deliberately lowering the relative prices and hence discouraging investment in those industries where the external economies or the nonfinancial returns are small, and raising prices and encouraging investment in those industries where the external economies or the nonfinancial returns are large.
> . . . (or) the general principle of the taxation of vice and the subsidization of virtue can be extended to include the taxation of those commodities the production of which we wish to discourage from the point of view of economic development and the subsidization of those the production of which we wish to encourage.[34]

The Soviets accomplished this end by subsidizing strategic materials and industries such as steel, engineering, chemicals, and electrical equipment; and taxing low priority products such as textiles and most consumer goods.[35]

In the context of economic development, "personal consumption should have a low claim on resources, and the static welfare criterion of equating price to marginal cost must recede in the background."[36] This the Soviets have done by imposing high turnover taxes on most consumer goods. Some consumer goods which have significance for development, such as paper which plays an important role in the spread of literacy, are favored.

Soviet pricing policies, therefore, make some sense in a development context. This only means, of course, that Soviet pricing policy has the same logic in a dynamic context that welfare theory has in a static context, and that neither can be proved to lead to an optimum resource allocation.

CENTRAL PLANNING IN SUMMARY

Soviet planning can be summed up by pointing out that it involves the determination by planners of final outputs and strategic inter-

---

34. Boulding and Singh, "The Role of the Price Structure in Economic Development," pp. 29, 33.

35. Subsidizing an industry has the same effect as increasing the price of its output, and, conversely, taxation has the same effect as decreasing price. Also, the effect of subsidization can be achieved by simply taxing some goods less than others. The effect is that some goods are priced below and others above what their relative equilibrium prices would be in a free market.

36. Boulding and Singh, "The Role of the Price Structure in Economic Development," p. 35.

mediate goods in physical terms; direct allocation of resources to desired objectives; reliance on a set of administrative commands concerning investment, outputs, and wage levels reinforced by adjusted prices to help implement the physical plan; utilization of market mechanisms for allocating labor and distributing consumer goods; and rough co-ordination between the physical and monetary balances concerning such macroeconomic magnitudes as investment, income, and consumption expenditures of households.[37]

Spulber summarizes the achievements of the Soviet planning system in promoting economic development:

> The achievement of high levels of capital accumulation by direct allocation of basic intermediate products, such as steel, at the place of production; the allocation of physical resources to the key branches in the quantities and qualities desired; the concentration of efforts integrally and sequentially according to priorities from the first to the next down the line; the introduction of the most advanced technology for the main processes in the leading branches; the continuous prodding of operational management and labor to keep in line—all these contributed to achieving the high defense and industrialization objectives set for the U.S.S.R. by its Communist leadership. These are typical 'war economy' methods; the uniqueness of the Soviet experience consists in the fact that they have never been applied on such a vast scale and for such a long time anywhere else.[38]

Again, it must be emphasized that the early Soviet planning methods may be applicable only for the period when a backward economy is attempting to initiate development. When the economy advances beyond this to the "drive to maturity," more sophisticated methods, involving greater use of monetary incentives, market mechanisms, and mathematical programming, may be necessary.[39]

THE RESULTS OF SOVIET INDUSTRIAL PLANNING

The index of industrial production in the Soviet Union is not reported on a value added basis. Instead, it is an index of gross in-

37. See Nicolas Spulber, *The Soviet Economy* (New York: W. W. Norton & Co., Inc., 1962), pp. 47-50.

38. Spulber, *Soviet Strategy for Economic Growth*, pp. 94-95.

39. See the debate in Harry G. Shaffer (ed.) *The Soviet Economy: A Collection of Western and Soviet Views* (New York: Appleton-Century-Crofts, 1963), pp. 340-421. Also Lange, "Role of Planning in Socialist Economy" in *Problems of Political Economy of Socialism*, ed. Lange, pp. 16-30. Lange's analogy of capitalism as an old fashioned balloon, early socialist planning as an airplane continuously guided by the pilot, and future socialist planning as an airplane operated mainly by an automatic pilot mechanism is interesting and instructive.

dustrial production. Therefore, the index includes a large amount of double-counting. This will not affect a time series index if the amount of vertical integration of enterprises matches the amount of disintegration. The process of industrialization, however, usually means a movement toward greater specialization and, therefore, greater ver-

*TABLE IV-3*

*Average Annual Growth Rates of Industrial Production for the U.S.S.R.*

| | 1928-40 | 1928-55 | 1928/40-1948/55[a] | 1955-65 |
|---|---|---|---|---|
| Official gross index | 15.8% | 11.5% | 16.7% | — |
| Strumilin value added index | 17.4 | 10.1 | 14.7 | |
| Western estimates of value added: | | | | |
| Seton index | 13.6 | 9.7 | 14.0 | — |
| Hodgman index | 12.9 | — | — | — |
| Jasny index | 10.7 | — | — | — |
| Clark index | 10.7 | — | — | — |
| Powell index: 1928-58 | | | | |
| 1928 price weights | 16.1 | 10.1 | 14.0 | — |
| 1937 price weights | 9.8 | 7.4 | 10.2 | — |
| 1950 price weights | 8.4 | 7.0 | 9.7 | — |
| Moorsteen-Kaplan index | 8.4 | 6.8 | 9.7 | — |
| Nutter index | 8.3 | 6.5 | 9.4 | — |
| Joint Economic Committee index-Cohn | — | — | — | 8.3% |

Sources:

TsSU, *Narkhoz, 1963*, p. 110. *Pravda* (January 22, 1960). Campbell, *Soviet Economic Power*, p. 48. N. M. Kaplan and R. H. Moorsteen, "An Index of Soviet Industrial Output," *American Economic Review*, Vol. L, No. 3 (June, 1960), p. 301. Raymond P. Powell, "Industrial Production," *Economic Trends in the Soviet Union*, p. 155. G. Warren Nutter, "The Structure and Growth of Soviet Industry: A Comparison with the United States," *Comparisons of the United States and Soviet Economies*, p. 97. U.S. Congress, Joint Economic Committee, *New Directions in the Soviet Economy*, 89th Cong., 2nd Sess., 1966, p. 282. The Hodgman, Jasny, and Clark indices are taken from Campbell. The Seton index is taken from Kaplan and Moorsteen.

[a] Excludes the war and reconstruction years of 1941-48.

tical disintegration. This has certainly been true in the case of the Soviet Union. Where it is true, a gross index will have an upward bias, over time, relative to a value added index. There is also the familiar index number problem which is important in comparing indices among countries. In addition, Soviet statisticians have not fully corrected for price level changes when entering new products into the index. Thus, their index has a further upward bias because of inflationary prices of new products.[40] For all of these reasons Western economists have reconstructed industrial production indices for the Soviet Union on a value added basis. Table IV-3 presents a number of these attempts along with the official index.

The widely varying results attained by the different investigators is due primarily to the extent of coverage and the weighting systems used. The impact of different weighting systems can be most clearly seen in the three Powell indices. However, even the lowest of these independently constructed indices shows very rapid growth. Which of the indices is the best is difficult to say. Campbell's remark should be kept in mind: ". . . perhaps the wiser course is to view the lowest indexes with a degree of skepticism. If one wants strongly enough to believe that Soviet industrial output has not grown too fast, it is always possible to find a weighting system which gives this conclusion."[41]

Table IV-4 compares industrial growth in the U.S.S.R. with selected other countries. Time periods were chosen wherever possible to correspond with each country's beginning period of industrialization. For the U.S.S.R., both the Seton and the Nutter indices are used. These are the high and low Western estimates of Soviet industrial growth. Even the Nutter index yields a growth rate that exceeds that of every country in Table IV-4 except Japan. The Japanese growth rate, however, is based on a gross index and is, thus, overstated relative to the Soviet rate. If the Japanese index were computed on a value added basis, the growth rate would most likely be somewhat less.[42] If only the "effective" years of 1928-40 and 1948-63 are used in computing the Soviet growth rate, then the disparity with other rates is even more marked. Since the Soviet

40. For all of these problems concerning the Soviet index of gross industrial production, see Campbell, *Soviet Economic Power*, pp. 34-47.

41. *Ibid.*, p. 48.

42. Professor Lockwood details reasons similar to those mentioned in regard to the Soviet index. See W. W. Lockwood, *The Economic Development of Japan* (Princeton: Princeton University Press, 1954), pp. 114-16.

*TABLE IV-4*

*Average Annual Growth Rates of Industrial Production
in the U.S.S.R. and Selected Other Countries*

| Countries and Years | % Growth Rates |
|---|---|
| U.S.S.R.:[a] | |
| 1928-1965: | |
| Seton index | 9.3 |
| Nutter index | 6.9 |
| 1928-1940 and 1948-1965 | |
| (Effective years) | |
| Seton index | 12.3 |
| Nutter index | 9.0 |
| U.S.A.: | |
| 1839-1869 | 5.6 |
| 1869-1899 | 5.5 |
| GREAT BRITAIN: | |
| 1760-1800 | 1.9 |
| 1801/11-1831/41 | 4.7 |
| GERMANY: | |
| 1870-1913 | 4.4 |
| FRANCE: | |
| 1860-1900 | 2.5 |
| SWEDEN: | |
| 1870-1910 | 3.9 |
| 1900-1925/29 | 2.7 |
| JAPAN:[b] | |
| 1905/09-1930/34 | 6.9 |
| MEXICO: | |
| 1940-1960 | 6.2 |

Sources:

Table IV-3. U.S. Bureau of the Census, *Historical Statistics of the United States: Colonial Times to 1957* (Washington: Government Printing Office, 1960), p. 139. Phyllis Deane and W. A. Cole, *British Economic Growth: 1688-1959* (Cambridge: Cambridge University Press, 1964), pp. 78, 170. Surendra J. Patel, "Rates of Industrial Growth in the Last Century, 1860-1958," in *The Experience of Economic Growth*, ed. Barry E. Supple (New York: Random House, 1963), p. 70. W. W. Lockwood, *The Economic Development of Japan* (Princeton: Princeton University Press, 1954), p. 115. Robert L. Bennett, *The Financial Sector and Economic Development: The Mexican Case* (Baltimore: The Johns Hopkins Press, 1965), p. 187.

[a] The growth rates were extended to 1965 by splicing the Joint Economic Committee index to the Seton and Nutter indices.

ᵇ The index is for gross industrial production and is subject to all the limitations mentioned about the Soviet gross index. A value added index would yield a lower growth rate.

index of industrial production only regained the prewar level by 1948, a rate computed over the "effective" years seems the most logical one to use.

The explanation for these high growth rates of industrial production lies in the combination of central planning outlined in this chapter and the strategies of industrial development discussed in the next.

## V. THE SOVIET STRATEGY OF DEVELOPMENT

---

Strategies are ways of using resources in order to attain a given long-run objective. In the Soviet Union the overriding objective has been rapid economic development. As in market economies in wartime, all resources were mobilized and allocated to activities that furthered the attainment of the primary objective. Activities that detracted from that objective were suppressed or neglected.

The atmosphere and terminology during the 1930's was that of a wartime economy—bottlenecks, campaigns, assaults, and victories. As in wartime, mistakes were made and there was a great deal of waste. Economic criteria were often ignored and entire sectors of the economy, mainly the consumer sectors, were neglected.[1] Yet, despite the lack of balance and other shortcomings in Soviet development, significant progress in the transformation of the Soviet economy to a modern economy was made in a very brief period of time.

The main features that distinguished Soviet industrial development strategy may be summarized as follows:[2]

(1) Industry was treated as the leading sector in the development program and investment in agriculture held to the minimum necessary to allow agriculture to provide industry with a growing marketed surplus of agricultural products and an expanding source of labor supply.

(2) A very high investment (and savings) rate was maintained, because of the planners' propensity to discount the future at a low rate.

(3) An unbalanced growth pattern was adopted of allocating a very large share of industrial investment to heavy industry.

1. See Oscar Lange, "The Working Principles of the Soviet Economy," *U.S.S.R. Economy and the War* (New York: Russian Economic Institute, 1943), p. 43.
2. The features selected for examination are those considered to be most broadly characteristic of Soviet industrial development. Many other more specific or less distinctive features are, of necessity, omitted.

76

(4) In choosing among alternative productive techniques, the most advanced technology was utilized, while at the same time, the scarcest inputs—capital and skilled labor—were economized.

(a) A mixed or dual technology was adopted. Advanced Western technology with a high capital-labor ratio was favored in the basic production processes while old-fashioned methods and techniques with a low capital-labor ratio were favored in auxiliary and subsidiary processes.

(b) They utilized multiple shift operation and plants and equipment were typically kept in operation long after they would have been retired in the more advanced countries of the West.

(c) Strong preference was shown for the construction of integrated, large-scale plants, specialized with respect to product and having a high fixed cost to variable cost ratio.

(5) During the industrialization drive heavy emphasis was placed upon vocational and technical training to build up the stock of human capital and the factory itself was used as a major training device.

(6) An import-substitution policy of international trade was adopted.

Certain other aspects of Soviet strategy have been discussed in previous chapters. Soviet attempts to create enthusiasm and release the energies of the population (however abortive) by social change were outlined in Chapter II. The related strategy of forming human capital was also introduced there and will be further elaborated in this chapter. The use of surplus agricultural labor for capital formation was discussed in Chapter III, and the use of administrative measures to ensure plan fulfillment was examined in Chapter IV.

INDUSTRY AS THE LEADING SECTOR IN THE SOVIET DEVELOPMENT
PROGRAM

In the Soviet Union, industry has been treated as the leading sector in the development program. Consequently, investment in agriculture has been held to the minimum necessary to allow agriculture to provide industry with food, raw materials, and labor. Gross investment in agriculture accounted for 16.1 per cent of total gross investment during the period 1928-32, 12.6 per cent during 1933-37, 11.4 per cent during 1938-41, 12.8 per cent during 1946-50, 15.5 per cent during 1951-55, 17.6 per cent in 1956, 16.3 per cent in 1957, 15.8 per cent in 1958, and 15.8 per cent during the period 1959-64.[3] In 1928, at the beginning of industrialization, 49.2 per cent of the net national product originated in agriculture, forestry, and fisheries. By 1958, the share of agriculture in net national product had declined to 22.1 per cent.[4] Agriculture has continuously received, therefore, a smaller share of gross investment than its share of net national product. In addition, agriculture's share in net investment has been much lower. Naum Jasny estimates that up to 1938 net investment was zero, because of the vast decline in livestock, and that half of the prewar investment in agriculture was lost during World War II.[5]

As was demonstrated in Chapter III, Soviet investment in agriculture was sufficient to generate enough agricultural output to feed the growing industrial work force, to provide the required raw materials for industry, to provide for export needs, and to release the labor necessary to fill the new jobs. This enabled the modern industrial sector to be constructed. However, as was also pointed out in Chapter III, the Soviets probably went too far in emphasizing industry and minimizing investment in agriculture. That is, more investment in agriculture would probably have increased the growth rate of national income. At the same time, however, it should be remembered that the agricultural investment picture would look much better if the blunders of livestock collectivization and World War II had not occurred.

There is, of course, no a priori way of determining the proper percentage share of investment that should be allocated to agriculture in a development program.[6] A country's resource endowment,

3. TsSU, *Narkhoz, 1961*, pp. 540-41. TsSU, *Narkhoz, 1964*, p. 514.

4. Simon Kuznets, "A Comparative Appraisal," in *Economic Trends in the Soviet Union*, eds. Abram Bergson and Simon Kuznets (Cambridge: Harvard University Press, 1963), p. 343.

5. Naum Jasny, *The Socialized Agriculture of the U.S.S.R.: Plans and Performance*, Grain Economic Series No. 5 (Stanford: Stanford University Press, 1949), pp. 61-63.

6. Because the agricultural sector accounts for a larger share of gross national product than in the Soviet Union, China has devoted a larger share of gross investment to agriculture. During the period 1953-55, agriculture received 27.6 per cent of total investment, 27.0 per cent during 1956-57, and 26.6 per cent in 1959. This compares with India, a non-Soviet type economy, where 26.5 per cent of total investment during 1951-57 was allocated to agriculture. Wilfred Malenbaum, "India and China: Contrasts in Development Performance," *American Economic Review*, Vol. XLIX, No. 3 (June, 1959), p. 300; and W. W. Hollister, "Capital Formation in Communist China,"

size, existing stock of capital, and so on are important in determining the exact percentage share. Most underdeveloped countries today undoubtedly need a higher rate of agricultural investment than the Soviet Union managed to get by with. However, the general Soviet position that industry should be the leading sector has some merit. There are, of course, countries so small in land area and population that any such program of industrialization first would be impossible. As was pointed out in Chapter I, the Soviet model has little relevance for these countries. It is quite possible that no model has relevance for these countries unless they join with other countries in some form of common market program.

It has been argued that before agricultural productivity can be increased the industrial sector must provide the necessary means. "Rationalization of agriculture (is) . . . conditioned . . . by industrial advance. The growth of industry . . . would provide the means for supplying agriculture with more power, better transport facilities, marketing, and similar services."[7] Industry performed just such services in the Soviet Union. Both sectors of the economy must be developed, of course, but a faster rate of growth can be attained if the industrial sector is the prime mover. Historically, agricultural growth rates have been much lower than industrial. One important reason is that advanced industrial technology faces less resistance in a traditional society. Agricultural science and technology must take into account different soils, crops, and climate. Because "linkages" with other domestic economic activity are tenuous, the potential external economies are smaller in agriculture. Increased agricultural activity does not have the educational and cultural conditioning effects that industrialization brings. It is for these reasons that in nineteenth-century European economic development "the more backward a country, the less likely was its agriculture to play any active role by offering to the growing industries the advantages of an expanding industrial market based in turn on the rising productivity of agricultural labor."[8]

If, as seems reasonable, the marginal productivity of capital and/or the marginal propensity to save are higher in the industrial than

*Industrial Development in Communist China*, ed. Choh-Ming Li (New York: Frederick A. Praeger, Inc., 1964), pp. 42-45.

7. K. Mandelbaum, *The Industrialization of Backward Areas* (Oxford: Basil Blackwell, 1945), p. 3.

8. Alexander Gerschenkron, *Economic Backwardness in Historical Perspective* (New York: Frederick A. Praeger, Inc., 1965), p. 354.

in the agricultural sector, economic growth will be lower under an agriculture-first development program.[9] The marginal propensity to save is lower in agriculture because of the conspicuous consumption habits of the semi-feudal upper strata and the subsistence level of incomes received by the bulk of the peasantry. The problem would still exist, though in a different form, under a collective farm system. Urban-rural wage differentials would have to be narrowed, and with the peasants' high propensity to consume, this would mean a sharp reduction in the savings rate.[10] The argument for the marginal productivity of capital being higher in industry rests on the greater possibilities for capturing external economies. Also many agricultural investment projects are much more capital using than is usually assumed.[11] This is particularly true when it is realized that successful extension work in agriculture has occurred in those countries where a developed industrial sector and an extensive network of social overhead capital were in existence. When this capital (such as agricultural colleges) is taken into account, capital/output ratios in agriculture are higher and the marginal productivity of capital lower.[12]

It has often been argued that if agricultural development is stressed and the increased production exported to pay for imports of capital goods, economic growth will be maximized.[13] There is no question that, where possible, agricultural products should be exported to obtain capital goods that are unavailable from domestic production. The smaller the country the more international trade will be necessary. The Soviet Union, in spite of its great size, exported large quantities of agricultural products in the early 1930's

---

9. W. Arthur Lewis, "Economic Development with Unlimited Supplies of Labor," *The Manchester School of Economic and Social Studies*, XXII (May, 1954), 139-91; and Kenneth K. Kurihara, "Theoretical Objections to Agriculture-Biased Economic Development," *Indian Journal of Economics*, Vol. XXXIX, No. 153, Part II (October, 1958), pp. 163-70.

10. This was one of the main points of discussion in the famous industrialization debate in the 1920's. See Alexander Erlich, *The Soviet Industrialization Debate, 1924-1928* (Cambridge: Harvard University Press, 1960).

11. Walter C. Neale, "Must Agriculture Come First?" *Co-Existence*, No. 3 (May, 1965), pp. 40-48.

12. W. B. Back, "The Economic and Institutional Forces," in *Land Use Policy and Problems in the United States*, ed. Howard W. Ottoson (Lincoln: University of Nebraska Press, 1963), pp. 189-92.

13. See William H. Nicholls, "The Place of Agriculture in Economic Development," in *Agriculture in Economic Development*, eds. Carl Eicher and Lawrence Witt (New York: McGraw-Hill Book, Co., 1964), pp. 11-44; and Jacob Viner, *International Trade and Economic Development* (Oxford: Oxford University Press, 1957).

and would have exported more if the terms-of-trade had not been so unfavorable.[14] The real question is whether increasing agricultural production for export purposes should have priority over domestic industrialization.

There are two lines of argument to the agriculture-first position. The first is that since agriculture employs the vast bulk of the work force it is only common sense that it must be developed first. What is more important, however, is the proportion of national product originating in the agricultural sector. In recent years, the share of agriculture, forestry, and fishing in gross domestic product has been 20 per cent in Argentina (1961), 27 per cent in Brazil (1959), 14 per cent in Chile (1960), 34 per cent in Colombia (1960), 37 per cent in Ecuador (1961), 33 per cent in Egypt (1956), 48 per cent in India (1960), 34 per cent in the Philippines (1960), and 38 per cent in Thailand (1961).[15] In discussing this argument, Dr. Hans Singer points out that ". . . it is only with reference to employment and not with reference to national income that agriculture can, in strict truth, be described as the 'basic' activity in underdeveloped countries. This point is worth making since reports of missions and similar documents abound with statements that improvements in agriculture are in some sense 'more important' than non-agricultural improvements since agriculture is the 'basic activity.' "[16]

The second argument maintains than a country should utilize its comparative advantage in primary products by expanding their production and exportation. Here again, however, the pace of industrial development is being tied to the pace of agricultural development. Furthermore, the comparative advantage argument is a static one. Current comparative advantages do not necessarily coincide with potential comparative advantages. Most important, however, are the problems of terms-of-trade and fluctuation for primary products in the world market.

Economists such as Hans Singer and Raul Prebisch[17] have argued

14. Franklyn D. Holzman, "Foreign Trade," in *Economic Trends in the Soviet Union*, eds. Bergson and Kuznets, pp. 283-306.

15. U.S. Bureau of the Census, *Statistical Abstract of the United States, 1963* (Washington: Government Printing Office, 1963), p. 912.

16. H. W. Singer, "The Mechanics of Economic Development," in *The Economics of Underdevelopment*, eds. A. N. Agarwala and S. P. Singh (Oxford: Oxford University Press, 1958), p. 384.

17. H. W. Singer, "The Distribution of Gains Between Investing and Borrowing Countries," *American Economic Review*, Vol. XL, No. 2 (May, 1950), pp. 473-85; and Raul Prebisch, "The Role of Commercial Policies in

that the long-run trend has been for the terms-of-trade to turn against primary products. While the statistical evidence on the historical movement of the terms-of-trade is somewhat ambiguous,[18] prospects for primary products in the future are not good.

> . . . the longer-term, if not immediate, prospects of cheaper domestic production of many manufactured products, together with the prospect or reality of deterioration in the terms of trade underscore the fact that heavy and prolonged reliance on exports of primary commodities has serious drawbacks. . . . The projections for 1970 made by Goreau and his associates at FAO certainly suggest a persisting tendency for agricultural exports to increase more rapidly than the demand for imports. In view of the rather low price and income elasticities of demand for primary products, deterioration of the terms of trade of exporters of such products seems to be the realistic expectation in a world economy characterized by widespread concern with efforts to accelerate economic development, including well-nigh universal preoccupation with the expansion of export crops.[19]

Probably more important than the long run terms-of-trade is the problem of instability in the prices of primary products.[20] This instability results in violent fluctuations in foreign exchange earnings for those countries whose exports are concentrated in a few primary products. These fluctuations are a serious impediment to economic development because long-range investment planning is almost impossible. If primary products are being exported to obtain imports of capital goods then investment planning becomes dependent on the vagaries of the international market. Compensatory financing schemes and other supplementary financial measures may help alleviate this problem in the future.

To conclude, therefore, the Soviet position of treating industry as the leading sector in a development program has merit. The degree of emphasis that should be given to industry, however, cannot be determined solely on a priori grounds. Population, factor endowments, and a host of other variables must be taken into account in

---

Underdeveloped Countries," *American Economic Review*, Vol. XLIX, No. 2 (May, 1959), pp. 251-73.

18. For a brief review of the literature, see Benjamin Higgins, *United Nations and U.S. Foreign Economic Policy* (Homewood, Illinois: Richard D. Irwin, Inc., 1962), pp. 38-40.

19. Bruce F. Johnston and Soren T. Nielson, "Agricultural and Structural Transformation in a Developing Economy," *Economic Development and Cultural Change*, Vol. XIV, No. 3 (April, 1966), p. 295.

20. See Higgins, *United Nations and U.S. Foreign Economic Policy*, pp. 50-51, for the statistical evidence on price changes of primary products.

making the final decision about degree of emphasis. A first approximation to an answer and more-or-less what the Soviets did is to allocate to the agricultural sector just enough investment so that there will be no food, raw material, or labor shortages to slow down the advance of industry.[21]

## THE CHOICE OF AN INVESTMENT RATE

Once having made the decision to embark upon a development program, the choice of an appropriate investment rate assumes prime importance.

The Soviet Union has had a high rate of investment because the planners discounted the future at a very low rate. This is a major reason why the Soviet Union has grown faster than private enterprise economies.

In the Soviet Union, the rate of gross investment increased from 12.5 per cent of gross national product in 1928 to 25.9 per cent in 1937 and 28.1 per cent in 1955.[22] Over fairly long periods in the past in Argentina, Canada, Germany, Norway, the United States, and the Union of South Africa, the gross investment rate exceeded 20 per cent.[23] What is distinctive about the Soviet experience is the speed at which the rate was increased. Furthermore, in comparison with underdeveloped countries generally, investment rates over 20 per cent are very high.

The reason that a high investment rate is desirable, of course, is because it rapidly increases the stock of capital in the economy. The size of the stock in any period, in turn, is a main determinant of total output in that period. If the capital-output ratio does not significantly increase, higher rates of investment will yield higher growth rates of total output.[24] In the Soviet Union, incremental

21. In an excellent article, Johnston and Mellor have commented on ". . . the importance of developing agriculture in such a way as to both minimize its demands upon resources most needed for industrial development and maximize its net contribution to the capital required for general economic growth." Bruce F. Johnston and John W. Mellor, "The Role of Agriculture in Economic Development," *American Economic Review*, Vol. LI, No. 4 (September, 1961), pp. 590-91.

22. Abram Bergson, *The Real National Income of Soviet Russia Since 1928* (Cambridge: Harvard University Press, 1961), p. 128.

23. Kuznets, "A Comparative Appraisal," in *Economic Trends in the Soviet Union*, eds. Bergson and Kuznets, p. 354.

24. For an elaboration, see Wassily Leontief, "Theoretical Note on Time-Preference, Productivity of Capital, Stagnation and Economic Growth," *Readings in Economic Development*, eds. Theodore Morgan, George W. Betz, and

capital-output ratios only increased, on a gross basis, from 3.53 in 1928-40 to 3.69 in 1950-58, and actually declined on a net basis from 2.76 to 2.60.[25] No capitalist economy has combined over long periods relatively low incremental capital-output ratios with high investment rates. Kuznets has pointed out that ". . . the distinctive feature of the USSR record is that so much capital formation was possible without an increase in the capital-output ratio to uneconomically high levels."[26] The choice of technology embodied in the Soviet strategy of industrial development which explains this combination of high investment rates and low capital-output ratios will be covered later in the chapter.

What was the optimum rate of investment for the Soviet Union in the 1930's and by extension for a poor country beginning a development program today? There is no uniquely determinate economic solution to this question. Increasing the rate of investment today means lowering the share of consumption in gross national product (though not necessarily the absolute amount) in the present in exchange for a larger income and consumption in the future. A lower rate of investment will yield greater consumption in the present, but lower amounts in the future, than would higher rates of investment. The key to the solution, therefore, is the trade-off between present and future consumption contained in a community's social time preference function.

A central planning board cannot simply imitate the rate of investment that would emerge from individual time preferences. The social perspective of the future and the time horizon of a community differ significantly from those of an individual.[27] What rate of in-

N. K. Choudry (Belmont: Wadsworth Publishing Co., Inc., 1963), pp. 113-19; and Joseph S. Berliner, "The Economics of Overtaking and Surpassing," *Industrialization in Two Systems: Essays in Honor of Alexander Gerschenkron*, ed. Henry Rosovsky (New York: John Wiley & Sons, Inc., 1966), pp. 159-85.

25. Kuznets, in *Economic Trends in the Soviet Union*, eds. Bergson and Kuznets, p. 353.

26. *Ibid.*, p. 357.

27. See Stephen A. Marglin, "The Social Rate of Discount and the Optimal Rate of Investment," *Quarterly Journal of Economics*, Vol. LXXVII, No. 1 (February, 1963), p. 111. Also, see Franklyn D. Holzman, "Consumer Sovereignty and the Rate of Economic Development," *Economia Internazionale*, Vol. XI, No. 2 (1958), pp. 3-17; Maurice Dobb, *An Essay on Economic Growth and Planning* (London: Routledge & Kegan Paul, 1960), pp. 15-28; A. K. Sen, "On Optimising the Rate of Saving," *The Economic Journal*, Vol. LXXI, No. 283 (September, 1961), pp. 479-96; Roy Harrod, *Towards a Dynamic Economics* (London: Macmillan & Co., Ltd., 1961), p. 40; S. S. Wagle, *Technique of Planning* (Bombay: Vora & Co., 1961), pp. 165-69; G. L. S.

vestment does the planning board choose? Holzman says it is indeterminate between the lower limit set by the present evaluation of the present versus the future and the upper limit set by the future evaluation of the present versus the future.[28] The hindsight of the future evaluation of the present versus the future overcomes the "weakness of imagination" and "defective telescopic faculty" of the present evaluation of the present versus the future and, thus, would yield a higher rate of investment. Sen argues that the investment rate is indeterminate between a lower limit set by the rate necessary to utilize existing productive capacity and to maintain a constant consumption level for a growing population and an upper limit set by that rate of investment which maintains the present level of consumption[29] and does not yield negative marginal returns.[30] The indeterminacy in practice, however, is not so great as these limits might imply. The rate of investment is not determined in isolation. The past allocation between consumption and investment production will physically limit the present alternatives. The rate of investment chosen in the present will, in turn, limit the alternatives in the future.[31] More importantly, the choice of investment rate cannot be determined independently of the choice of investment projects and technique.

Once the specificity of productive capacity is recognized to have an important bearing on the question, the problem of the *allocation* of investment between different sectors becomes the present-day equivalent of choosing future rates of saving. If, for example, we assume that investment goods are of two types, viz., those that make consumer goods and those that produce investment goods, the present-day allocation of

---

Shackle, *Time in Economics* (Amsterdam: North-Holland Publishing Co., 1958), p. 37; and Branko Horvat, "The Optimum Rate of Investment," *The Economic Journal*, Vol. LXVIII, No. 272 (December, 1958), pp. 747-67.

28. Holzman, "Consumer Sovereignty and the Rate of Economic Development," pp. 8-10.

29. He adds that "one of the advantages that a post-revolutionary government has compared with the pre-revolutionary government in the same society is a certain relaxation of this barrier. By eliminating a certain high-consumption class from the top of the social hierarchy, which previously enjoyed a big part of the cake, a revolution might lead to a raising of the upper social limit of saving given by the difference between productive capacity and the socially accepted limit of maximum consumption." Sen, "On Optimising the Rate of Saving," p. 491.

30. *Ibid.*, pp. 492-95.

31. If the allocation between consumption and investment is changed too abruptly, excess capacity will appear in the sector receiving the reduced allocation.

productive *capital* between these two sectors comes to very much the same thing as the determination of the future division of national output between consumption and investment. The allocation of *investment* between the two becomes the means of influencing the rates of investment in the future.

If one assumes further specificity, so that investment goods to make investment goods to make consumer goods are different from investment goods to make investment goods to make investment goods, the decision has to be taken one further step backwards, and so on.[32]

Thus, the decision on the investment rate, is dependent on the *allocation* of investment and vice versa. In the Soviet Union particularly, the decision on allocation greatly affected the final determination of the rate of savings and investment. This problem of allocation between sectors and projects is the next aspect of the Soviet experience to be considered.

THE ALLOCATION OF INVESTMENT AND UNBALANCED GROWTH

Investment allocation in the Soviet Union provides an historical example of the unbalanced growth strategy advocated by economists such as Hirschman.

Exponents of unbalanced growth have stressed that if a country decides to industrialize, the correct development strategy is not to seek an optimal allocation of resources at any given time nor to dissipate scarce resources by attempting to advance on all fronts simultaneously but, rather, to concentrate on a few major objectives most conducive to transforming the economy to a higher stage. Efficiency is attained in the dynamic sense of finding the most effective sequences for converting a stagnant, backward economy into one which is dynamic and modern. In other words, to be breathlessly climbing a peak in a mountain range is considered more important than standing poised on the crest of a ridge in the foothills.

There is not an infinite number of alternative investment allocation patterns. Because of complementarities and indivisibilities each individual investment project cannot be evaluated in isolation. The construction of a steel industry requires increased coal mining and investment in steel using industries. The capture of external econ-

32. Sen, "On Optimising the Rate of Saving," pp. 493-94. Also, see H. B. Chenery, "Comparative Advantage and Development Policy," *American Economic Review*, Vol. LI, No. 1 (March, 1961), p. 41; and Maurice Dobb, *Some Aspects of Economic Development*, Occasional Paper No. 3 (Delhi: Delhi School of Economics, 1951), pp. 52-53.

omies requires that the entire range of investment projects be evaluated as a whole.

". . . problems of economic planning seem to acquire a resemblance to the problems of military strategy, where in practice the choice lies between a relatively small number of plans, which have in the main to be treated and chosen between as organic wholes, and which for a variety of reasons do not easily permit of intermediate combinations. The situation will demand a concentration of forces round a few main objectives, and not a dispersion of resources over a very wide range."[33]

The Soviet Union pursued a "shock" strategy of bottlenecks successively created and resolved. Thus, Soviet planning concentrated on certain key branches in each plan to overcome particular bottlenecks. Scarce capital and managerial talent were then concentrated on these key targets. This gave Soviet planning its peculiar nature of planning by "campaigning."[34] During the first Five-Year Plan the main target was heavy industry with particular emphasis on machine building. During the second and third Five-Year Plans the target was again heavy industry with metallurgy, machine building, fuel, energetics, and chemicals singled out for emphasis. This emphasis on key branches yielded high growth rates. The average annual rates of growth in Soviet heavy industry between 1928/29 and 1937 were 18.9 per cent for machinery, 18.5 per cent for iron and steel, 14.6 per cent for coal, 11.7 per cent for petroleum products, 22.8 per cent for electric power, and 17.8 per cent for all heavy industry.[35] Sectors which did not contribute directly to further growth (consumption) were neglected while sectors which enhanced growth (capital goods) were emphasized.

Growth tempos such as these caused acute shortages and strains. The industrial bottlenecks which appeared then became the new targets. This is unbalanced growth with a vengeance. Much of the balanced growth versus unbalanced growth debate boils down to the question of where external economies are the greatest. One of the key questions in choosing investment criteria, in turn, hinges on how best to take advantage of external economies and avoid external

33. Maurice Dobb, *Soviet Economic Development Since 1917* (London: Routledge & Kegan Paul, Ltd., 1960), p. 6.

34. See Alec Nove, *The Soviet Economy* (New York: Frederick A. Praeger, Inc., 1961), pp. 288-95.

35. Alexander Gerschenkron, "Soviet Heavy Industry: A Dollar Index of Output, 1927-1937," in *Economic Backwardness in Historical Perspective*, p. 247.

diseconomies. Economic theorists usually argue that investment should be allocated in such a way that its social marginal product (SMP) is equal in all uses. While this is true as a formal statement it has no meaning unless the "empty box" entitled SMP can be filled with some content. To date no one has done so. One advantage of the unbalanced growth strategy is that it provides a practical signal for reallocating investment. When bottlenecks appear, the planner can be sure that the SMP of investment is not equal in all uses. The industries that are the bottlenecks will have a high SMP and thus should receive large investment allocations in the next period. In this sense the SMP will be equated in all uses through time, that is, in a dynamic sense. Thus the campaign method of unbalanced growth, though crude, does have a logic. It also entails a large risk of waste. If the bottlenecks are not quickly opened they can seriously retard economic growth.[36]

The logic of the campaign method does not ensure that any particular campaign is the right one. The search is for industries which are particularly potent in starting a chain reaction through the capture of external economies. An indication of which industries these are may be found, according to Hirschman, by calculating the backward and forward linkage effects of the industry. Backward linkage represents the degree of input requirements or derived demand which every nonprimary economic activity generates. Forward linkage represents the degree to which output is utilized as an input for activities other than final demand. Thus, the establishment of a new industry with a high backward linkage will provide a new and expanding market for its inputs, whether supplied domestically or from abroad. Similarly, the domestic production of a product will tend to stimulate the development of industries using this product. Of course, the domestic availability of a product will not "compel" the construction of industries using the product, but it will create conditions favorable to their development. Hirschman admits that backward linkages are much more clear cut in their stimulating effects than forward linkages. While backward linkage creates demand, forward linkage is dependent upon the existence or anticipation of demand. Therefore, forward linkage cannot be regarded as an independent inducement mechanism. It acts, however, according to Hirschman, as an important and powerful reinforcement to backward

36. Albert O. Hirchman, *The Strategy of Economic Development* (New Haven: Yale University Press, 1958), pp. 98-119.

linkage. Industries with a high combined backward and forward linkage should, therefore, play a powerful role in inducing industrial development through "creating the demand" or "paving the way" for other supplier or user industries. Indeed, examination of the process of development of a number of mature economies such as Great Britain, Germany, and the United States reveals the crucial role in development played by leading sectors with high linkage effects.

The identification of high-linkage industries should make it possible to discover the crucial sectors or subsectors whose growth, through the realization of external economies, has a maximum impact on an economy's development. Data prepared by Chenery and Watanabe based on input-output tables for the United States, Italy, and Japan indicate that industries with the highest combined linkage effect include (in order of rank) iron and steel (144 of a possible combined 200); nonferrous metals (142); paper and paper products (135); petroleum products (135); grain mill products (134); coal products (130); chemicals (129); textiles (124); metal mining (114); petroleum and natural gas (112); and coal mining (110). Two other industries, transportation equipment (80) and machinery (79), would certainly have scored substantially higher and been included among the above group of industries had the sales of these industries not been construed in input-output tables as final demand under capital formation, but as inputs into other industries.[37]

This list of industries, derived without reference to Soviet experience, is very similar to a list of the "leading sectors" given priority in Soviet development. The Soviet Union did not give high priority to paper and paper products, and textiles. In the case of grain mill products the high linkage effect, in this case largely backward, is explained by the industry being a satellite of agriculture. It is an outgrowth rather than a cause of agricultural development and for this reason could properly be excluded from the original list. Of the industries given high priority by the Soviet Union, only electric power production is omitted from the list. The relatively low combined linkage effect (86) would not apply in the Soviet Union, however, where a much smaller share of electric power output is used by households or for municipal lighting.[38] When these qualifi-

37. Hollis B. Chenery and Tseunehiko Watanabe, "International Comparisons of the Structure of Production," *Econometrica* (October, 1958), p. 493, quoted in *ibid.*, pp. 106-7.

38. The United States uses about half of its electric power for industrial

cations are taken into account, the lists very nearly overlap and the similarity of the two lists is surely not coincidental.

While linkage is not the same thing as external economies, it is probably a good indicator of where they lie. Hirschman, however, stresses the incentive effect of linkage. The creation of bottlenecks forces entrepreneurs to invest in the bottleneck industries. Presumably an over-all plan would account for linkage effects and thus the incentives of linkage would be minimized. However, economic planning of the type used by the Soviet Union during the industrialization period, and by extension in less developed countries today, is a relatively crude affair. "Campaigns," with their ensuing bottlenecks, substitute for the profit motive in keeping the planning bureaucracy on its toes.

". . . the entire *rationale* of the Soviet 'campaign' approach to economic planning rests upon . . . the need to stimulate not only the executants but also the controllers. . . . Campaigns are among other things, a means of goading the goaders, of mobilizing the controllers, of providing success indicators for officials at all levels.

". . . Hence the vital role of campaigns as controller mobilizers. Hence the value of bottlenecks as stimulators to effort."[39]

The Soviet campaign method of planning thus has logic when viewed in the light of Hirschman's unbalanced growth theory and concept of linkage. When the SMP of investment is viewed as containing the return on external economies, allocation of investment to bottleneck industries as they arise through time appears to be not only good practice but possibly good theory as well. This does not imply that the Soviets deliberately created bottlenecks or that they understood the meaning of unbalanced growth. Rather, the bottlenecks and unbalanced growth were necessary by-products of the high growth tempos that the planners adopted. It is also true that the Soviets have pushed unbalanced growth so far at times that

purposes while the Soviet Union uses perhaps 80 per cent. W. W. Rostow, "Summary and Policy Implications," *Comparisons of the United States and Soviet Economies*, Part III (Washington: Joint Economic Committee, GPO, 1959), p. 291.

39. Nove, *The Soviet Economy*, p. 292. Also, see Gregory Grossman, "Soviet Growth: Routine, Inertia and Pressure," *American Economic Review*, L (May, 1960), 62-72. Preplanned co-ordination of investment projects through central planning does not conflict with unbalanced growth and "campaigns." Unbalanced growth is a strategy designed to obtain a dynamic equilibrium through time, and "campaigns" are a means of implementing the plan.

waste occured with a consequent reduction in the potential growth rate.[40]

As an economy becomes more sophisticated, "campaign" planning becomes less appropriate. The number of products multiply and "balance" becomes more important. Since structural change is slower, and firms and industries are operating closer to equilibrium, marginal calculations become more feasible. This seems to be the present situation of the economy of the Soviet Union. Failure to pull up lagging sectors, particularly agriculture, and to develop more sophisticated planning methods is causing the Soviets severe problems and slowing their growth tempo.

Soviet emphasis on the development of leading sectors has relevance for the industrialization of less developed economies. If less developed countries were to follow the Soviet example of stressing leading sectors, they would very nearly maximize the combined forward and backward linkage effects along the lines advocated by Hirschman. The "leading links" of Soviet development should be evaluated in terms of their feasibility and potential effect on the development of a specific country. Hirschman freely admits that, "industrial development clearly cannot be started everywhere with an iron and steel industry. . . ."[41] The present analysis suggests, however, that the preoccupation of many less developed countries with the development of basic metallurgical and capital goods industries is not as foolish as has often been thought. On the contrary, where feasible these policies appear consistent with the achievement of a rapid transformation of the economy to a higher stage of development.

CHOICE OF TECHNOLOGY AND SOVIET DEVELOPMENT STRATEGY

Another feature of Soviet industrial strategy involves choice of technology in production. In Soviet literature this problem resolved into

40. The Soviets frequently blundered in their implementation of the strategy. Not only was the rate of investment in heavy industry as a whole overambitious but overinvestment in certain industries, such as metal-fabricating, caused under-uitilization of capacity and created bottlenecks that were not quickly closed. See David Granick, *Soviet Metal-Fabricating and Economic Development: Practice versus Policy* (Madison: The University of Wisconsin Press, 1967); and Alexander Erlich, "Development Strategy and Planning: The Soviet Experience," in *National Economic Planning*, ed., Max F. Millikan, NBER (Columbia University Press, New York, 1967), pp. 233-78.

41. Hirschman, *The Strategy of Economic Development*, pp. 180-9.

a question of whether capital should be devoted to large-scale units using advanced and expensive technology or to smaller-scale enterprises using simple tools and employing relatively more workers. It is often argued in Western economic writings that since, practically by definition, there is a shortage of capital and a surplus of labor in less developed countries, labor-intensive techniques should be used wherever possible so as to conserve on capital and provide as much employment as possible. But, to a large extent, this is a false issue. The decision on the type of technology to use cannot be divorced from the decision regarding the allocation of investment. Once the allocation of investment to sectors and industries has been decided the choice of technologies is severely limited. The range of processes available for the production of steel, electric power, tractors, and machine tools is not a continuous function where capital and labor are substitutable at the margin in infinitesimal increments. More realistically, the production function in these key industries is sharply discontinuous with probably only two or three alternative processes which make any sense from the purely engineering point of view. Further, many of the most modern technologies tend to be both labor and *capital* saving, as witnessed by the declining capital-output ratios of the advanced countries during their industrialization. Using 1900 as a base of 100, the capital-output ratio of the American automobile industry declined to 55 in 1909 and to 16 by 1929.[42] The situation is usually such that there is a distinction between labor-intensive techniques of production and those which are more productive in the sense of contributing more to the increase of national income. While labor-intensive methods will provide more employment in the short run, by choosing the method of production which increases national income more rapidly, even if it is less labor-intensive, over a longer time period national income will have grown to such an extent that the total amount of investment will be large enough to provide more employment. Zauberman has put the problem facing underdeveloped countries in sharp focus. "As a rule in modern industry, variation limits of capital-to-labour proportions are becoming

42. Based on data giving fixed capital in Table 16 of Daniel Creamer, *Capital and Output Trends in Manufacturing Industries, 1880-1948* Occasional Paper 41 (New York: National Bureau of Economic Research, Studies in Capital Formation and Financing, 1951), pp. 72-74. Declines in the capital-output ratios of other industries were not as spectacular. Nonetheless, in the various branches of the machine industry, in iron and steel and their products, in chemical and allied products, and others, the decline from 1919 to 1948 ranged from 40 to 50 per cent.

increasingly narrow, hence the dilemma facing promoters of initial industrialization is one of Hobson's choice: either to condemn the industry to technological backwardness at birth, or to deepen structural underemployment."[43]

Since Great Britain each succeeding country to industrialize has capitalized on its ability to borrow the most advanced technology from the more developed countries. Gerschenkron points out that "borrowed technology . . . was one of the primary factors assuring a high speed of development in a backward country entering the stage of development."[44]

In the late 1920's, most Soviet industrial plants were old, but great new increments were needed to speed up industrialization. In the debates among planners and engineers about the proper technology to adopt for new plants during this period the problem was posed as a choice between American mass-production techniques versus European small-batch production methods.

The above mentioned decline in the American capital-output ratio over a period of only three decades represented the kind of alternatives open to the Soviet planners in the late 1920's when existing technology in the automotive industry was very much like that in the United States in 1900. The European alternative can be considered as represented by the United States industry in 1909, and the most advanced techniques open to the Soviets represented by the American industry in 1929.

A crucial step in the resolution of the debate in favor of American techniques was the decision to model the Stalingrad tractor plant, the first large-scale, modern, mass-production manufacturing plant in the Soviet Union, after the most advanced American plants. It was decided to leap to the most advanced technical level without passing through intermediate stages of development characterized by the European technology. Although the plant scarcely functioned at all during its first year of operation, mass-production techniques were finally mastered by workers and management and their successful adoption set an example followed by other industries.

Confirmation of the advantages available is provided by a comparison of the capital-output ratio of an old-fashioned, small-scale Soviet tractor plant and a giant plant employing the latest American technology. The modern plant provided not only very substantial

43. Alfred Zauberman, "Soviet and Chinese Strategy for Economic Growth," *International Affairs*, Vol. XXXVIII, No. 3 (July, 1962), p. 347.
44. Gerschenkron, *Economic Backwardness in Historical Perspective*, p. 8.

savings in labor but also savings in capital per unit of output.[45] While the automotive industry undoubtedly offered unusually favorable opportunities for capital savings through modern technology, similar but more modest savings were available in other industries. The substantial capital savings combined with even greater savings in labor which the most advanced technique provided made its adoption the only sensible course for the Soviet planners.

Wholesale borrowing of the most advanced technologies that are labor-saving *but not* capital-saving would be desirable, however, only if the factor proportions in the less developed country were somewhere near those in the developed country. This is seldom the case, however. Where it is not, redesigning and adapting the most advanced technology to its own factor proportions will yield a larger output.[46]

*Dual Technology.* Soviet development policy has been aware of this conflict between requirements of progress and factor endowment and has dealt with it by adopting the strategy of a "dual technology." On the one hand, in the key industries, they utilized to the maximum the advantage of borrowing the most advanced technologies developed in economies with very different factor endowments. On the other hand, they allowed for these differences by utilizing manual labor in auxiliary operations and by aiming at high performance rates per unit of capital instead of per man.[47] In this fashion they obtained the best of two worlds and achieved the over-all effect of saving capital.

In many Soviet plants it is common to find the most advanced capital equipment in the basic processes and, at the same time, the

45. Norton T. Dodge, *Trends in Labor Productivity in the Soviet Tractor Industry: A Case Study in Industrial Development* (Ph.D. dissertation, Harvard University, 1960), chap. VIII.

46. For fuller theoretical treatment of this, see Joseph Berliner, "The Economics of Overtaking and Surpassing," in *Industrialization in Two Systems,* ed. Rosovsky, pp. 170-74. R. S. Eckaus, "Factor Proportions in Underdeveloped Areas," *American Economic Review,* Vol. XLV, No. 4 (September, 1955), pp. 539-65. Hirschman, *The Strategy of Economic Development,* pp. 150-52.

47. See Zauberman, "Soviet and Chinese Strategy for Economic Growth," pp. 347-49. Berliner, "The Economics of Overtaking and Surpassing," in *Industrialization in Two Systems,* ed. Rosovsky, pp. 173-74. Gregory Grossman, "Scarce Capital and Soviet Doctrine," *Quarterly Journal of Economics,* LXVII (August, 1953), 311-43. Professor Granick's study cites evidence for these Soviet policies but his evaluation is much more negative. See David Granick, *Soviet Metal-Fabricating and Economic Development.*

most primitive labor-intensive methods in maintenance, intra-plant transport, and materials handling. In such enterprises as the Gorky Automotive Plant, which was a direct copy of the Ford River-Rouge plant, they allowed for their lower level of labor skills by redesigning job descriptions so that each worker performed fewer and simpler tasks.[48] Thus, the Soviets obtained the advantages of advanced technology, conserved scarce capital in auxiliary operations that did not limit output, and utilized their relatively abundant unskilled labor.

In addition, the Soviets aimed at high performance rates per unit of capital instead of per man in further adapting advanced technology to their factor endowments. Typical are their records in output of pig iron per cubic meter of blast furnace. In 1958 they obtained 1.25 tons of pig iron per cubic meter of blast furnace capacity per day compared with about 0.92 tons per cubic meter in the United States. Without this utilization differential they would have needed an additional 39 blast furnaces to produce the same output.[49] Thus, again, they economized on the scarce factor.

The Soviet Union also used the same approach in transportation. More intensive usage was substituted to a large extent for new construction. Railroad traffic density increased in the Soviet Union from 1,215 thousand metric ton-kilometers per kilometer of road in 1928 to 4,363 thousand in 1938. American railroads in the 1890's carried about 500 thousand metric ton-kilometers per kilometer of road per year.[50] In terms of freight car capacity, utilization productivity in the Soviet Union in 1954 was 17.96 thousand ton-miles per ton of capacity. For the United States in 1955 the figure was 7.0 thousand ton-miles per ton of freight car capacity.[51]

*Multi-shift Operation.* Another way capital was used intensively was by multi-shift operation of plants. In both the prewar and postwar periods, many Soviet industrial plants operated on a two-shift basis. Three-shift operation, although introduced in manufacturing plants in the early 1930's, has been discarded except in those industries where the technology demands it. It was soon discovered

48. Berliner, "The Economics of Overtaking and Surpassing," in *Industrialization in Two Systems,* ed. Rosovsky, p. 172.

49. Robert W. Campbell, *Soviet Economic Power* (Boston: Houghton Mifflin Co. 1960), p. 61.

50. Holland Hunter, "Transport in Soviet and Chinese Development," *Economic Development and Cultural Change,* Vol. XIV, No. 1 (October, 1965), p. 79.

51. Campbell, *Soviet Economic Power,* p. 60.

that the third shift was needed for repairs, clean up, and the production of deficit parts. Multi-shift operation reached a peak in the Soviet Union in 1932 when the shift coefficient (the ratio of total man-days worked to those in the main shift) reached 1.73. It declined slightly in the mid-1930's. When figures were next published in 1959 the coefficient for all industry had declined to 1.55.[52] These figures may be compared with figures for United States manufacturing in 1959-60 of 1.30.[53] In England and leading European industrial countries the ratio is even lower. It is clear that Soviet practice regarding multi-shift operation of her plants deviated from the pattern in the United States and other advanced Western countries.[54]

The difference in multi-shift operations stems partly from the relative scarcity of capital in the Soviet Union and the concern of Soviet planners to minimize the use of capital. With labor and output measured as flows and capital as a stock, two-shift operation, for example, reduces the capital-labor ratio by one-half. If capital is also measured as a flow of services to take account of more rapid physical wear and tear under multi-shift operation the reduction would be somewhat less. As a consequence of multi-shift operation the Soviets have been able to adapt a more advanced technology with a higher capital-labor ratio than would have been possible with single shift operations. Although there are disadvantages to multi-shift operation,[55] the Soviet pattern of widespread two-shift operation would seem superior to single shift operation for most underdeveloped economies. Indeed, a distinct tendency toward multi-shift operation has already been observed in underdeveloped countries which would seem to bear out the lesson of Soviet experience.[56]

Both the use of labor-intensive techniques in auxiliary operations

52. See *Sotsialisticheskoe stroitel 'stvo SSSR* (Moscow: TsUNKU Gosplana SSSR, 1935), p. 503, and *Narkhoz, 1959*, p. 601.

53. Otto Hollberg and Alexander Jarrell, "Supplementary Wage Benefits in Metropolitan Areas, 1959-60," *Monthly Labor Review*, Vol. 84, No. 4 (April, 1961), pp. 379-87. The data are from a sample survey of 188 metropolitan areas covering all parts of the United States.

54. See Professor Granick's *Soviet Metal-Fabricating and Economic Development*, pp. 95-110, for a critical evaluation of Soviet implementation of multi-shift operation. He also argues that it was not extensively used in the metal-fabricating industry because of lack of technicians and supervisors.

55. *Ibid.*, pp. 95-110.

56. See Economic Commission for Latin America, *Labor Productivity of the Cotton Textile Industry in Five Latin American Countries* (New York: United Nations, April 23, 1951).

and the intensive utilization of capital tended to lower the capital-output ratio or at least keep it from rising. Thus, the benefits of modern technology were reaped while at the same time minimizing the demand for capital, which is the scarce factor.

The Soviets have also used another means to obtain this result. While progressively adding the newest capital equipment they have continued to operate obsolescent plants far beyond the time possible in a competitive market system. Here again, within limits, the factor endowment of the Soviet Union was taken into consideration.

Undoubtedly the Soviets did not perfectly accommodate modern technology. There are many examples where they did not adapt borrowed technology but instead imitated it exactly.[57] Of greater consequence was the planned undermining of the traditional small handicraft workshops in the 1930's. The Chinese seem to have learned a lesson from this, and alongside the modern sector have consciously tried to preserve and promote small-scale and cottage-type sectors that have smaller capital requirements per man.[58] Zauberman notes that this is ". . . a rational way of mitigating the inherent conflict between the basic factor-configuration of the economy and the desire to set in motion a spiral of modern technological advancement."[59]

As indicated in the preceding examples, the key to adoption of this dualistic technology was the desire of Soviet planners to conserve scarce capital. It has seemed strange to many observers that the adoption of advanced technology in the basic production processes has been the result. There is no inconsistency, however. The spectacular labor saving effect of advanced technology in the basic production processes has tended to overshadow the very real but more limited capital saving effect. In many instances, the choice of advanced technology could be made on purely engineering grounds rather than economic grounds, since both labor and capital were saved.

57. See Berliner, "The Economics of Overtaking and Surpassing," in *Industrialization in Two Systems*, ed. Rosovsky, p. 173. M. Gardner Clark, *The Economics of Soviet Steel* (Cambridge: Harvard University Press, 1956), pp. 65-66, 84.

58. Professor Eckaus' two sector model, wherein one sector is by nature capital-intensive and limited substitutability prevails, and the other is characterized by variable coefficients of production, provides an excellent theoretical base for this policy. See Eckaus, "Factor Proportions in Underdeveloped Areas," pp. 539-65.

59. Zauberman, "Soviet and Chinese Strategy for Economic Growth," p. 349.

*Plant Scale and Design.* Another consideration regarding Soviet choice of technique concerns the scale and design of fixed plants. The Soviets exhibited a strong preference for large-scale, integrated plants with high fixed-to-variable cost ratios and specialized with respect to product. This emphasis upon size has often been pointed to by Western economists as an apt illustration of the irrationality of Soviet planning. In a number of instances this was undoubtedly the case.[60] Indeed, the Soviet leadership itself became concerned with wastes involved and roundly condemned the "gigantomania" of the early 1930's. There is a good rationale for this practice in a planned economy with a specific goal of rapid economic development.

A stock of capital is adaptable if it is capable of being combined with different amounts of the variable factors. It is flexible if it approximates the best technology for a wide range of output. High efficiency at many possible levels of output is attained at the cost of not attaining the highest possible efficiency at any one level of output. Flexibility is built into plants in order to overcome imperfect adaptability, because without flexibility production at any level other than the optimum would involve unprofitably high marginal costs. That is, a flexible plant would be characterized by a shallow, bowl-shaped average cost curve and an inflexible plant by a deep, U-shaped curve with the bottom of the curve lying below the lowest point of the flexible plant's curve.[61]

In a capitalist economy it is rational to build flexibility into the plant. This is so because of uncertainty about the level and composition of future output. In a planned economy oriented to attaining a particular goal, uncertainty is considerably reduced and the construction of plants which yield minimum average cost only over a narrow range of output becomes rational.

The concept of plant size needs to be pursued further. Research by Joe Bain and others on the relationship between scale of plant and unit costs in the United States suggests that cost differences ex-

---

60. Also, the interdependence of many new plants with long gestation periods meant that a delay in completing one plant was likely to hold back completion or full operation of others. See Erlich, "Development Strategy and Planning," in *National Economic Planning,* ed. Millikan, pp. 243-44 and 248-49.

61. See George Stigler, "Production and Distribution in the Short Run," *Readings in the Theory of Income Distribution,* eds. William Fellner and Bernard Haley (Philadelphia: Blackiston, 1946). Also Berliner, "The Economics of Overtaking and Surpassing," in *Industrialization in Two Systems,* ed. Rosovsky pp. 174-76.

ceeding 3 per cent, due to quadrupling the scale, are to be found in a number of machinery industries.[62] Accordingly, this suggests that unless the gestation period of a large-scale plant is appreciably longer and the interest rate or time preference very high, large-scale plants are likely to be fully warrented. This was true of the Soviet tractor industry in the 1930's.[63]

Other factors such as difficulties in co-ordinating the activities of a large plant, of staffing it with adequate managerial personnel, and so forth, may provide overriding reasons for favoring smaller plants.[64] Soviet experience suggests, however, that it pays to raise the skills of management and workers to the level of the best technology rather than to saddle the economy for a lengthy period with an inefficient, small-scale technology. This point will be developed later in the section on human capital.

In addition to building large plants, the Soviets intended to build highly integrated plants. During the early stages of the Soviet industrialization drive in the late 1920's and early 1930's, the Soviet economy lacked the well developed system of separate supplier plants necessary to support a complex, highly specalized industrial economy. The transport system was overloaded, as well, and the delivery of parts or materials from other plants could not be relied upon. Under such circumstances new plants, if they were to operate successfully, had to be constructed along highly integrated, less specialized lines than was originally intended by Soviet planners. In the automotive industry, for example, the major plants included every process from the pouring of metal to shipping the finished product. They also manufactured repair parts for machine tools and even made their own special tools and equipment in the absence of other suppliers.

Since most less developed countries also suffer from lack of a fully developed complex of supply and service industries, the Soviet policy of integrated plants suggests a logical initial pattern of development for them. However, as the industrial base broadens and deepens and supplies of parts become more certain, plants which are more highly specialized with respect to production processes can sensibly

62. Joe S. Bain, *Barriers to New Competition: The Character and Consequences in Manufacturing Industries* (Cambridge: Harvard University Press, 1956).

63. Dodge, *Trends in Labor Productivity in the Soviet Tractor Industry*, Appendix V.

64. *Ibid.*, Appendix U.

be built. In recent years, for example, the Soviets have devoted considerable attention to the construction of tractor assembly plants and to plants producing motors for several types of tractors and combines.

A high degree of product specialization is another major feature of Soviet choice of production techniques.[65] The motive behind this policy was, of course, to achieve the economies provided by economies of scale and mass production. In addition, by keeping the number of product types or models small, problems of repair and replacement parts were simplified. Nevertheless, in evaluating the merits of this policy, the advantages of producing and servicing a limited number of models must be weighed against the reduced utility of models insufficiently tailored to differing conditions or requirements in use. There can be little doubt that the Soviets pushed product specialization too far in a number of industries. In the tractor industry, for example, only three basic tractor models were produced during the 1930's although there were four major plants in production which might have produced four different models as efficiently as three. As a result, the varied needs of agriculture and other users such as the construction industry were not properly met. Despite such specific weaknesses in application, the policy of favoring simplification of the product-mix and interchangeability of various components was more appropriate to the Soviet economy than the practice in advanced Western countries of producing a multiplicity of models differentiated as much in superficial as fundamental respects.

Are the advantages of a dual technology which we have enumerated for the Soviet economy significant for less developed economies today? Since many conditions, such as a shortage of capital, are common to all of these economies, there should be a considerable carry-over in Soviet experience to the less developed countries. The degree of carry-over depends, of course, on the type of development undertaken in each country. A partial list of the industries in which capital saving possibilities through the use of advanced technology in the basic production processes are possible would include the automotive industry, agricultural machinery, petroleum refining, heavy chemicals, fertilizers, iron and steel, cement, pulp and paper, and many "modern" industries producing consumer goods ranging from radios and light bulbs to toothpaste and aspirin. These latter in-

65. *Ibid.*, pp. 481-83. See Granick, *Soviet Metal-Fabricating and Economic Development*, chap. 2, for a more detailed and more critical treatment.

dustries are "new" industries which are seldom found in less developed countries in the initial stages of their development.

Capital saving possibilities among a second group of industries whose products compete with "old" industries are less certain. Textiles, particularly the spinning phase, is a classic example of this type of industry. In these "old" industries, there are greater possibilities for the substitution of labor for capital than in the "new" industries. Despite this limitation on the applicability of a dual technology, it is apparent that for most countries capable of a substantial industrial sector the Soviet lessons regarding the advantages of a dual technology have widespread relevance.

It is doubtful that the more recent Soviet experience with automation can be so generally applied. A much higher level of technological accomplishment is required for the introduction of automated technology than many of the less developed economies can muster alone. However, with outside aid, as the development of many enclave industries have shown, very complex technology can be employed.

THE ROLE OF VOCATIONAL AND TECHNICAL TRAINING IN THE
FORMATION OF HUMAN CAPITAL

A basic feature of Soviet development strategy is the stress upon vocational and technical training and the use of the factory itself in the educational process. From the outset of the industrialization drive the Soviets have indicated a profound appreciation of the importance of human capital in the development process and have shown a willingness to commit substantial sums and effort to build up not only a skilled labor force but also professionals able to lead and direct the industrial effort.[66]

Since the initial labor force for the plants completed in the late 1920's and early 1930's was largely drawn from peasant and urban youths who had no background or legacy of skills, it was unavoidable that the Soviets should develop extensive training facilities. Many of these raw recruits could neither read nor write and had never held a wrench or screwdriver in their hands before.[67] Having such raw human material to work with, the plants initially were required not only to train workers to handle their machines and to conform to the

66. See Granick, *Soviet Metal-Fabricating and Economic Development,* pp. 107-10.
67. *Ibid.,* pp. 29-30.

factory regime but also to provide the rudiments of an elementary education. As a result, extensive educational and training programs were established at the factories themselves.

Most of the training was on-the-job in character, but numerous schools known as F.Z.U. (factory and work apprentices' schools) were opened at the factories to train apprentices for skilled trades. During the first Five-Year Plan the F.Z.U. schools trained over 450 thousand skilled workers.[68] Each year since the first Five-Year Plan about 100 thousand skilled workers have been trained through these factory apprentice schools. In addition, an annual average of 2.5 million workers and employees between 1940 and 1959 were taught new trades and specialities on the job, and an additional 5.0 million were trained to improve their skills each year.[69] Also, many workers learned their "three R's" in factory-run evening schools.

Eason points out that "the experience of the Soviet Union lends support to the view that major strides in raising the quality of labor can be made without elaborate and extensive educational facilities."[70] The advantage of on-the-job training, particularly during the early industrialization period, is that it conserves scarce resources. The use of scarce capital in constructing special education facilities is minimized. In addition, the educational gestation period is shortened. If the quality of the educational output is not high, at least the training is wasteful only of the relatively abundant factor of unskilled labor. In the 1930's, on-the-job training was combined with a major overstaffing of jobs in the factories. While this was wasteful of labor, it did have great educational value. This overstaffing combined with the usage of advanced technology was a stimulus to the creation of a disciplined industrial work force.

"New technologies do much to educate industrial labour to become a reliable and disciplined social stratum, psychologically adjusted to the requirements of the modern factory. In order to operate with modern machinery some attitude of responsibility and some habits of punctuality are necessary. The education of such a stratum is a protracted process and involves no less difficulties than the

68. U.S. Department of Education, *Education in the U.S.S.R.* Bulletin 1957, No. 14 (1957), p. 130.

69. TsSU, *Narkhoz, 1959*, p. 624. While it is difficult to know exactly what these figures mean, they do evidence a continuing concern with upgrading skill levels.

70. Warren W. Eason, "Labor Force," in *Economic Trends in the Soviet Union,* eds. Bergson and Kuznets, p. 62.

creation of the necessary savings."[71] The Soviets seemed to recognize the importance of this factor in choosing modern techniques of production. In 1934, Stalin commented on this factor when he said: "True, we destroyed many machines . . . but at the same time we won the most important thing—time—and we created the most precious thing in the economy—cadres."[72] In effect, the Soviets' decision was to "trade-off" scarce physical capital in return for even scarcer human capital. Indeed, trained industrial workers were possibly the most important output of the new factories.[73]

This policy of overstaffing and on-the-job training would be difficult to transfer to an underdeveloped country with a capitalist economy because of the nonappropriability of the returns by private firms. It is possible, however, that a tax-subsidy scheme could be devised to make the policy feasible.

In the Soviet Union, formal education has been devoted principally to those subjects most amenable to classroom methods of instruction and which are considered to be especially important for economic development. The natural sciences and engineering have been particularly emphasized. Night schools for adults have been extensively used to train technicians. Table V-1 summarizes the Soviet emphasis on development oriented subjects at the higher educational level.

THE ROLE OF INTERNATIONAL TRADE

The final question that arises in a discussion of development strategy is the role of international trade in the Soviet model.[74] Foreign

71. S. Swianiewicz, *Forced Labour and Economic Development: An Inquiry into the Experience of Soviet Industrialization* (London: Oxford University Press, 1965), p. 263.

72. *Pravda*, December 29, 1934. Quoted in Berliner, "The Economics of Overtaking and Surpassing," in *Industrialization in Two Systems,* ed. Rosovsky, p. 173.

73. This is an interesting idea. It might be more appropriate to calculate the value added in production *and* the educational value added to the work force to obtain industrial output for a developing country. The differential education effect is one of the primary reasons it is so difficult to estimate the SMP of investment in different uses. Also see Granick, *Soviet Metal-Fabricating and Economic Development,* chap. 3.

74. The three most important sources used for this section are: Frederic L. Pryor, "Foreign Trade Theory in the Communist Bloc," *Soviet Studies,* Vol. XIV, No. 1 (July, 1962), pp. 41-61; Franklyn D. Holzman, "Foreign Trade," in *Economic Trends in the Soviet Union,* eds. Bergson and Kuznets, pp. 283-332; and Franklyn D. Holzman, "Foreign Trade Behavior of Centrally Planned Economies," in *Industrialization in Two Systems,* ed. Rosovsky, pp. 237-65.

TABLE V-1
*U.S.S.R., 1928-1959, and U.S.A., 1926-1958:*
*Number of Graduates of Higher*
*Educational Establishments*

| Field | U.S.S.R. | U.S.A. | U.S.S.R. as per cent of U.S.A. |
|---|---|---|---|
| Engineers | 1,117,800 | 620,300 | 180.0 |
| Science majors | 430,000 | 704,400 | 61.0 |
| Medical doctors | 420,000 | 181,700 | 231.2 |
| Agricultural specialists | 389,200 | 166,400 | 233.9 |
| Sum of above fields | 2,357,000 | 1,672,800 | 140.9 |
| Humanities, social sciences, etc. | 1,772,300 | 5,198,600 | 34.1 |
| All fields | 4,129,300 | 6,871,400 | 60.1 |

Source:
Eason, "Labor Force," in *Economic Trends in the Soviet Union,* eds. Bergson and Kuznets, p. 63.

trade in the Soviet Union has always been subordinated to the requirements of economic development and central planning. It is seen as a means to an end—the end being the attainment of needed imports. Alexander Gerschenkron has argued that "Russia exports solely in order to obtain the wherewithal for payments for imports. In this sense, she is likely to live up to the classical doctrine of foreign trade and to reject the tenets of mercantilism. This, no doubt, sounds paradoxical, but is undeniable. From the Russian point of view exports are a loss and not a gain."[75]

Both political and economic considerations shaped Soviet trade policy. The Soviet Union undoubtedly would have preferred to increase its imports through long-term credits but in the world situation of the 1930's was unable to do so. A high degree of self-sufficiency was deliberately pursued because of fear (rightly or wrongly) of further foreign attack.[76] Because of the large size and varied resource endowment of the Soviet Union, foreign trade as a proportion of GNP has naturally tended, as in the United States, to be small. Table V-2 summarizes the exports, imports, and terms-of-trade of the Soviet Union during the period 1929-59. During the first years

75. Quoted in Holzman, "Foreign Trade Behavior of Centrally Planned Economies," in *Industrialization in Two Systems,* ed. Rosovsky, p. 240.
76. See *ibid.,* p. 313.

TABLE V-2

### Indices for Exports, Imports, and Terms-Of-Trade in the U.S.S.R., 1929-1959

| Year | Exports | | Imports | | Terms-of-trade index |
|------|----------------|----------------|----------------|----------------|----------------|
| | Volume index | Price index | Volume index | Price index | |
| 1929 | 100.0 | 100.0 | 100.0 | 100.0 | 100.0 |
| 1930 | 135.7 | 82.7 | 141.3 | 85.1 | 97.2 |
| 1931 | 146.1 | 60.1 | 161.5 | 77.1 | 77.3 |
| 1932 | 127.8 | 48.7 | 115.8 | 68.0 | 71.6 |
| 1933 | 118.5 | 45.2 | 62.5 | 63.2 | 71.5 |
| 1934 | 102.9 | 44.0 | 47.1 | 56.0 | 78.6 |
| 1935 | 90.5 | 44.0 | 51.5 | 52.8 | 83.3 |
| 1936 | 68.2 | 49.3 | 59.4 | 54.1 | 91.1 |
| 1937 | 71.5 | 60.4 | 54.5 | 63.9 | 94.5 |
| 1946 | 64.9 | 125.2 | 95.7 | 111.3 | 112.4 |
| 1950 | 189.1 | 119.1 | 160.4 | 124.3 | 95.8 |
| 1959 | 571.2 | 119.1 | 525.8 | 132.6 | 89.7 |

Source:

Holzman, "Foreign Trade," in *Economic Trends in the Soviet Union*, eds. Bergson and Kuznets, pp. 289, 305.

of industrialization foreign trade expanded, but, as the terms-of-trade worsened and productive-capacity increased, a withdrawal to a greater degree of autarky occurred.

The actual trade policy adopted by the Soviet Union was one of import substitution. Capital goods, blueprints, prototypes, and technicians were imported in exchange for traditional exports until this imported capital could be used to construct industries whose output would replace the imports. For example, the import of machinery and equipment increased from 917.6 million rubles (at the 1950 exchange rate) in 1929 to 1,354.6 million rubles in 1932 and then decreased to 242.8 million rubles in 1937. The share of machinery and equipment in total imports increased from 29.9 per cent in 1929 to 55.2 per cent in 1932 and then declined to 23.9 per cent in 1937.[77] Further evidence of this import substitution policy is presented in Table V-3 which sets forth data on the percentage share of imports in total consumption of particular commodities. As Table V-3

77. *Ibid.*, pp. 288, 296.

TABLE V-3

*U.S.S.R.: Share of Imports in Total Consumption,*
*Various Years (Per cent)*

| Commodity | 1928 | 1930 | 1932 | 1935 | 1937 |
|---|---|---|---|---|---|
| Lead | — | 88.4 | 64.4 | 46.0 | 54.8 |
| Zinc | — | 90.3 | 43.6 | 3.0 | 4.0 |
| Aluminum | 100.0 | 100.0 | 74.1 | 0.3 | — |
| Rubber | 100.0 | 100.0 | 100.0 | 60.3 | — |
| Cotton | 30.2 | 15.4 | 5.5 | 2.8 | 1.8 |
| Rolled ferrous metals | — | — | 17.0 | 2.0 | 0.7 [a] |
| Iron and steel pipes and tubing | 29.0 | 10.7 | 11.4 | 5.5 | — |
| Turbines, generators, boilers | — | 89.0 | 77.0 | 19.0 [b] | — |
| Machine tools | — | — | 66.0 | 14.0 | 10.0 |
| Metal-cutting machines | 66.4 | 58.1 | 54.5 | — | 2.0 [c] |
| Machinery | — | 19.0 | 7.3 | 1.0 | — |
| Automobiles, buses, trucks | — | 66.4 | 3.9 | 0.2 | — |
| Tractors | 75.4 | 81.2 | 0.0 | 0.0 | — |

Source:

Holzman, "Foreign Trade," in *Economic Trends in the Soviet Union*,
eds. Bergson and Kuznets, p. 299.

[a] 1938         [b] 1933         [c] 1955

demonstrates, during the 1930's domestic production replaced imports as the major source of supply. During this period the Soviets imported many prototypes, blueprints, and technicians with the aid of which they constructed their domestic industry. This was an inexpensive way to obtain access to the most modern technology of the developed countries.

Viewed from static equilibrium analysis the Soviet strategy of import substitution—substituting higher cost domestic production for imports—led to a misallocation of resources and a reduction in real national income. However, if the Soviet policy of allocating investment to import-replacing industries instead of to export-oriented industries is viewed dynamically, it is possible that this policy increased the rate of growth enough to cover any static allocation losses. In the case of the Soviet Union, the import-replacing industries were the heavy capital-goods industries and the export-oriented industries were in nondurable consumer goods, wood products, and agriculture.

The dynamic rationale for Soviet policy is simply a variant of the infant industry argument. Assume the Soviet Union has a choice between (a) investing in export-oriented consumer goods, wood products, and agriculture, and then exporting the output in exchange for capital goods; or (b) investing in import-replacing capital goods. Assume also, as was the case, that planners' preferences determine the configuration of demand. If the Soviet Union pursued the first policy, the international trade/national income ratio would increase as would, presumably, the gains from trade.[78] Productivity would increase in these industries because of the increased investment. However, the increase would be relatively slow because of the absence of large "linkages" and economies of scale. Adoption of the second policy, while decreasing the international trade/national income ratio and the gains from trade,[79] would result in larger productivity increases because of the greater prevalence of "linkages," external economies, and internal economies of scale in the heavy capital goods industries.[80]

During the first Five-Year Plan the Soviet Union exported relatively large quantities of agricultural products, consumer goods, and wood products in return for capital goods that enabled them to expand their import-replacing industries. Holzman notes that "had it not been for the adverse shift in terms of trade and high cost of borrowing abroad, such a policy might have been adopted more broadly," and he concludes by saying that "While the Soviet Union does not fully exploit foreign trade to its profitable limits, the losses are not as large as would appear from the point of view of static comparative advantage; further, . . . its policy has reduced the profitable limits of trade below what they would otherwise have been had it followed more normal trade and investment policies."[81]

78. If the terms-of-trade turned against the Soviet Union, as they did in the 1930's, then the gains from trade could be wiped out. This possibility was treated at length in the first section of this chapter. This would reinforce the desirability of the second policy.

79. If comparative advantages shift as the new industries are constructed, there might be an actual increase in the gains from trade.

80. The problem of the location of "linkages," external and internal economies, was discussed earlier in the chapter. Consumer durable goods would be similar to capital goods but these were not the type of consumer goods the Soviet Union was capable of producing. Capital goods industries are needed before the production of consumer durables is possible.

81. *Ibid.*, pp. 324-25.

While the Soviet Union probably pushed its import-substitution policy too far, there is no reason why other countries must pursue the strategy to the same *degree*. International trade can certainly alleviate some of the difficulties of economic development. Trade is particularly important for smaller countries because it can enable them to develop without establishing the entire range of modern industry. But, at a minimum, industrialization in those areas of *potential* comparative advantage seems necessary. Comparative advantage shifts over time with changes in relative development patterns between countries. This makes static equilibrium analysis inapplicable in the context of economic development.

The potential for large foreign trade does not change the essence of the Soviet model presented in this paper. As the above illustration on import-substitution demonstrated, export industries, regardless of the nature of their product, can become "capital goods" industries if their output is sold for foreign exchange, which is then used to import capital goods. In what degree such a strategy is wise depends, among other things, on the particular country's natural resource endowment, on the comparative possibilities of increasing productivity in the capital goods and export industries, and the terms of trade that will prevail after the expansion of exports.

It is necessary in ending this chapter on Soviet development strategy to emphasize again that the policies comprising this strategy have application mainly to a backward economy trying to achieve the one overriding goal of economic development. The methods are basically those of a war economy. As such, when the economy has reached some level of sophistication, the time for war economy methods has passed. The required economic strategy then changes from one of maximum concentration of available resources on a few main goals towards successively greater dispersion.

# VI. THE SOCIAL COST OF DEVELOPMENT

In the previous chapters a model of economic development was constructed based on the historical experience of the Soviet Union and modified in certain respects by the later experience of other Soviet-type economies. An important question remains to be considered: how high is the cost of development in the Soviet model in terms of living standards, excess mortality, and human values (freedom, dignity, etc.)? This chapter attempts to evaluate that question.

Any writer begins a discussion of the human cost of Soviet industrialization with a certain amount of trepidation. In Western industrialization, the human costs are detailed but are usually treated as mere aberrations from a basically sound and moral system. On the other hand, the same human cost in Soviet industrialization is viewed as an essential part of the Soviet social system. Therefore, one system merely needs reform while the other is essentially evil and can never be anything but evil. E. H. Carr has formulated this problem clearly:

> Let us take the story of the industrialization of Great Britain between, say, about 1780 and 1870. Virtually every historian will treat the industrial revolution, probably without discussion, as a great and progressive achievement. He will also describe the . . . abuses (that) occurred in the working of the system. . . . But he will assume, again probably without saying it, that measures of coercion and exploitation, at any rate in the first stages, were an unavoidable part of the cost of industrialization. . . . This example is of particular interest to me, because I hope soon in my history of Soviet Russia to approach the problem of the collectivization of the peasant as a part of the cost of industrialization; and I know well that if, following the example of historians of the British industrial revolution, I deplore the brutalities and abuses of collectivization, but treat the process as an unavoidable part of the cost of a desirable and necessary policy of industrialization, I shall incur charges of cynicism and of condoning evil things.[1]

1. E. H. Carr, *What is History?* (New York: Alfred A. Knopf, 1962), pp. 103-4.

But an evaluation must be made if an honest appraisal of the Soviet industrialization model is to be attempted.

The first section of the chapter considers changes in living standards in the Soviet Union. The second section considers the loss of life incurred during collectivization and the industrialization drive. The third section discusses the question of freedom and other human values during economic development. In all three sections, comparisons with other countries are used to attain historical perspective. The final section takes up the question of whether the social costs incurred in the Soviet Union are an inherent part of the Soviet model of development and thus must be repeated by underdeveloped countries adopting the model.

CHANGES IN LIVING STANDARDS

There seems to be little doubt that living standards declined during the first Five-Year Plan. There is no accurate quantitative measure of the over-all decline but it is evident from the 18 per cent reduction in net agricultural output between 1928 and 1932 and the sharply increased exportation of agricultural products.[2]

However, since the second Five-Year Plan, with the exception of the World War II period, per capita consumption has increased. Table VI-1 gives estimates of the average annual increase in per capita consumption between 1928 and 1958. Four weighing systems have been used to estimate consumption in the Soviet Union. Professor Bergson believes that "1937 adjusted market prices" and "composite, 1937 base" are the most soundly based. In the former, adjusted market prices for 1937 are used as weights in all years. In the latter, with 1937 as the base year, the index for 1928 is weighted by adjusted market prices of 1928; the indices for 1955 and 1958 by adjusted market prices of 1950. Bergson has not been able to decide which of these is the best so he uses both. Both will be used in this chapter in comparison with other countries. The only decline recorded in Table VI-1 is for the period 1928-37 using 1937 adjusted market prices. And this is only for household consumption of private goods. If communal consumption is added, consumption increases of all periods seem respectable (between 1928 and 1932, however, consumption decreased). Communal consumption pri-

2. D. Gale Johnson and Arcadius Kahan, "Soviet Agriculture, Structure and Growth," in *Comparisons of the United States and Soviet Economies,* Joint Economic Committee, 86th Cong., 1st Sess., 1960, p. 205.

TABLE VI-1

Estimates of Average Annual Increases in Per Capita
Consumption in the U.S.S.R.: Various Years

| | % 1928-37 | % 1928-58 | % 1928-40 and 1948-58 |
|---|---|---|---|
| CONSUMPTION OF PRIVATE GOODS: | | | |
| 1928 adjusted market prices | 2.2 | 3.4 | 4.7 |
| 1937 " " " | −0.3 | 2.1 | 2.9 |
| 1950 " " " | 0.1 | 2.1 | 2.9 |
| Composite, 1937 base | 2.2 | 2.7 | 3.8 |
| COMMUNAL SERVICES: | | | |
| 1928 adjusted market prices | 16.1 | — | — |
| 1937 " " " | 14.6 | 5.6 | 7.7 |
| 1950 " " " | 14.7 | 6.3 [a] | 9.0 [a] |
| Composite, 1937 base | 16.1 | 6.1 | 8.4 |
| TOTAL CONSUMPTION: | | | |
| 1928 adjusted market prices | 3.8 | — | — |
| 1937 " " " | 1.1 | 2.4 | 3.3 |
| 1950 " " " | 1.5 | 2.1 [a] | 2.9 [a] |
| Composite, 1937 base | 3.8 | 3.1 | 4.3 |

Sources:
   Abram Bergson, *The Real National Income of Soviet Russia Since 1928* (Cambridge: Harvard University Press, 1961), pp. 225, 237, 252. Janet S. Chapman, "Consumption," in *Economic Trends in the Soviet Union*, eds. Abram Bergson and Simon Kuznets (Cambridge: Harvard University Press, 1963), pp. 238-39. The 1928-40 and 1948-58 period is used so as to exclude the war and reconstruction of 1940-47. The CIA estimated that per capita consumption increased at an annual rate of 2.8% between 1959 and 1965. See David W. Bronson and Barbara S. Severin, "Recent Trends in Consumption and Disposable Money Income in the U.S.S.R.," in *New Directions in the Soviet Economy*, U.S. Congress, Joint Economic Committee, 89th Cong., 2nd Sess., p. 521.
   [a] The ending year is 1955.

marily consists of education and medical services received from the state.

Table VI-2 compares changes in consumption for the Soviet Union and the United States. The rate of increase in the Soviet Union appears respectable when viewed against the experience of the United States. The increase of per capita consumption in the Soviet Union over the period 1928-58 was between 2.4 per cent and 3.1

*TABLE VI-2*

### Average Annual Increases in Per Capita Consumption in the U.S.S.R. and the U.S.A.: Various Years

| Country and Period | %<br>Annual Rate |
|---|---|
| U.S.S.R.: | |
| 1928-1937, 1937 adjusted market prices | 1.1 |
| 1928-1937, Composite, 1937 base | 3.8 |
| 1928-1958, 1937 adjusted market prices | 2.4 |
| 1928-1958, Composite, 1937 base | 3.1 |
| 1928-1940 and 1948-1958, 1937 adjusted market prices | 3.3 |
| 1928-1940 and 1948-1958, Composite, 1937 base | 4.3 |
| U.S.A.: | |
| 1869-1899 | 3.0 |
| 1869-1958 | 2.0 |
| 1870/79-1900/09 | 2.4 |
| 1880-1894 | −0.1 |
| 1899-1929 | 2.0 |
| 1928-1937 | −0.2 |
| 1928-1958 | 1.4 |

Sources:

Table VI-1 and Chapman, "Consumption," in *Economic Trends in the Soviet Union*, eds. Bergson and Kuznets, pp. 246-47. The consumption data for the United States are Simon Kuznets' "flow of goods to consumers" and include final government services to consumers. These are taken from Chapman. The weights are 1954 dollars.

per cent depending on the weighing system used. The increase in the United States over the period 1869-99 was 3.0 per cent. Janet Chapman concludes from her study of consumption in the Soviet Union that "In terms of the American experience the Soviet achievement looks quite respectable, particularly since the American progress was achieved in a peaceful world . . . while the 1928-58 period for the Soviet Union was characterized by the upheavals of the revolution in agriculture and the devastation of a major war fought largely on Russia's own soil."[3] In addition, if the Soviet industrialization period

3. Janet Chapman, "Consumption," in *Economic Trends in the Soviet Union*, eds. Abram Bergson and Simon Kuznets (Cambridge: Harvard University Press, 1963), p. 245.

is compared to the similar period of 1869-99 in the United States, the Soviet record appears better in a number of respects. In the Soviet Union, much less child labor was used, working hours were fewer, working conditions were superior, social security provisions were far better, and income was more equally distributed and steadier.[4]

Changes in living standards in the Soviet Union compare favorably with the experience of other countries during their period of industrialization. For most countries, good statistical data are lacking, but some rough comparisons can be made.

Per capita consumption declined in the Soviet Union between 1928 and 1932. However, similar decreases have occurred in many other countries. Table VI-2 shows that there was a decline in the U.S. between 1880 and 1894. There were several periods during the English industrial revolution when per capita consumption declined for a few years.[5] In Japan, too, there were years when per capita consumption declined.[6]

Table VI-3 compares some components of the standard of living in the Soviet Union, Mexico, and Japan. Japan began her industrialization in 1868. Mexico marked time from the revolution in 1910 until the development program really got started in 1940. The Soviet Union began industrializing in 1928. If 1960 is taken as the comparison date, and if the World War II period is excluded for Japan and the Soviet Union, then the Soviet Union has had 24 years,

4. *Ibid.*, pp. 245, 254, 261, 268-70. Real wages per urban worker declined between 17 and 43 per cent during the 1930's and did not regain their 1928 level until after Stalin's death. While real urban wages in the United States increased rapidly after 1890, Stanley Lebergott's work suggests almost no rise between 1800 and 1880. He also shows a decline of 10 to 30 per cent between 1800 and 1830, as well as other declines for shorter periods. This stagnation in real wage rates does not seem to be important for living standards because in both the Soviet Union and the United States the work force in the beginning period was very small and grew rapidly by transfers of workers from lower paid agricultural work. See Janet Chapman, *Real Wages in Soviet Russia since 1928* (Cambridge: Harvard University Press, 1963), pp. 142-88. Stanley Lebergott, "Wage Trends, 1800-1900," *Trends in the American Economy in the Nineteenth Century*, A Report of the National Bureau of Economic Research, Vol. 24 of Studies in Income and Wealth (Princeton: Princeton University Press, 1960), pp. 493, 499.

5. A. J. Taylor, "Progress and Poverty in Britain, 1780-1850: A Reappraisal," in *Essays in Economic History*, ed. E. M. Carus-Wilson (London: Edward Arnold Ltd., 1962), III, 391.

6. W. W. Lockwood, *The Economic Development of Japan: Growth and Structural Change, 1868-1938* (Princeton: Princeton University Press, 1954), pp. 34, 148-49.

TABLE VI-3

*Some Indicators of the Standard of Living in the*
*U.S.S.R., Mexico, and Japan: 1958-1962*

|  | U.S.S.R. | Mexico | Japan |
|---|---|---|---|
| Actual caloric intake as percentage of individual country minimum standards | 112 | 105 | 100 |
| Actual protein intake as percentage of individual country minimum standards | 145 | 113 | 117 |
| Average number of persons per room in residential housing | 1.5 | 2.9 | 1.4 |
| Life expectancy at birth, in years | 67.4 | 51-55 | 67.5 |
| Infant mortality rate | 32.0 | 70.2 | 26.5 |
| Number of physicians per 10,000 inhabitants | 30.3 | 5.8 | 10.6 |
| Proportion of illiterates in the population 15 years and older | 2 | 43 | 2 |
| Number of students in higher educational establishments per 100,000 population | 689 | 111 | 470 |
| Per capita consumption of fibers, kilograms | 8.5 | 4.0 | 8.3 |
| Per capita consumption of energy, kilowatt hours | 2,847 | 1,012 | 1,164 |
| Movies attended per capita | 17.7 | 10.4 | 7.0 |
| Stock of radios, per 1,000 population | 202 | 97 | 107 |
| Stock of television sets, per 1,000 population | 28 | 25 | 98 |

Sources:
U.S. Department of Agriculture, *The World Food Budget, 1970* (Washington: Government Printing Office, 1964), pp. 25-26. U.S. Bureau of the Census, *Statistical Abstract of the United States, 1963* (Washington: Government Printing Office, 1963), pp. 932-33. United Nations, *The Economic Development of Latin America in the Post-War Period* (New York: United Nations, 1964), pp. 56-61. United Nations, *Statistical Yearbook, 1963* (New York: United Nations, 1964), pp. 52-53, 641, 647, 682-83. While movie attendance and stocks of radios and television sets may not be the best indicators of consumption levels, they are the only ones available for all three countries.

Mexico 20 years, and Japan 84 years to attain the consumption levels shown in Table VI-3. The Soviet Union ranks first on eight of the indicators, ties for first on one, and is second on four. Given the relative time spans since industrialization began in the three countries, Soviet performance has been quite respectable.

### THE HUMAN COSTS OF DEVELOPMENT

*Excess Mortality in the U.S.S.R.* The major loss of life occurred during the collectivization of agriculture. Possibly the majority of poor peasants would have peacefully, if not willingly, joined the collective farms except for the opposition of the "well-to-do" peasants.[7] They actively and forcibly resisted by killing party cadres and burning their crops, and, through their traditional leadership positions in the villages, by persuading great numbers of poorer peasants to resist, also. This brought brutal and ruthless retaliation by the Soviets. An observer has vividly pictured the results.

The more well-to-do peasants continued to resist the movement, and, to dispose of their opposition, the Soviets proceeded to liquidate them. . . . Only those who visited Russian villages in those stormy days can appreciate the human tragedy that liquidation brought in its train. *Koolacks* had their property unceremoniously taken from them, and were cast out of their homes on to some barren or swampy piece of land outside their own, or in some other village, to wrest a living from a niggardly soil as best they could. Or, with their families, they were packed into overcrowded freight cars, sometimes with scanty food supplies, and exiled to some northern region—to start life over again on virgin lands, in a lumber camp, or in some new construction project.[8]

What did "liquidation" of the kulaks mean? Sir John Maynard says it meant that ". . . persons numbering, with their families, some five millions, were to be dispossessed of their properties, and in many cases driven from their homes."[9] This certainly caused untold suf-

7. Sir John Maynard writes that the great majority of peasants did or would have joined willingly because ". . . collectivization is a step up on the social ladder, and I err greatly if this has not been an element of importance in the acceptance of the change. It was otherwise, of course, with the prosperous peasant, who desired no such change; but the prosperous peasant, in his character of *kulak* was condemned beyond reprieve," Sir John Maynard, *The Russia Peasant: And Other Studies* (New York: Collier Books, 1962), p. 388. See also Maurice Hindus, *The Great Offensive* (New York: Harrison Smith and Robert Haas, 1933). For an opposing view, see M. Fainsod, *Smolensk under Soviet Rule* (Cambridge: Harvard University Press, 1958).

8. Hindus, *The Great Offensive*, pp. 146-47.

9. Maynard, *The Russian Peasant*, p. 366.

fering among these people, but it did not cause the death of all of them. After the good harvest of 1935 confirmed the victory of collectivization ". . . it became possible to 'amnesty' a large number of the liquidated kulaks."[10] That is, many kulaks were allowed to return and join the collective farms.

Many commentators estimate that the deaths among all classes of peasants due to collectivization and the attendant famine were about 5.5 million. There are, however, no reliable data to substantiate this or any other figure. The 5.5 million figure is based on a population study prepared by Frank Lorimer for the League of Nations.[11] Arguing from these data, Naum Jasny states that the decline in the excess of births over deaths from 20 per 1,000 before 1928 to 10.7 per 1,000 between 1928 and 1938 cannot be talked away.[12] The major reason for this decrease is a fall in the birth rate, but it does not necessarily follow, as Jasny argues, that it fell because of starvation. It is just as possible that the decline in the birth rate was due to a lowered desire for children during a period of great upheaval and uncertainty[13] and the use of abortion (which was legal at this time).

Jasny's use of population statistics to estimate excess mortality is open to a more damaging criticism. How accurate is a population census taken by an inexperienced government in an underdeveloped country such as Russia? Of course, possible errors could work either way. The above is not written to deny that there was a great loss of human life, but only to show that the quoted 5.5 million figure is not hard fact. The best that can be said for this figure is that it serves as the upper limit on possible losses.[14]

There are normally two causes given for the deaths: the famine of 1932-34 and the liquidation of the kulaks. It has been shown conclusively that there was a famine, but the only quantitative evidence is composed of estimates by Western journalists. These esti-

10. *Ibid.*, p. 379.

11. Frank Lorimer, *The Population of the Soviet Union: History and Prospects* (Geneva: League of Nations, 1946).

12. Naum Jasny, *The Socialized Agriculture of the U.S.S.R.: Plans and Performance*, Grain Economic Series No. 5 (Stanford: Stanford University Press, 1949), pp. 322-24.

13. This is what happened in the United States during the Great Depression. The birth rate fell from 21.3 in 1925 to 16.9 in 1935. U.S. Bureau of the Census, *Statistical Abstract of the United States, 1963* (Washington: Government Printing Office, 1963), p. 52.

14. The 5.5 million figure must be the upper limit unless birth rates were *higher* and/or death rates *lower* in the 1930's than the trend of the 1920's.

*TABLE VI-4*

Per Capita Net Output of Selected Agricultural
Products in the U.S.S.R.
(Kilograms Per Capita)

|            | 1926-1929 | 1931-1934 | 1935-1938 |
|------------|-----------|-----------|-----------|
| Grains     | 241.4     | 218.9     | 247.3     |
| Potatoes   | 102.1     | 133.5     | 144.1     |
| Vegetables | 49.8      | 64.6      | 57.9      |
| Milk       | 176.2     | 111.6     | 131.6     |
| Meat       | 32.7      | 16.7      | 19.8      |
| Eggs       | 64.2      | 25.7      | 41.6      |

Sources:
D. Gale Johnson and Arcadius Kahan, "Soviet Agriculture: Structure and Growth," in *Comparisons of the United States and Soviet Economies,* 86th Cong., 1st Sess., 1960, p. 210.

mates range from a few thousand deaths to 10 million.[15] Indirect evidence of famine conditions is the sharp reduction in agricultural output during the early 1930's. Table VI-4 presents per capita net output figures for various agricultural products over the period 1926 to 1938. These figures do not represent per capita consumption because industrial uses, exports, and changes in stocks are not accounted for.

The agricultural data presented in Table VI-4 lend support to the position that there was a sharp reduction in food consumption in the Soviet Union. In addition, food exports were increased in the early 1930's. However, the data throw no light on the extent or severity of the food shortage. Even if there were few deaths from outright starvation, it is probable that the debilitating effects of widespread hunger caused a large number of premature deaths among children and elderly people. To this writer's knowledge there have been no attempts to measure this abnormal mortality except by the previously mentioned population statistics.

The "liquidation of kulaks *as a class*" was not designed to kill them but rather to liquidate their power as property owners. While it is true that thousands of them were shot, most of those who died did so from the hardships of transportation to and working in the

15. See Dana G. Dalrymple, "The Soviet Famine of 1932-1934," *Soviet Studies,* Vol. XV, No. 3 (January, 1964), pp. 250-84.

Siberian regions. Also some, especially in the Cossack areas, died of starvation and related diseases due to the fact that after they destroyed their livestock and seed grain, and refused to plant, the Soviets denied them relief.[16] Here again there is no evidence as to the extent of these practices. It can be concluded, however, that excess mortality in the Soviet Union during the 1930's was certainly high, exactly how high, however, is unknown.

It has sometimes been argued that, because of the tremendous social cost of economic development, industrialization should not be attempted. Rather, increased welfare through heightened agricultural efficiency should be aimed for; or industrialization, if followed, should proceed very slowly. Some would disagree that what is needed is *rapid* economic development. They ask why the hurry— why this "obsession" with economic growth?

*The Cost of Underdevelopment.* While it is true that social revolution and industrialization have always entailed a high price, the price of underdevelopment is also very high. E. H. Carr has remarked that "the cost of conservation falls just as heavily on the underprivileged as the cost of innovation on those who are deprived of their privileges."[17] The cost of underdevelopment is high indeed; chronic disease, hunger, famine, premature death, and degradation of the human spirit which lasts not for a few years, but century after century. For example, it is estimated that prior to 1949, 50 per cent of Chinese mortality was directly or indirectly caused by chronic malnutrition, and some four million persons died every year as a result of contamination by human excrement.[18] And the Chinese suffered 1,829 famines during the last 2,000 years—an average of almost a famine a year.[19] Famine in China extending from 1876 to

16. "Ukrain [*sic*] villages which failed to deliver their quotas to the collectors were punished by the confiscation of all grain, and the stoppage of relief supplies: a measure of ruthless reprisal which was doubtless the cause of some of the local mortality." Maynard, *The Russian Peasant*, p. 377.

17. Carr, *What Is History?* p. 102. One cannot refrain from quoting Mark Twain (*A Connecticut Yankee in King Arthur's Court*), on this subject. "There were two 'Reigns of Terror,' if we would but remember it and consider it; the one wrought murder in hot passion, the other in heartless cold blood; the one lasted mere months, the other lasted a thousand years; the one inflicted death upon 10,000 persons, the other upon a hundred millions; but our shudders are all for the 'horrors' of the minor Terror; the momentary Terror, so to speak whereas, what is the horror of swift death by the axe, compared with life-long death from hunger, cold, insult, cruelty, and heart-break?"

18. See Josué de Castro, *The Geography of Hunger* (Boston: Little, Brown and Co., 1952), pp. 29, 151.

19. *Ibid.*, p. 29.

1879 is believed to have caused 9 million deaths, and a famine in China's Hunan Province in 1929 led to 2 million fatalities.[20] As another example, ten major famines in India between 1860 and 1900 resulted in 15 million deaths.[21] The 1918 influenza epidemic killed between 15 and 20 million Indians; as recently as the winter of 1942-43, the bodies of the famished littered the streets of Calcutta so profusely that their mere removal became impossible.[22] In the days of the Czars, Russia was known throughout the world as the country of the great famines, and as late as the middle of the nineteenth century, Western Europe was still subject to frequent famines.[23] These are just a few examples of the cost of nondevelopment.

Table VI-5 brings together three indicators of the human cost of underdevelopment. As an example, of the estimated 22 million children born each year in the Group VI countries, approximately 4.0 million die before they reach their first birthday. If these countries had the infant mortality rate of Group I countries then the mortality of infants would be approximately 0.5 million. This means that because of underdevelopment, 3.5 million infants die *each year* in the Group VI countries.

The "mathematics of suffering" may be morbid, but it does give perspective to the human costs of economic development. Holzman faces the problem of human cost squarely. His consideration of the problem is worth quoting at length.

Let us turn now to the case of the nation caught in the "Malthusian trap," nations in which: 1) there has been no increase in the standard of living for centuries—perhaps there has even been a decline—2) increases in output lead to a corresponding fall in the death rate so that no change in the standard of living occurs, i.e. those who live remain at subsistence 3) the death rate is so high relative to the death rate in nations which have experienced secular economic progress that it is fair to say the inability to escape the "Malthusian trap" is responsible for the (premature) death of most of those born, and finally 4) escape from the "trap" requires a rate of investment so high that increases in productivity outrun increases in population. With such nations the case for a high rate of investment for a long period of time (one which enables the nation to escape the "trap") becomes much easier to justify and value judgements easier to make. The essential distinction between this case and that of the progressive economy is that loss of life can no

20. *Colliers Encyclopedia*, 1962, Vol. 9, p. 552.
21. *Ibid.*
22. Castro, *The Geography of Hunger*, p. 177. Except for American grain shipments, there would probably have been famine in India during 1966-68.
23. *Ibid.*, p. 277. *Colliers Encyclopedia*, 1962, Vol. 9, p. 552.

*TABLE VI-5*

### The Human Costs of Underdevelopment

| Countries grouped by national income per capita | Infant mortality rate (average 1955-1958) | Life expectancy (average 1955-1958) | Caloric intake per capita (1960-1962) |
|---|---|---|---|
| Group I: $1,000 and more | 24.9 | 70.6 | 3,153 |
| Group II: $575 to $1,000 | 41.9 | 67.7 | 2,944 |
| Group III: $350 to $575 | 56.8 | 65.4 | 2,920 |
| Group IV: $200 to $350 | 97.2 | 57.4 | 2,510 |
| Group V: $100 to $200 | 131.1 | 50.0 | 2,240 |
| Group VI: Less than $100 | 180.0 | 41.7 | 2,070 |

Source:
United Nations, *The Economic Development of Latin-America in the Post-War Period*, p. 62.

longer be considered an "absolute," i.e. an infinite disutility. It was reasonable to consider it in this way in the progressive economy because loss of life is not comparable, by any measure, with other changes in the level of individual welfare. In the case of the "Malthusian trap" nation, however, one is put in the position of having to compare losses of life between periods. That is to say, failure to attempt to escape the "trap" may be considered equivalent to condemning to death, needlessly, members of future generations. Under these circumstances, loss of life would seem to become a legitimate and measurable datum of the system. The question facing the planner is: shall we raise the rate of investment in the present to a point high enough to escape the "trap" even though this will involve a rise in the death rate of the present generation if we know that it will increase the life expectancy and raise the standard of living of countless future generations? No matter what his decision, the planner faced with such a question is responsible for imposing the death sentence on someone. When life and death are compared on this plane, escape from the trap might well seem to be the superior alternative since by simple addition it becomes obvious that more lives would be saved than lost in the process.[24]

24. Franklyn Holzman, "Consumer Sovereignty and the Rate of Economic Development," *Economia Internazionale*, Vol. XI, No. 2 (1956), pp. 15-16.

Most of the peoples of the world exist in conditions of poverty which are difficult for the affluent West to understand. And the effect on the dignity of the individual, the degradation of his very being, cannot be measured.[25]

*The Cost of Industrialization under Capitalism.* What was the human cost of industrialization in the capitalist countries? This is probably an unanswerable question. Much depends on the viewpoint adopted, since precise causal relationships cannot be established between industrialization and social costs. In what follows, no attempt is made to establish cause and effect. However, the following material must at least be considered in evaluating the human cost of capitalist development relative to the human cost of Soviet development described above.

The human costs incurred in England during the industrial revolution were not small. The use of women and children in factories during the industrial revolution was notorious. Even though adult males were not treated with quite the same cruelty, their life in the factory was hard enough. They, too, suffered from too many working hours, from overcrowded and unhealthy working conditions, and from tyrannical employers.

Adding to, and a partial cause of, the evils was the absolute and uncontrolled power of the factory owner. This power was acknowledged, admitted and even proclaimed with brutal candor. It was the employer's own business and this was justification enough for his conduct. He owed his employees wages, and once those were paid he had no further obligations.

The first result of the industrial revolution "was deplorable, for, instead of creating a happier, wiser, and more self-respecting society, this revolution led to the degradation of large masses of people and the rapid growth of a town life in which everything was sacrificed to profit."[26] The reaction of the English government in the face of the destitution and degradation of the working classes is instructive. The Poor Law Reform of 1834 was its answer. The Poor Law abolished outdoor relief for the able-bodied. To receive relief the worker and his family had to move to the workhouse. The Act attempted to

25. For illuminating views on the effect of poverty on the human spirit see: Maria Carolina de Jesus, *Child of the Dark* (New York: E. P. Dutton & Co., 1962), and Oscar Lewis, *The Children of Sanchez* (New York: Random House, 1961).

26. J. L. and B. Hammond, *The Town Labourer, 1760-1832* (London: Longmans, Green & Co., 1932), p. v.

make the receipt of relief shameful. Unemployment, for instance, was considered to be due to laziness, which could, therefore, be cured by the threat of the workhouse. This, of course, was a complete misunderstanding of cyclical unemployment, which was becoming important.

The working classes did not accept their situation quietly, but there was little they could do about it. There was protest, as can be seen in the massive proportions of unrest. "Luddism, the abortive march of the 'Blanketeers' in 1817, the Peterloo massacres two years later, the revolt of the agricultural workers in 1830, the meteoric rise and precipitous decline of the Grand National Consolidated Trades Union, Owenite socialism, the Ten Hours Movement, and Chartism,"[27] all testify to the discontent of the growing industrial working class. These attempts to revolt were suppressed in two ways: explicitly by the police power of the state and implicitly through the market mechanism. The Luddite movement was crushed after Parliament made the breaking of machines a capital offence.[28] In 1819, the passage of the Six Acts restricted civil liberties by increasing the power of magistrates to punish "subversion." Workers who protested against conditions and those convicted of petty crimes were often exiled to penal colonies such as Australia.[29]

In spite of the very poor conditions described above, there was not great loss of life among Englishmen. However, mention must be made of the human cost incurred by others. Here, again, no direct cause and effect relationship is implied; only that these costs place the costs in the Soviet Union in better perspective.[30] During

27. Karl De Schweinitz, "Economic Growth, Coercion, and Freedom," *World Politics*, Vol. IX, No. 2 (January, 1957), p. 176.

28. Frightened by these internal manifestations of discontent and by the revolutionary changes in America and France, Parliament added 63 new capital offenses between 1760 and 1810. "Not only petty theft, but primitive forms of industrial rebellion—destroying a silk loom, throwing down fences when commons were enclosed, and firing corn ricks—were to be punished by death." E. P. Thompson, *The Making of the English Working Class* (London: Victor Gollancz Ltd., 1964), p. 60. Professor Thompson also points out that an average of 50 to 60 persons were hanged each year for these "crimes against property." *Ibid.*, p. 61.

29. Between 1786 and 1869, some 160,000 persons were transported to Australia as convicts. Margorie Barnard, *A History of Australia* (New York: Frederick A. Praeger, Inc., 1963), p. 210.

30. As will be explained later, it is this writer's belief that the major human costs incurred in both the Soviet and capitalist development experience are not inherent in the systems and, therefore, need not be repeated by underdeveloped countries today.

the industrial revolution, England dominated the economy of Ireland. In the famine years of the 1840's, at least one and a half million Irish died and another one million were forced to emigrate.[31]

The period of the industrial revolution also saw great human cost in India, as Britain began to spread her power. After the battle of Plassey in 1757, British rule began to consolidate itself in Bengal, Bihar, Orissa, and eventually in all of India. British policy consisted of expropriation of Indian land and resources for English companies, high taxation of Indian manufactures and agriculture, and through political control, artificial turning of the terms-of-trade against Indian products. English products were allowed free entry, or virtual free entry, into India, but tariffs were erected against the entry of Indian industrial products into England, and direct trade between India and any other country was prevented by the operation of the Navigation Acts. These policies led to the destruction of Indian manufactures, which prior to 1757 had been competitive with British. By the early nineteenth century, India had been converted into an exporter of food and raw materials. In Nehru's opinion, this had important consequences for India.

The liquidation of the artisan class led to unemployment on a pro-digious scale. What were all these scores of millions, who had so far been engaged in industry and manufacture, to do now? . . . They could die of course. . . . They did die in tens of millions. . . . But still vast numbers of them remained. . . . They drifted to the land, for the land was still there. But the land was fully occupied and could not possibly absorb them profitably. So they became a burden on the land and the burden grew, and with it grew the poverty of the country, and the standard of living fell to incredibly low levels. . . . India became pro-gressively ruralized. . . . This, then, is the real, the fundamental cause of the appalling poverty of the Indian people.[32]

England was not the only industrializing country to possess col-onies. The Dutch had the East Indies, the French had Indo-China and parts of Africa, and Belgium had the Congo. Japan took over Taiwan and Korea as colonies, thus shifting some of the burden of capital accumulation to the people of these countries.

A large share of the human costs of capital accumulation in the

31. See Cecil Woodham-Smith, *The Great Hunger* (New York: Harper and Row, 1963). She places a large share of the blame for the high mortality on the English policy of laissez-faire and the land tenure system imposed by the English over the preceding years.

32. Jawaharlal Nehru, *The Discovery of India* (New York: Doubleday & Co., 1956), pp. 211-12.

Western countries was also borne by the Negroes caught in the African slave trade.[33] By the 1790's, the value of English incomes derived from trade with the West Indies was about four times larger than the income from trade with all the rest of the world. And the trade with the West Indies was in many respects the ideal colonial system, since it consisted in simple exchange of cheap manufactured goods for African slaves; of African slaves for West Indian foodstuffs and tobacco; and of these products for high return in cash from Europe.

There is no need to detail the cost in suffering to the slaves in providing this capital accumulation for the developing countries. The only question is how many Africans had to pay this price. "So far as the Atlantic slave trade is concerned, it appears reasonable to suggest that in one way or another, before and after embarkation, it cost Africa at least fifty million souls. This estimate . . . is certainly on the low side."[34]

Even in the United States, where conditions were the most advantageous for development, there was a high human cost. Too often the economic historian focuses only on the social cost to the white worker. But the role of the American Indian and the Negro slave must not be completely overlooked. In the nineteenth century, the American Indian stood in the way of capitalist expansion. Thus, a policy that can only be called genocide was embarked upon. "Disease, conquest, mass executions, oppression, decay and assimilation had by about 1900 reduced the number of Indians in the United States to some 250,000 or less than one-third of the estimated population in aboriginal time."[35] The same type of policy was followed in Canada, Australia, and New Zealand.

According to Douglass North, the main catalyst of United States industrialization in the 1820-40 period was exports of cotton which were produced by Negro slaves.[36] What cost did the American Negro

33. For a detailed analysis of the slave trades' contribution to European development, see Eric Williams, *Capitalism and Slavery* (Chapel Hill: The University of North Carolina Press, 1944); Basil Davidson, *Black Mother* (Boston: Little Brown & Co., 1961); and Daniel P. Mannix, *Black Cargoes* (New York: Viking Press, 1962).

34. Davidson, *Black Mother*, p. 80.

35. William Brandon, *The American Heritage Book of Indians* (New York: Dell Publishing Co., 1961), p. 360.

36. Douglass North, *The Economic Growth of the United States: 1790-1860* (Englewood Cliffs: Prentice-Hall, Inc., 1961), p. 189. See also Kenneth M. Stampp, *The Peculiar Institution: Slavery in the Ante-Bellum South* (New York: Vintage Books, 1964).

pay, both as a slave and later as a freedman for American economic development?

It should be noted again that none of the above is meant to prove a cause and effect relationship between capitalist development and the detailed human costs. The purpose of including these costs is to place the human cost of development in the Soviet Union in perspective. In both the Soviet and capitalist cases there is insufficient evidence to say that the *process* of development *required* these human costs. In fact, one of the goals of development policy today should be the attempt to minimize the attendant social costs.

## FREEDOM AND ECONOMIC DEVELOPMENT

*The Cost in the U.S.S.R.* The greatest drawback of the Soviet model has been its implementation by totalitarian communist regimes. It is true that communist parties have provided the coercive leadership and development ethic necessary to successfully carry out industrialization. But communism has not just been authoritarian, it has imposed a totalitarian *Weltanschauung* that has been economically counterproductive and that has generated appalling and unnecessary social costs. This totalitarian *Weltanschauung,* combined with the fear of "capitalist encirclement," led in the Soviet Union to the treatment of dissent as treason and of error as sabotage. In this atmosphere, a secret police, "corrective" labor camps, and purges were enabled to thrive.

It is true, of course, that this *Weltanschauung* was reinforced by the historical background of Russia. The vast bulk of the Russian people lost little freedom under the Soviet regime because they had little to lose. Secret police organizations to fight revolutionary activity had long been used in Tsarist Russia. Banishment and exile were old Tsarist institutions. Forced labor in the form of serfdom also had a long history.

Since the Russian Revolution the secret police have brought suffering and fear to millions of people. It is only in their colonial possessions that we see capitalist countries maintaining a secret police and using terror to maintain order.[37] The use of forced labor was widespread in the Soviet Union.[38] Capitalist countries utilized forced

37. See Wilbert E. Moore, *Industrialization and Labor* (New York: Cornell University Press, 1951); and J. C. Furnivall, *Colonial Policy and Practice* (New York: New York University Press, 1956).

38. Western estimates of the peak use of forced labor vary between 3 and 13 million. See S. Swianiewicz, *Forced Labour and Economic Development* (London: Oxford University Press, 1965), pp. 25-40.

labor in their colonies and through the institutions of slavery and indentured servitude.

Presumably the more pragmatic Communist leadership that has emerged since Stalin's death, combined with the decline in fear of "capitalist encirclement," will reduce these totalitarian social costs in the future. However, if the social costs of the Stalin era had to be repeated when utilizing the Soviet model, then almost any alternative would be preferable.

*The Cost in the Underdeveloped Countries.* In discussing the impact of rapid industrialization on freedom, it must be remembered that for the bulk of the people in underdeveloped countries, there is little freedom to be lost. Moreover, too often the meaning of freedom to Western observers is entirely unlike that understood by the masses of poor in the underdeveloped areas. The Brazilian economist, Celso Furtado, has argued:

> It must be recognized . . . that the masses in the underdeveloped countries have not generally put the same high valuation on individual liberty that we do. Since they have not had access to the better things of life, they obviously cannot grasp the full meaning of the supposed dilemma between liberty and quick development. Also, if we were to assert that rapid economic development of socialist countries was achieved only at the price of restricting civil liberties, we must then accept the corollary that the liberty enjoyed by the minority in our society is paid for by the delay in general economic development, hence is at the expense of the welfare of the great majority.[39]

The problem of how to obtain present sacrifices from the present generation for the benefit of the future cannot be ignored. It might very well involve a postponement of political freedom. In England, the working class did not receive the right to vote until 1867, after the "big push" stage of the industrial revolution was over. In both Germany and France, the lower classes were effectively excluded from the franchise until development was well on its way. In Japan, there were no political rights for the lower classes. Even in the United States, political rights were severely restricted during the crucial 1830-60 period. The American Negro, the American Indian, and imported foreign workers such as Chinese coolies had no political rights. In addition, property, residence, and literacy requirements effectively disenfranchised large segments of the lower classes. Still,

39. Celso Furtado, "Brazil: What Kind of Revolution," *Foreign Affairs,* Vol. 41, No. 3 (April, 1963), p. 530.

the Soviet record with regard to political freedom has been no better and possibly poorer than the capitalist countries of the West.

### SOCIAL COSTS AND THE SOVIET MODEL

There is no doubt that the social cost of economic development in the Soviet Union was very high. However, the important question for the purposes of this study is whether or not these costs are an inherent part of the Soviet model. A good case can be made for the position that not all of these costs are inherent in the model, but instead are due to specific historical circumstances and mistakes.[40] Still others were due to the totalitarian nature of Stalinist communism and thus need not be repeated.[41]

A portion of the social cost in the Soviet Union can be attributed to the extraordinary speed of industrialization which was necessitated by the fear (real or imagined) of foreign attack. Gerschenkron has pointed out:

Much of what happened at the turn of the third and fourth decades of the century was the product of that specific historical moment . . . it must not be forgotten that the smashing defeat of the country by Germany stood at the very cradle of the Soviet regime. Foreign intervention in the Civil War, however half-hearted, certainly left memories that were long in fading . . . after Hitler's advent to power . . . the threat of a military attack began to loom larger and larger each year. There is very little doubt that . . . Russian industrialization in the Soviet period was a function of the country's foreign and military policies.[42]

The adverse impact on the people of this rapid tempo of industrialization was increased by the sharp decline in the international terms-of-trade which required larger agricultural exports to obtain the same amount of capital imports. In addition, Gerschenkron points out that the Soviets' willingness to push rapidly ahead in spite of the social costs incurred was conditioned by the historical acceptance of force in Russia.

40. Professor Swianiewicz, however, argues that the rapid tempo of development adopted in the Soviet model necessarily causes a demand for labor that can be met at reasonable cost only through forced labor. See Swianiewicz, *Forced Labour and Economic Development*, pp. 189-207. However, this would be profitable only if the difference in consumption between free and forced labor exceeded the difference in output between the two kinds of labor.

41. For an interesting discussion of this point see Alec Nove, "Was Stalin Really Necessary?" in his *Economic Rationality and Soviet Politics* (New York: Frederick A. Praeger, Inc., 1964), pp. 17-39.

42. Alexander Gerschenkron, *Economic Backwardness in Historical Perspective* (New York: Frederick A. Praeger, Inc., 1965), pp. 147-48.

If Peter the Great had been called back to life and asked to take a good look at Russia, say, in the second half of the thirties . . . he might have found the purge trials unnecessarily cumbersome and verbose; and he might have upbraided Stalin for the unmanly refusal to participate physically in the act of conveying the modern *Strel'tsy* from life to death. Yet it should not have taken him long to understand the essentials of the situation. For the resemblance between Soviet and Petrine Russia was striking indeed. . . . He would no doubt have acquiesced in the tremendous human cost of the collectivization struggles, once it had been explained to him that the quantitative difference between the Soviet period and his own time in this respect was largely the result of the colossal growth in population in the two intervening centuries.[43]

The major cause of the famine in the early 1930's was the massive destruction of livestock that occurred at the beginning of the collectivization drive. This was caused by the attempt to collectivize all of the peasants' livestock. Rather than acquiesce, the peasants slaughtered and ate their livestock. The decision to collectivize livestock was probably the single most important mistake made in the Soviet Union during the 1930's. The Communist countries that began collectivization later did not repeat this mistake. The eastern European countries collectivized at a much slower rate and even stopped temporarily when resistance became strong.[44] In China, "the principal domestic animal, the pig, was left in private hands . . . the Chinese were able to avoid mass slaughter of livestock and famine in carrying through full-scale collectivization."[45]

In conclusion, while the social costs incurred in the industrialization of the Soviet Union need not be repeated to the same degree by an underdeveloped country adopting the Soviet model or some part thereof, some social costs seem almost inevitable regardless of what development model is followed.

There are a number of reasons why the industrialization process is not a painless one. First, there is the need in many countries for a radical change in social structure. In many cases, this can be

43. *Ibid.*

44. The percentage of cows in the private sector in 1964 was 90 per cent in Poland, 47 per cent in East Germany, 22 per cent in Czechoslovakia, 57 per cent in Hungary, 62 per cent in Rumania, 35 per cent in Bulgaria, and 95 per cent in Yugoslavia. U.S. Department of Agriculture, *The U.S.S.R. and Eastern Europe Agricultural Situation* (Washington: Government Printing Office, 1966), p. 60.

45. Alec Nove, "Collectivization of Agriculture in Russia and China," in *Symposium on Economic and Social Problems of the Far East*, ed. E. F. Szczpanik (Hong Kong: Hong Kong University Press, 1962), p. 19.

brought about only by a more or less violent social revolution. The old order will fight to maintain its dominance and the new will defend itself against possible counterrevolution. And the period of revolution is not restricted to just the time of open civil war (if there is one) but extends until the inhibiting features of the old social structure are eradicated. The American Civil War officially ended in 1865 but the social revolution that engendered it goes on today in the battles of Little Rock, Birmingham, Watts, Detroit, and Washington, D.C. The collectivization battles of the 1930's were a continuation of the Russian Revolution of 1917.

Second, and closely allied to the first, is the need to develop new social institutions and to educate people to new habits and values. Peasants must be turned into factory workers. A new kind of discipline must be learned. People must be convinced that new ways of doing things can be good and beneficial. This is often not easy. The Luddites rose up and smashed the new machinery in the British industrial revolution. The Russian peasant tried to sabotage the introduction of the kolkhoz. The type of labor discipline that is required in an industrial society is alien to the habits of a preindustrial society. It is difficult to convince people of the need for new habits and discipline exclusively by methods of persuasion. It is not so much that the need for discipline and change is not understood; but as often happens, what is understood is not yet sufficiently willed. Thus, the change-over from one set of habits and values to another is difficult, and some compulsion is often required. This compulsion took the form of the *explicit coercion* of the state police power to expedite the movement from individual to collective farms and to enforce factory discipline in the Soviet Union of the 1930's. In capitalist countries, the *implicit coercion* of the market mechanism transferred labor from rural to urban areas and imposed discipline through the threat of starvation and unemployment.

Third is the need to increase the rate of capital accumulation. This involves widening the margin between consumption and total output. Despite the fact that consumption levels are already deplorably low in underdeveloped countries, it is most unlikely that they can be substantially raised in the early stages of development. "Often it is argued that (the) more humane approach is what distinguished economic development under democratic conditions from what would take place under a Communist regime—in my opinion a rather dangerous assertion if, realistically, living standards will have to be kept low in order to allow development."[46] This need to restrain consumption in favor of capital accumulation can cause a rise in social discontent. The poorer classes will feel that after fighting for the recent revolution they are entitled to its fruits. The middle classes and the remaining upper classes will resent the curtailment of their former privileges and "luxury" consumption. To keep this unrest from upsetting the development plans or from leading to counterrevolution a powerful, even ruthless, government policy of coercion may be needed. This, while enabling capital to be accumulated, will increase the social cost of doing so. It is wrong to envision economic development as a smooth evolutionary process of change since ". . . the happy picture of a quiet industrial revolution proceeding without undue stir and thrust has been . . . seldom reproduced in historical reality."[47] The changes necessary to initiate economic development are more likely to resemble a gigantic social and political earthquake. Kuznets has pointed out:

> These changes do not occur in a vacuum; they are made in societies that usually have a long tradition of the premodern economic organization and social structure, and they must be directed by agents with the power to overcome resistance and incur necessary costs. . . .
> It is this dislocation and break with the old order that constitutes the major cost of the transition to modern economic growth. Moreover, the benefits of the innovation are not immediate, since it is during this period that the shift to higher proportions of capital formation may occur; and the rise in consumption per capita, if any, must be smaller than the rise in total product per capita. . . .
> In short, the transitions can be described as periods of controlled social and economic revolution. . . . Not every society can muster the necessary ingredients: a minority that can assume leadership and an organizational framework and set of values that can hold the population together and make it accept the costs and cooperate with the minority.
> . . . this innovating minority must have minimum cooperation from the population, and it may secure it by different means, ranging from authoritarian compulsion backed by powerful propaganda to instill allegiance to the "wave of the future," to a laissez-faire attitude with government setting the permissive conditions by removing obstacles and providing encouragement on the theory that the activities of the private enterpreneurial groups will redound to the benefit of society as a whole.[48]

46. Gunnar Myrdal, *An International Economy* (New York: Harper & Brothers Publishers, 1956), p. 164.
47. Gerschenkron, *Economic Backwardness in Historical Perspective,* p. 213.
48. Simon Kuznets, *Economic Growth and Structure* (New York: W. W. Norton & Co., Inc., 1965) pp. 106-8.

CONCLUSION

From the discussion in this chapter we can draw a number of conclusions. The social cost of development in the Soviet Union was high indeed—purges, Stalinist terror, forced labor, famine, and lack of freedom. The cost of capitalist development was high also—slavery, colonialism, genocide of native races, and lack of freedom. The extent of a cause and effect relationship is probably impossible to establish. It would seem, however, that particular historical circumstances, rather than the development process itself, account for the major share of the human costs. The human cost of either capitalist or Communist development appears less than the cost of continued underdevelopment. Still, some social cost seems inevitable if economic development is to take place.

Given the inevitability of some social cost, how does one evaluate the acceptability of this cost relative to the potential benefits of economic development? Seeking refuge in some predetermined ideological position does not solve the problem because as Richard Ohmann has pointed out:

A man who subscribes to a moral or social ideology runs the risk that someone will put it into practice and thereby burden it with a wretched freight of human error and venality. The guillotine becomes an argument against libertarianism, juvenile gangwars an argument against permissive parenthood, the carpetbaggers an argument against emancipation. When this happens, the ideologist may recant; or he may save his ideology by disowning the malpractice as irrelevant perversion. A third response is possible: to accept *la guillotine* along with *la liberté*; but in a man of good will, this requires a strong stomach and a certain obstinacy.[49]

None of these responses seems adequate to the problem. Possibly there is no adequate answer since our normal moral standards are so ambiguous. However, the problem at least can be made clearer by briefly discussing two factors that affect moral judgments.

First, there are the "objective conditions controlling the environment in which behavior takes place."[50] An example of this would be a state of war. Restrictions of civil liberties, for example, are usually judged more acceptable in wartime than in time of peace. Economic development is also an objective condition. The prevailing objective conditions will help determine what is acceptable behavior

49. Richard Ohmann, "GBS on the U.S.S.R.," *The Commonweal* (July 24, 1964), p. 519.
50. De Schweinitz, "Economic Growth, Coercion, and Freedom," p. 168.

on the part of the state and of individuals. This may be an ambiguous standard but it seems to be accepted by most people. For example, Bowles has pointed out that ". . . the death of a political enemy on a battlefield is approved, the domestic execution of a political prisoner is disapproved."[51]

Second, there is the "ideology affecting the norms by which man evaluates such behavior."[52] In the example cited above, a state of war is an objective condition, while the historical tradition and system of beliefs which shape peoples' attitudes about civil liberties comprise the ideology or value system. Obviously the two factors interact. The objective conditions can alter the ideological commitments. Given the situation of ruthless guerrilla warfare in South Vietnam, many Americans became willing to view torture and napalm bombing of peasant villages as acceptable conduct. Even with roughly similar objective conditions, a value system can yield different judgments of identical actions. In the aftermath of the Cuban revolution the execution of a few thousand Batista supporters was condemned by many Americans. The shooting of several hundred thousand Communists in the recent Indonesian revolution was received, if not with approval, at least with tolerance. Also, at least until recently, a government which did not allow white people to vote would be judged a dictatorship, while one that only disenfranchised colored people could be considered a democracy. In addition, of course, different value systems will judge the same actions or behavior differently. Raising the price of a good to take advantage of a temporary scarcity in its supply would have been condemned as a sin by Medieval Catholicism; in a capitalist society it would be considered good business practice.

The above discussion highlights the complexity of the problem of evaluating the social costs of economic development. Man seems to be faced with a dilemma. On the one hand, the failure to overcome underdevelopment *allows* untold human suffering to continue. On the other hand, the process of overcoming these human costs through speeding up development will most likely *generate* some new ones; and the faster the old human costs are overcome the more severe the new. Also, there is the danger that the centralized power needed to generate rapid development will be used, as with Stalin, to consolidate personal power and establish totalitarianism.

51. W. Donald Bowles, "Soviet Russia As a Model for Underdeveloped Areas," *World Politics*, Vol. XIV, No. 3 (April, 1962), p. 502.
52. De Schweinitz, "Economic Growth, Coercion, and Freedom," p. 168.

Let me close this discussion by quoting a written comment received from a close colleague, W. Michael Bailey, after he had read the chapter.

It seems most ironic that to be FREE (from want and privation) man must be made a SLAVE to some political and economic gyroscope that spins off goods in abundance while grinding away at moral freedom and the possibility of real human choices. In a sense your paper is the most immoral thing of all because it portrays so clearly the necessity for evil and provides the perfect motive for doing for good reasons what so many want to do for the sheer pleasure of it and for the terrible beauty of the awesome power machine that man can make. False gods beckon on every side; only a few see God within the shadows, faint like a mist but more real than man's most titanic creations, as good is.

*Part Two*

*AN APPLICATION OF THE SOVIET MODEL:*
*SOVIET CENTRAL ASIA*

# VII. SOVIET CENTRAL ASIA BEFORE 1928

In the previous six chapters a historical-theoretical model of Soviet economic development has been constructed. In this chapter, an actual application of the model to an underdeveloped area is studied. For this purpose, a case study of Soviet Central Asia is presented.

Some writers maintain that the U.S.S.R. is a poor model for underdeveloped areas because it was more developed in 1928 than the typical Asian or African country is today. Soviet Central Asia has been chosen as a case study because on the eve of the great industrialization drive it had all of the characteristics of an underdeveloped area. The following pages of this chapter will bring this out in detail.

The development of Central Asia by the Soviet regime is an excellent example of substantial economic development produced quickly and under governmental auspices. Soviet Central Asia is taken here in its broad sense as an over-all term for the five Soviet Socialist Republics of the U.S.S.R.—Kazakhstan, Uzbekistan, Kirgizia, Tadjikstan, and Turkmenistan—which lie to the each of the Caspian Sea. These five republics cover a vast region, extending almost 1,900 miles from east to west and totaling 1,542,000 square miles.[1] In 1959, the total population was 22,978,000[2] of which approximately 68 per cent were Asiatics.[3]

1. Tsentralnoye statisticheskoye Upravleniye pri Sovete Ministrov SSSR, *Narodnoye Khozyaystvo SSSR v 1961 godu: statisticheskiy yezhegodnik* (Moscow: Gosstatizdat, 1962), p. 33. Many writers do not include Kazakhstan because of the large Russian population in the republic. It is felt that for the purposes of this study that it is proper to include it because the five republics form a natural geographical and racial unit and to some extent have been treated as a separate geographical area for Soviet economic organization purposes. Wherever it seems desirable, Kazakhstan and the rest of Central Asia will be treated both together and separately.

2. *Ibid.*, p. 9.

3. J. P. Cole and F. C. German, *A Geography of the U.S.S.R.: The Background to a Planned Economy* (London: Butterworths, 1961), p. 58.

Soviet Central Asia is divided into four natural or geographical regions.[4] First, there is the steppe region of northern Kazakhstan which is a continuation of the south Russian and southern Siberian steppe. It is a more or less level, treeless expanse, without surface water or swamps, and covered with grass on black-earth soil. It has a continuous cover of feather grass interspersed with occasional bare patches. In the extreme north of Kazakhstan is a forest-steppe. The steppe lies in the lower limit of precipitation necessary for agriculture. Thus nonirrigated agriculture is feasible under favorable circumstances. Second is the semi-desert or steppe desert which lies south of the steppe and extends in a continuous belt across the North Caspian Lowland to the Altay Mountains. It is a transitional zone between desert and steppe. Feather grass, interspersed with desert plants and extensive bare patches, make up the plant cover. The soil is saline to a high degree, with many salt lakes and expanses of alkali flats. Nonirrigated agriculture is possible but unreliable. Third is the desert proper. This is a region of low precipitation and high evaporation which lies south of the semi-desert and stretches from the Volga Delta north and east of the Caspian Sea to the Persian Highlands, then east to the Pamir and Tien-Shan Mountain ranges along the Chinese-Russian border. Vegetation growth is limited by seasons to the few days of spring rain. Along the banks of lakes and rivers are *tugays,* or jungle thickets. Finally, there is the mountain region which lies almost entirely in the southeastern corner, along the Chinese and Afghan borders. The main ranges are the Pamir and Tien-shan. The highest point in the U.S.S.R., 24,700 feet, is Mount Communism in the Pamirs.

Soviet Central Asia is for several reasons "a very desirable area in which to observe the Soviet economic programme in action."[5] As pointed out above, it forms a natural geographical and racial unit. It has always to some extent been treated as a separate geographical area for Soviet economic organization purposes. Its resources are varied enough to illustrate Soviet economic activity in many fields. The level of cultural attainment and the strength of historical tra-

4. Bureau of Social Science Research, American University, *Handbook of Central Asia*, Subcontractors monograph HRAF-49 (3 vols.; New Haven: Human Relations Area Files, Inc., 1956), I, 43-46.

5. Paul B. Henze, "The Economic Development of Soviet Central Asia to the Eve of World War II: An Examination of Soviet Methods As Applied to a Semi-Colonial Area," *Royal Central Asian Society Journal*, Part I, Vol. XXXVI (July, 1949); Part II, Vol. XXXVII (January, 1950); Vol. XXXVI (July, 1949), p. 279.

ditions is much more similar to the important underdeveloped areas of the world today than is, for example, Siberia, which until recently was in a primeval, almost uninhabited state. And, finally, Soviet Central Asia is a kind of "showcase" of socialist development methods.

Asia and Africa—and Latin America—are far more interested in the people of Soviet Central Asia than in the other non-Russian areas of the U.S.S.R. This is because Central Asia was the colonial hinterland of the Tsar's empire. The American or European is prone to overlook the fact that what has happened there is an inspiration to Asians.

To Asians, the important thing is that, with rare exceptions, Soviet Central Asian women are no longer veiled; people are clothed and no longer in rags; there is milk for children—all children; there are hospitals—good hospitals; there are enough Asian doctors to staff them.

American visitors to Soviet Central Asia see a living standard not to be compared with that of the United States. Asians see that there are no beggars; people have jobs. Americans are depressed by the fact that city people are crowded a whole family to one room, and farm families in two—or three—room cottages. Asians see that there is no one sleeping in the streets, no sewage in the gutters, no scooping of drinking or washing water from open ditches.[6]

## THE HISTORICAL BACKGROUND OF SOVIET CENTRAL ASIA[7]

Traditional Central Asian society developed between the sixteenth and the twentieth centuries. A rather fluid set of states and principalities were characteristic of the period. In one sense, these were the succession states of the Mongol empire. These states were of two basic types—nomadic and sedentary.

The sedentary or agricultural state was ruled by a khan or sultan from one of the major cities of the region. His khanate was not an empire; it usually comprised no more than one or two of the fertile river valleys of Central Asia. The khanate was divided among a group of local lords or *beks,* who supported the khan through payments of tax and tribute. Also, the khan or central ruler owned land

6. William Mandel, *Russia Re-Examined: The Land, The People and How They Live* (New York: Hill and Wang, 1964), pp. 57-58.

7. The following sources were consulted in preparing this section: Richard A. Pierce, *Russian Central Asia, 1867-1917* (Berkeley: University of California Press, 1960); William Mandel, *The Soviet Far East and Central Asia,* Institute of Pacific Relations Inquiry Series (New York: The Dial Press, Inc., 1944), pp. 97-118; Michael Rywkin, *Russia in Central Asia,* Russian Civilization Series (New York: Collier Books, 1963), pp. 15-32; Bureau of Social Science Research, *Handbook on Central Asia,* I, 6-33.

in the territories of his *beks*. The Uzbeks, the Tadjiks, the Karakal-paks, and part of the Turkmens were governed by this system of rule.

The chief representative of the nomadic form of state was the Kazakhs. The nomadic Kirgiz never developed a state form. The Kazakhs were divided into three hordes, each with a separate khan. The khans ruled from their steppe localities and rarely settled down in a city.

The leader on the steppes had his retinue, just as did the feudal lord. The leader supported his retainers, and they in turn fought at his command and otherwise helped him keep the peace within his domain and defend it from external enemies. The steppe ruler had a council of his immediate subordinates corresponding to the concilium of the European feudal lord. The steppe nomadic rulers were separated from their subjects as aristocracy and commoners; and the feudal lord in turn was differentiated from the commoners by different family trees. The feudal lord exacted from his serfs the *corvee*, or feudal due in labor, as well as payment in agricultural products or kind.[8]

This description of Central Asian society is accurate right up to the time of the Russian conquest of the nineteenth century. "Between the time of the Mongol dynasties of the 13th and the 15th centuries and the Russian conquests in the 19th there was little change in the system of rule."[9]

Russian Tsarism did not undertake the conquest of Central Asia until the sixties of the nineteenth century. The social structure of the area remained largely unchanged during the half century of Russian rule. Its system of land tenure, which lay at the base of its economy and history, was feudal, and yield and population rose and fell with the changing relationships between beks and khans. When the khan was strong, the irrigation canals were maintained and agriculture flourished. When the beks felt themselves strong enough to challenge the khan, agriculture declined, particularly if the wars were of long duration. Pierce sums up the situation as follows:

Political power in the Central Asian State was of a feudal nature similar to that of medieval Europe. Hereditary rulers had nominal control, but the provincial beks (governors) were practically independent and carried on constant wars against their neighbors or their sovereigns. The government was tyrannical and oppressive and meted out cruel punishments. The clergy dominated thought, and illiteracy and superstition were widespread.

8. Bureau of Social Science Research, *Handbook of Central Asia*, I, 15.
9. *Ibid.*, p. 13.

The economy of the settled population was based on agriculture, chiefly the growing of grain. Most of the land was worked by peasants on shares, and many of the peasants were so heavily in debt that they were in virtual serfdom. Unbelievers were enslaved. Trade was poorly developed and sapped by heavy taxes. Caravans were prey to the nomads. Almost constant warfare between the khanates or the bekdoms placed a heavy burden on inhabitants. Irrigation systems could not be repaired or expanded, flocks were driven off, and sown areas varied in extent depending on the ability of the inhabitants to defend them. Thus, though Central Asia had achieved a high level of prosperity in earlier times, by the middle of the nineteenth century the region was in a state of decay, isolated from the modern world, its population static, and its economy depressed.[10]

After the Russian conquest two problems emerged which were to dominate the Russian development of Central Asia. The first was the need of the Russian and Polish textile industry for cheap domestic cotton. The fertility of the Fergana valley and the successful introduction of American cotton in 1894 made cotton a key product of Central Asia. Although the economy changed rapidly from one that was self-sufficient in food products to a one-crop system (the area under cotton cultivation grew from 13,200 hectares in 1886 to 597,200 hectares in 1914), the bek-dekkan (lord-peasant) relationship remained.[11] In fact, this relationship was strengthened because the independent peasantry rapidly lost most of their land under the usurious terms of credit and became sharecroppers, often retaining only one-fourth of the crop. The Russian textile industry, which imported 96 per cent of all its cotton needs in 1886, was importing only 48.7 per cent by 1914.[12] The cotton boom had a decisive influence on other areas of the economy. Industrial development was centered around cotton. Cotton mills, employing two-thirds of all industrial workers, accounted for over three-fourths of total industrial output of the area.[13] By 1907, Central Asia had become an important buyer of grains, sugar, lumber, iron and steel products as well as of manufactured goods from European Russia.

Second was the problem of the so-called "surplus lands" in the Kazakh Steppe and in Kirgizia. There land that was suitable for agriculture was "bought, seized or expropriated by the Russians . . . the natives, like the American Indians, were forced to move out into less

10. Pierce, *Russian Central Asia, 1867-1917*, pp. 12-13.
11. Rywkin, *Russia in Central Asia*, p. 29.
12. *Ibid.*
13. *Ibid.*

desirable areas."[14] The taking over of "surplus lands" was most often done under harsh administrative pressure, and not only nomads, but even settled Kazakhs and Kirgizes were deprived of their lands. It is estimated that between forty and forty-five million hectares of Kazakh land alone were taken over prior to 1917.[15] Driven into the desert, the nomads' cattle died off, and the nomads themselves died in large numbers. Between "1902 and 1907, the Kirghiz' cattle herds decreased by 27 per cent, and the number of Kirghiz people itself is estimated to have dropped by 7 to 10 per cent in the years 1903-1913."[16] In the same area the average Russian farm had an annual income twice that of the average Kazakh farm. The real difference was much greater, however, because much of the Kazakh wealth was held by that 4 per cent of the population that comprised the tribal aristocracy.[17]

CENTRAL ASIAN ECONOMY AND SOCIETY ON THE EVE OF THE 1917 REVOLUTION

The state of the economy and the level of social and cultural development at the end of Tsarist rule in Central Asia is the question that must be investigated next.[18] "There is no doubt that Central Asia had almost, if not all, the characteristics generally attributed to underdeveloped areas: low productivity, antiquated technology, widespread poverty, little or no modern intensive, or mechanized agriculture, wide-spread illiteracy, and so forth."[19] The industrial de-

14. *Ibid.*, p. 28. See also Mandel, *The Soviet Far East and Central Asia,* pp. 101-2; Pierce, *Russian Central Asia, 1867-1917,* pp. 107-38; Olaf Caroe, *Soviet Empire: The Turks of Central Asia and Stalinism* (London: Macmillan & Co., Ltd., 1954), pp. 82-86.

15. Rywkin, *Russia in Central Asia,* p. 31. Mandel estimates the amount at 100 million acres in Kazakhstan. See Mandel, *The Soviet Far East and Central Asia,* p. 101.

16. *Bolshia Sovetskaia Entsiklopedia,* Vol. 32, p. 377, cited by Mandel, *The Soviet Far East and Central Asia,* p. 101. Also the "land expropriation resulted in yearly famines among the Moslems between 1910 and 1913," S. D. Asfendiarov, *Natsionalno-osvoboditelnoe vosstania 1916 g. v. Kazakhstane* (Alama Ata-Moscow: Kazakhskoe Kraevoeizd., 1936), p. 184, cited in Rywkin, *Russia in Central Asia,* p. 31.

17. Rywkin, *Russia in Central Asia,* p. 31.

18. The estimated population at this time, 1914, was 13,579,000. Frank Lorimer, *The Population of the Soviet Union: History and Prospects,* Series of League of Nations Publications–Economic and Financial (Geneva: League of Nations, 1946), p. 36.

19. Walter McKenzie Pintner, "Initial Problems in the Soviet Economic Development of Central Asia," *Royal Central Asian Society Journal,* XL (July/October, 1953), 284.

velopment of Central Asia began with the Soviet era. In the present area of Uzbekistan the primitively equipped cotton-ginning and cotton oil industry accounted for 86.7 per cent of total industrial production in 1913, and for 54.2 per cent of all industrial workers; and in all of Central Asia this industry accounted for three-fourths of total industrial production and two-thirds of all industrial workers.[20] Even the industrially most developed region of pre-revolutionary Kazakhstan, Akmolinsk, "had a per capita industrial output of less than one-third of the average for Russia as a whole, and the number of workers per 100,000 population was only about one-fifth of the country's average."[21] In 1913, in the five republics of Central Asia and in Azerbaijan, Georgia, and Armenia, a total of "30 primitive machine-tools (1.7 per cent of Russia's total) were produced."[22] The food industry in Kazakhstan comprised 62.6 per cent of total industrial production according to the census of 1913. The production of spirits, vodka, and beer equaled the total output of all branches of heavy industry.[23] In the whole of Uzbekistan before 1917, there were only 425 primitive workshops and factories. There was not a single textile mill, although the main crop was cotton.[24] In 1913, Kirgizia had only a small number of handicraft shops with primitive machinery which employed fewer than 1,500 workers.[25] Prior to the 1917 Revolution, the industry of Turkmenistan was composed mainly of small enterprises in industry.[26] Tadjikstan was one of the most backward regions in Tsarist Russia. Its industry was confined to semi-artisan workshops chiefly devoted to processing agricultural raw materials.[27]

The system of fuel supply was extremely backward. In all of

20. P. Alampiev, *Where Economic Inequality Is No More: Progress of the Soviet Eastern Republics As Exemplified by Kazakhstan* (Moscow: Foreign Languages Publishing House, 1959), p. 35. Also Rywkin, *Russia in Central Asia*, p. 29.

21. Alampiev, *Where Economic Inequality Is No More*, pp. 33-34.

22. *Ibid.*, p. 70.

23. *Ibid.*, pp. 95-96.

24. Arif Alimov, *Uzbekistan*, The Fifteen Soviet Socialist Republics Today and Tomorrow (London: Soviet Booklets, 1960), p. 6.

25. Kazy Dikambayev, *Kirgizia*, The Fifteen Soviet Socialist Republics Today and Tomorrow (London: Soviet Booklets, 1960), p. 6.

26. Balysh Ovezov, *Turkmenia*, The Fifteen Soviet Socialist Republics Today and Tomorrow (London: Soviet Booklets, 1960), p. 8.

27. Central Statistical Board of the U.S.S.R. Council of Ministers, *Forty Years of Soviet Power: In Facts and Figures* (Moscow: Foreign Languages Publishing House, 1958), p. 126.

Central Asia, in 1913, 131,100 tons of coal, 260,000 tons of oil, and 7.1 million kilowatts of electric power were produced.[28] Uzbekistan and Turkmenistan produced no coal and Kirgizia and Tadjikstan no oil or electric power.[29] The fuel supply was not only inadequate, but erratic, which required enterprises to resort to fuels such as rushes, camels' thorn, saksaul, pressed sheep dung, and the dung of camels, cows, and horses.

With approximately 10 per cent of the population and 18.4 per cent of the area of the U.S.S.R. in 1913, Central Asia accounted for only 1.8 per cent of railway freight tons originated and 2.1 per cent of the tons terminated. Kirgizia had no railway system and Kazakhstan had a total of 2,042 kilometers of railway track on January 1, 1913, or 0.87 kilometers per 1,000 square kilometers.[30]

As late as 1926, 80 per cent of the Uzbek people lived in rural areas, 98 per cent of the Kazakhs, 99 per cent of the Kirgiz, 85 per cent of the Tadjiks, and 99 per cent of the Turkmens.[31]

The total number of students in all educational institutions in Central Asia, in 1914, was 137,100, of which less than 10 per cent were non-Europeans.[32] Thus, in Soviet Central Asia, 1.1 per cent of the population was attending school as against 5.7 per cent in Russia as a whole.[33] Only 19,200 students were in grade levels above the fourth.[34] There were no institutions of higher learning prior to the 1917 Revolution.[35] In 1897, the illiteracy rate of the age group nine to forty-nine was 96.4 per cent in Uzbekistan, 91.9 per cent in Kazakhstan, 96.9 per cent in Kirgizia, 97.7 per cent in Tadjikstan,

28. E. I. Lagovskaya, *Soyuznye Respubliki Sredney Azii* (Moscow: Gosudarstvyennoye, Uchyebno-Pyedagogichyeskoye Izdatyelbstvo, Ministyerstva Prosvyeshchyeniya RSFSR, 1959), p. 188; TsSU, *Forty Years of Soviet Power*, pp. 117-18, 125-26, 128. Rywkin, *Russia in Central Asia*, p. 68.

29. Lagovskaya, *Soyuznye Respubliki Sredney Azii*, p. 118.

30. Tsentralnoye statisticheskoye upravleniye pri Sovete Ministrov SSSR, *Transporti i svyaz SSSR: statisticheskiy sbornik* (Moscow: Gosudarstvyennoye Statisticheskoye Izdatyelstvo, 1957), pp. 68-69.

31. Bureau of Social Science Research, *Handbook of Central Asia*, I, 202.

32. Tsentralnoye statischeskoye upravleniye pri Sovete Ministrov SSSR, *Kulturnoye stroityelstvo SSSR: statisticheskiy sbornik* (Moscow: Gosudarstvyennoye Statisticheskoye Izadatyelstvo, 1956), pp. 16, 18, 30, 32, 36. Bureau of Social Science Research, *Handbook of Central Asia*, II, 451, 460, 468, 478, 488.

33. In the United States, 24 per cent attended school in 1930. U.S. Bureau of the Census, *Statistical Abstract of the United States, 1963* (84th annual edition; Washington: Government Printing Office, 1963), pp. 5, 113.

34. TsSU, *Kulturnoye stroityelstvo SSSR*, pp. 16, 18, 30, 32, 36.

35. *Ibid.*, pp. 208-10.

and 92.2 per cent in Turkmenistan.[36] As late as 1926 the illiteracy rate for all of Soviet Central Asia was 83.8 per cent.[37]

There were 408 doctors for all of Central Asia in 1913. This provided one doctor for every 33,000 persons. In the same year, there were 3,240 hospital beds or one for every 4,200 persons.[38] In all of Tadjikstan there were 40 hospital beds. In Bukhara and the Khiva khanate, there were no doctors or hospital beds.[39] As late as 1926, the infant mortality rate in Central Asia was approximately 230.[40] ". . . By the end of the Tsarist regime the life of the rural hinterland had changed very little from centuries-old patterns. The bulk of the population was still desperately poor. Agricultural implements and methods were largely those of ancient times. Illiteracy and disease had not been reduced significantly. The native barbers were still removing parasitic worms from the limbs of the people as they had in Marco Polo's day."[41]

INITIAL PROBLEMS IN THE SOVIET ECONOMIC DEVELOPMENT OF CENTRAL ASIA[42]

Central Asia was the first part of Tsarist Russia to given open evidence of discontent during World War I. Rebellion broke out in 1916 after the tsarist government, in need of manpower, decreed

36. Tsentralnoye statischeskoye upravleniye pri Sovete Ministrov SSSR, *Itogi vsyesoyuznoi pyeryepisi nasyelyeniya 1959 goda, SSSR* (Moscow: Gosstatizdat, 1962), p. 89.

37. Computed from Lorimer, *The Population of the Soviet Union*, p. 70.

38. Tsentralnoye statischeskoye upravleniye pri Sovete Ministrov SSSR, *Narodnoye khozyaystvo SSSR v 1959 godu: statisticheskiy yezhegodnik* (Moscow: Gosstatizdat, 1960), pp. 788, 796.

39. Alimov, *Uzbekistan*, p. 19.

40. Estimated from Lorimer, *The Population of the Soviet Union*, pp. 82, 119.

41. Warren Wilhelm, "Soviet Central Asia: Development of a Backward Area," *Foreign Policy Reports*, XXV (February 1, 1950), 219.

42. This section's discussion of Central Asia in the 1920's is drawn from the following sources: Caroe, *Soviet Empire*, pp. 95-161; Mandel, *The Soviet Far East and Central Asia*, pp. 89-118; W. P. Coates and Zelda K. Coates, *Soviets in Central Asia* (New York: Philosophical Library, 1951), pp. 67-93; Rywkin, *Russia in Central Asia*, pp. 33-63; Henze, "The Economic Development of Soviet Central Asia to the Eve of World War II, pp. 281-83; Walter Kolarz, *Russia and Her Colonies* (London: George Phillip and Son, 1952); and Alexander G. Park, *Bolshevism in Turkestan, 1917-1927* (New York: Columbia University Press, 1957). After this manuscript was finished, Violet Conolly's, *Beyond the Urals: Economic Developments in Soviet Asia* (London: Oxford University Press, 1967), was published. Some minor amendments were made throughout this case study in light of her research.

the mobilization of Central Asian Moslems, traditionally free from draft obligation, into labor units. Though the rebellion was suppressed by November, 1916, Central Asia was in a general state of ferment from this time on. After the November, 1917, Revolution, Lenin and the Bolsheviks ". . . aimed both at holding Central Asia because of its value as a source of cotton and at winning the support of its people and thereby making the region a base for the 'emancipation of the East.' "[43]

But the native populations were extremely anti-Russian, White or Red, and in the confusion of civil war and foreign intervention the Soviets were unable to maintain their authority in most parts of Central Asia. With transportation disrupted, grain deliveries from European Russia failed and there resulted famine conditions in many parts of the area in 1918-19. This increased the hostility toward Russians since it was tsarist policy which destroyed Central Asia's earlier self-sufficiency in food production.

The major native resistance to Soviet rule was concentrated in the famous Basmachi Revolt of the 1920's. In its origins the revolt was basically a nationalist movement against Russian domination of Central Asia. But the leadership was mainly that of the traditional rulers—the *beks* and *mullahs*. The revolt received support from the White armies and the intervening foreign powers. Thus the purely nationalist aim of the revolt was heavily compromised. After the defeat of the White Russian armies and the departure of British forces, the main military threat was eliminated. Land reform in the 1920's helped to separate the native peasants from their traditional leaders and helped to gain their acceptance of the Soviet regime.

The Central Asian economy emerged from World War I and the 1917 Revolution in a state of almost total collapse. In many areas production declined to 20 per cent of the 1913 level.[44] However, Lenin's New Economic Policy stimulated reconstruction, despite the continuing Basmachi revolt. Other than reconstruction, the only major economic activity of the 1920's was land reform. It consisted of "confiscating lands and water rights belonging to local *bais* (landlords) and distributing them to the *dekhane* (Moslem peasants)."[45] Started in 1921, then expanded in 1926-27, it brought little practical economic result. But by destroying the economic base of the tra-

43. Henze, "The Economic Development of Soviet Central Asia to the Eve of World War II," p. 281.
44. Rywkin, *Russia in Central Asia*, p. 63.
45. *Ibid.*

ditional ruling class's power, land reform cleared the way for rapid economic and social change. It also contributed greatly to the peasants' acceptance of the Soviet regime. By 1927, 60 per cent of peasant households had voluntarily organized into *Koshchi* unions (farmer's co-operatives).[46] They aided the peasants in buying necessary farm equipment and in marketing their products. Thus, until the industrialization drive began in 1928-29, the 1920's were a period of reconstruction and stabilization for the Central Asian economy.

The preceding pages have shown that Soviet Central Asia, on the eve of the great industrialization drive, was an underdeveloped area with all the characteristics of such. To further document this contention, Table VII-1 and VII-2 compare the state of economic development of Soviet Central Asia in 1926-28 with selected underdeveloped countries in 1960-62.

Since national income figures are unobtainable for Soviet Central Asia and generally are highly unreliable for underdeveloped countries, a composite index of fourteen nonmonetary indicators has been selected as the base for comparison.[47]

For comparison with Soviet Central Asia in 1926-28, the countries selected are mainly geographic neighbors with many of the same social and cultural characteristics. These are India, Iran, Pakistan, and Turkey. Colombia, a Latin American country, has also been selected so as to include a country with different social and cultural traditions, and a generally more advanced economy.

The nonmonetary statistical series deemed more or less useful as indicators of relative levels of economic development are as follows: (1) Wheat yields, 100 kilograms per hectare. (2) Number of tractors per 1,000 hectares of cultivated land. (3) Production of cotton and woolen fabrics, meters per capita. (4) Electricity generation, kilowatt-hours per capita. (5) Production of steel, metric tons per 1,000 population. (6) Consumption of petroleum, metric tons per 1,000 population. (7) Consumption of coal, metric tons per 1,000 population. (8) Million freight-ton-kilometers per 100,000 population. (9) Per cent of population in cities of 20,000 and more. (10) Per cent of population in secondary and higher education. (11) Per cent of adults (over 9) literate. (12) Daily newspaper

46. *Ibid.*
47. For an elaboration of this nonmonetary index, see Charles K. Wilber, "A Nonmonetary Index of Economic Development," *Soviet Studies*, Vol. XVII No. 4 (April, 1966), pp. 408-16.

TABLE VII-1

*Nonmonetary Indicators of Economic Development for*
*Soviet Central Asia and Selected Underdeveloped*
*Countries: Absolute Data*

| Country | (1) Wheat yields, 100 kg. per ha. | (2) Tractors per 1,000 ha. of cultivated land | (3) Prod. of cotton and woolen fabrics, m per capita | (4) Electricity generation, kwh per capita | (5) Prod. of steel, MT per 1,000 pop. |
|---|---|---|---|---|---|
| Soviet Central Asia (1926-28) | 8.7 | .25[a] | .01 | 4 | .0 |
| Colombia (1960-62) | 9.1 | 4.56 | 17.52[d] | 259 | 12.2 |
| India (1960-62) | 8.5 | .23 | 10.64 | 51 | 9.2 |
| Iran (1960-62) | 7.8 | .73[b] | 7.11 | 44[e] | .0 |
| Pakistan (1960-62) | 8.2 | .18[c] | 6.82 | 15 | .1 |
| Turkey (1960-62) | 9.1 | 2.68 | 18.88 | 99 | 9.9 |

Sources:

(1) Food and Agricultural Organization, *Production Yearbook, 1962,* Vol. 16 (Rome: Food and Agricultural Organization, 1963), pp. 35-36; Vladimir P. Timoshenko, *Agricultural Russia and the Wheat Problem,* Grain Economic Series No. 1 (Stanford: Food Research Institute and the Committee on Russian Research of the Hoover War Library, 1932), pp. 534, 538, 540, 542.

(2) FAO, *Production Yearbook, 1962,* pp. 3, 266-69; A. H. Steinberg (ed.), *The Stateman's Yearbook, 1961-1962* (New York: St Martin's Press, 1961), pp. 210, 911, 1,128, 1,149; TsSU, *Narkhoz, 1961,* p. 414; Henze, "The Economic Development of Soviet Central Asia to the Eve of World War II," I, 286

(3) United Nations, Department of Economic and Social Affairs, *Statistical Yearbook, 1962* (New York: United Nations, 1963), pp. 222, 226; Steinberg, *The Stateman's Yearbook, 1961-1962,* pp. 1, 129; TsSU, *Forty Years of Soviet Power,* pp. 117-18, 125-26, 128.

(4) UN, *Statistical Yearbook, 1962,* pp. 310-18; TsSU, *Forty Years of Soviet Power,* pp. 117-18, 125-26, 128.

(5) UN, *Statistical Yearbook, 1962,* p. 257; TsSU, *Forty Years of Soviet Power,* pp. 117-18, 125-26, 128.

(6) UN, *Statistical Yearbook, 1962,* pp. 147-48; UN, *Yearbook of International Trade Statistics, 1961* (New York: United Nations, 1963), pp. 158-60, 317, 320, 331-32, 476, 493, 639; TsSU, *Forty Years of Soviet*

| (6) | (7) | (8) | (9) | (10) | (11) | (12) | (13) | (14) |
|---|---|---|---|---|---|---|---|---|
| Cons. of oil, MT per 1,000 pop. | Cons. of coal, MT per 1,000 pop. | Million freight ton-km. per 100,000 pop. | Per cent of pop. in cities of 20,000 and more | Per cent of pop. in secondary and higher education | Per cent of adults (over 9) literate | Daily newspaper cir. per 1,000 pop. | Physicians per 100,000 pop. | Reciprocal of infant mortality rates |
| 27.7 | 35.4 | 55.5[h] | 9.3 | .16 | 16 | 35 | 17.4 | 4.3[k] |
| 223.8 | 186.9 | 5.3 | 22.4 | 1.88 | 62 | 56 | 41.3 | 11.2 |
| 19.5 | 125.0 | 16.4 | 11.9 | 2.34 | 24 | 11 | 17.4 | 6.8[m] |
| 317.9 | 12.2 | 9.8 | 15.0[j] | 1.53 | 15 | 15 | 25.4 | 5.0 |
| 15.8[f] | 28.1[g] | 8.8 | 8.0 | 1.77 | 16 | 7 | 11.4 | 15.9[n] |
| 57.0 | 188.4 | 13.0 | 14.5 | 2.00 | 30 | 45 | 34.4 | 6.1 |

*Power*, pp. 117-18, 125-26, 128; TsSU, *Transport i svyaz SSSR*, p. 71; Robert N. Taaffe, *Rail Transportation and the Economic Development of Soviet Central Asia*, Department of Geography Research Paper No. 64 (Chicago: The University of Chicago Press, 1960), pp. 120-24.

(7) UN, *Statistical Yearbook, 1962*, pp. 143-46; *Yearbook of International Trade Statistics, 1961*, pp. 158-60, 317, 320, 331-32, 476, 493, 639; TsSU, *Forty Years of Soviet Power*, pp. 117-18, 125-26, 128; TsSU, *Transport i svyaz SSSR*, p. 70; Taaffe, p. 118.

(8) UN, *Statistical Yearbook, 1962*, pp. 345-349; TsSU, *Transport i svyaz SSSR*, p. 67; Taaffe, *Rail Transportation and the Economic Development of Soviet Central Asia*, pp. 139, 164.

(9) Figures are for 1955. Norton Ginsburg, *Atlas of Economic Development* (Chicago: The University of Chicago Press, 1961), p. 34; TsSU, *Itogi vsyesoyuznoi pyeryepisi nasyelyeniya 1959 goda, Kazakh SSR* (Moscow: Gosstatizdat, 1962), p. 18; TsSU, *Itogi vsyesoyuznoi pyeryepisi nasyelyeniya 1959 goda, Uzbek SSR* (Moscow: Gosstatizdat, 1962), p. 16; TsSU, *Itogi vsyesoyuznoi pyeryepisi nasyelyeniya 1959 goda, Tadjik SSR* (Moscow: Gosstatizdat, 1962), p. 14; TsSU, *Itogi vsyesoyuznoi pyeryepisi nasyelyeniya 1959 goda, Turkmen SSR* (Moscow: Gosstatizdat, 1962), p. 14.

(10) UN, *Statistical Yearbook, 1962*, pp. 623-40; TsSU, *Kulturnoye stroityelstvo SSSR*, pp. 124, 126, 128, 130, 208, 210, 232, 234.

(11) United States, Agency for International Development and De-

partment of Defense, *Proposed Mutual Defense and Assistance Programs, FY1964: Summary Presentation to the Congress* (Washington: Government Printing Office, 1963), pp. 181-84; Lorimer, *The Population of the Soviet Union*, p. 70; TsSU, *Itogi vsyesoyuznoi pyeryepisi nasyelyeniya 1959 goda, SSSR*, p. 89.

(12) UN, *Statistical Yearbook, 1962*, pp. 649-50; TsSU, *Forty Years of Soviet Power*, pp. 273, 275, 281, 283, 287.

(13) UN, *Statistical Yearbook, 1962*, pp. 603-6; TsSU, *Forty Years of Soviet Power*, pp. 273, 275, 281, 283, 287.

(14) UN, *Demographic Yearbook, 1962* (New York: United Nations, 1962), pp. 502-15; Ginsburg, *Atlas of Economic Development*, p. 24; Lorimer, *The Population of the Soviet Union*, pp. 82, 119. *Iran Almanac* (3rd ed.; Tehran, 1963).

Notes:

[a] The number of tractors, 2,000 was estimated from Henze, "The Economic Development of Soviet Central Asia to the Eve of World War II," p. 288, and TsSU, *Narkhoz, 1961*, p. 414.

[b] Figure is for 1959.

[c] Figure is for 1956.

[d] Figure is for 1959.

[e] Figure is for 1959.

[f] Figure is for 1959.

[g] Figure is for 1959.

[h] This figure is only a rough estimate. Total freight originations and terminations in 1928 were obtained from TsSU, *Transport i svyaz SSSR*, p. 67. These had to be corrected for double counting of interregional traffic statistics which were obtained from Taaffe, *Rail Transportation and the Economic Development of Soviet Central Asia*, p. 139. To convert from a freight-ton basis to a freight-ton-kilometer one, average length of haul statistics for 1952 were used. These were obtained from *ibid.*, p. 164.

[j] Estimated from Ginsburg, *Atlas of Economic Development*, p. 34.

[k] The infant mortality rate of 230 per 1,000 live births was estimated from Lorimer, *The Population of the Soviet Union*, pp. 82, 119.

[m] Figure is for 1958-59.

[n] Figure is for 1954.

circulation per 1,000 population. (13) Physicians per 100,000 population. And (14) reciprocals of infant mortality rates.

Table VII-1 sets forth these indicators in absolute terms. Care should be exercised in evaluating these figures. For a few, they are estimates, and, for many, the quality of the underlying statistical data is questionable.

If economic development took place in exactly the same way in every country the problem of measuring relative levels of development would be simple. By definition any indicator, such as infant mortality rates, would be the same in any country which was at the same level of economic development. But, of course, this is not the case. The various sectors of an economy develop at different rates in different countries. Thus, an array of indicators is needed to account for differential growth patterns.

The important question then is why select these particular indicators and not some others. The overriding consideration, of course, is data limitations. Certain indicators are just unavailable for underdeveloped countries. A further limitation is imposed on the index presented here by the fact that the primary concern is with a *region,* Soviet Central Asia, not with a sovereign country. Because of inadequate interregional trade statistics, consumption data—as opposed to production figures—are impossible to obtain for many commodities. Thus, additional indicators can be used if the comparison is among national states only.

Another important question relates to the definition of "economic development." If per capita national income is used as the measure, then economic development has been defined as the growth in this indicator. Similarly, if these fourteen nonmonetary indicators are chosen as the measure, then economic development has been defined as the increase in these indicators. Thus, inescapably, an element of personal bias enters into the definition. Why select infant mortality rates as an indicator instead of per capita tobacco consumption? It is possible, of course, that these indicators will give the same measurement of economic development as per capita national income. This will be taken up later in the chapter.

With the above limitations in mind the justification for selecting each individual indicator must now be briefly considered. (1) Wheat yields: This indicator was selected as a measure of the efficiency of agriculture. Because of different resource endowments it is not a highly sensitive discriminator among nations of greater or lesser economic development, but it is one of the few agricultural statistics available. (2) Number of tractors per 1,000 hectares of cultivated land: This was selected as an indicator of the degree of mechanization in agriculture. Different agricultural product mixes (e.g., fruits *vs.* grains) affect the sensitivity of this indicator. (3) Production of cotton and woolen fabrics per capita: This indicator measures to some extent the development of light industry and the production of some important consumer goods. (4) Electricity

TABLE VII-2

### Nonmonetary Indicators of Economic Development for Soviet Central Asia and Selected Underdeveloped Countries: Relative Data[a]

| Country | (1)[b] | (2) | (3) | (4) | (5) |
|---|---|---|---|---|---|
| Soviet Central Asia (1926-28) | 95.6 | 5.5 | .1 | 1.5 | .0 |
| Colombia (1960-62) | 100.0 | 100.0 | 92.8 | 100.0 | 100.0 |
| India (1960-62) | 93.4 | 5.0 | 56.4 | 19.7 | 75.4 |
| Iran (1960-62) | 85.7 | 16.0 | 37.7 | 17.0 | .0 |
| Pakistan (1960-62) | 90.1 | 3.9 | 36.1 | 5.8 | .8 |
| Turkey (1960-62) | 100.0 | 58.8 | 100.0 | 38.2 | 81.1 |

Notes:

[a] Highest-ranking country = 100.0, each indicator.
[b] For sources and definitions of indicators, see Table VII-1.

generation per capita: This statistic gives some indication of the over-all development of industry. It is a measure of energy inputs into industry and of household use. (5) Production of steel per 1,000 population: Steel is the basic foundation of any modern economy. Production statistics measure the degree of development of the domestic industry. Because of international trade, steel consumption might be a better indicator, but interregional trade statistics for steel in Soviet Central Asia are unavailable. It is worth noting that the removal of steel production from the index does not change the rankings. (6) and (7) Consumption of petroleum and coal per capita: These supplement electricity generation as indicators of the over-all development of industry. (8) Million freight-ton-kilometers per 100,000 population: This statistic is intended to give an indication of transportation development. Its sensitivity, however, is affected by several factors such as land area, population density, and the availability of alternative means of transport. It also measures to some extent the efficiency of railroad usage. (9) Per cent of population in cities of 20,000 or more: Urbanization is generally correlated with economic development. In the absence of labor force statistics, this indicator serves as a rough measure of labor force distribution between industry and agriculture. (10) through (14): All of these indicators measure both the development of living standards and investment in human capital. Education and health are two of

| (6) | (7) | (8) | (9) | (10) | (11) | (12) | (13) | (14) | Total |
|---|---|---|---|---|---|---|---|---|---|
| 8.7 | 18.8 | 100.0 | 41.5 | 6.8 | 25.8 | 62.5 | 42.1 | 27.0 | 435.9 |
| 70.4 | 99.1 | 9.5 | 100.0 | 80.3 | 100.0 | 100.0 | 100.0 | 70.4 | 1,222.5 |
| 6.1 | 66.3 | 29.5 | 53.1 | 100.0 | 38.7 | 19.6 | 42.1 | 42.8 | 648.1 |
| 100.0 | 6.5 | 17.7 | 67.0 | 65.4 | 24.2 | 26.8 | 61.5 | 31.4 | 556.9 |
| 5.0 | 14.9 | 15.9 | 35.7 | 75.6 | 25.8 | 12.5 | 27.6 | 100.0 | 449.7 |
| 17.9 | 100.0 | 23.4 | 64.7 | 85.5 | 48.4 | 80.4 | 83.3 | 38.4 | 920.1 |

the most important components of the standard of living. It is this writer's belief that economic development should be defined to include increases in education and health. Also, the argument that investment in human capital is the major source of economic growth seems convincing. Literacy is a basic prerequisite of an industrial work force. It seems reasonable that those countries that invest heavily in education, particularly in postprimary education, are building solid foundations for economic growth and cultural change, whereas those countries that do not do so will continue to be faced with serious problems in the mobilization and utilization of their human resources. The per cent of population in secondary and higher education is affected by the age distribution of population—statistics which are unavailable. Newspaper circulation is a major means of disseminating ideas and innovations and thus enables change to proceed more rapidly. Also, it is the most important instrument for maintaining literacy among a population. Good medical care is not only a major item in living standards, but is a prerequisite for a healthy and productive work force. With a few exceptions, increases in education and health seem to depend upon increases in economic development, and in turn expanded education and medical care aid economic growth.

To obtain a single measure of economic development, an attempt is made in Table VII-2 to construct a "sort of aggregate" of these fourteen nonmonetary indicators. The basic problem is whether or not to assign weights to the individual indicators so as to allow for probable differences in importance. This writer knows of no basis

TABLE VII-3

*Alternative Nonmonetary Indices of Economic Development
for Soviet Central Asia and Selected
Underdeveloped Countries*

| | (1) Unweighted index | | (2) "Welfare" weighted index | | (3) "Industrial" weighted index | |
|---|---|---|---|---|---|---|
| Country | Index | Rank | Index | Rank | Index | Rank |
| Colombia (1960-62) | 1,222.5 | 1 | 1,666.0 | 1 | 1,601.5 | 1 |
| Turkey (1960-62) | 920.1 | 2 | 1,275.7 | 2 | 1,099.5 | 2 |
| India (1960-62) | 648.1 | 3 | 928.1 | 3 | 845.1 | 3 |
| Iran (1960-62) | 556.9 | 4 | 777.1 | 4 | 698.1 | 4 |
| Pakistan (1960-62) | 449.7 | 5 | 714.8 | 5 | 492.1 | 6 |
| Soviet Central Asia (1926-28) | 435.9 | 6 | 537.7 | 6 | 564.9 | 5 |

for asssigning weights that is not arbitrary.[48] Accordingly, the indicators have been expressed as relatives, taking the highest national figure as 100. With respect to any single indicator, a given country can then score a maximum of 100 points. With fourteen indicators, the maximum score of any country is 1,400 points. As indicated in Table VII-2, Soviet Central Asia in 1926-28 ranks last with a score a little more than one-third of Colombia's. To test the reliability of the rankings in Table VII-2, Table VII-3 was constructed. Column 1 repeats the summation of the unweighted (which means, of course, that equal weights are implied) indicators from Table VII-2. Column 2 reflects the attempt to weight the index on some kind of "welfare" basis. This is done by giving a weight of two to indicators (3), (10), (11), (13), and (14), and a weight of one to all the others. The index in Column 3 reflects an "industrial" bias. Indicators (4), (5), (6), (7), and (8) are given a weight of two and all others a weight

48. Bennett concurs and what follows is based on his approach to a similar problem. See M. K. Bennett, "International Disparities in Consumption Levels," *American Economic Review,* Vol. LI, No. 4 (September, 1951), pp. 632-49.

of one. Neither of these alternative weighting systems gives rise to any significant changes from the unweighted index. Soviet Central Asia is ranked sixth on the unweighted index, sixth on the "welfare" biased index, and fifth on the "industrial" biased index. The only change in ranking occurs in the "industrial" weighted index, where Pakistan and Soviet Central Asia change positions. But the change is so small that it carries little significance. Thus the original unweighted index, if due precaution is taken, can serve as a rough measure of relative levels of economic development.[49]

The one conclusion that can be safely drawn is that Soviet Central Asia was an underdeveloped area, with the characteristics of underdeveloped countries today, on the eve of the Soviet industrialization drive.

The remaining chapters of this case study analyze the success of Soviet strategy in modernizing the economy of Central Asia. Chapter VIII focuses on social change and human capital formation. Chapter IX discusses agricultural development. Chapter X analyzes the industrial sector. Chapter XI evaluates changes in living standards since 1928 and concludes with a general evaluation of the development program in Central Asia.

49. It is worthwhile to note that the coefficient of rank correlation between the unweighted index and Gross National Product per capita in dollars for 1961, omitting Soviet Central Asia for which no Gross National Product data exists, is .70. There would be a perfect rank correlation except for the relatively high, $211, per capita Gross National Product of Iran. This deviation can be explained in one word—oil.

# VIII. SOCIAL CHANGE AND THE FORMATION OF HUMAN CAPITAL

INTRODUCTION

The Soviet development program began in 1928, although certain important measures had been taken earlier, especially the Central Asian land reform of the middle 1920's. Soviet policy for Central Asia was determined by a number of objectives.

First was the urgent requirement of expanding cotton production. In 1927-8 the U.S.S.R. had been forced to allocate one-sixth of its total foreign expenditure to purchases of cotton, mostly American. Second, a number of considerations appeared to demand that the region be industrialized. There was the preconception that an industrial proletariat furnishes the most reliable Communists. There were preoccupations stemming from long-range policies toward Asia. The region was to be a graphic demonstration of how well Asians could fare under Communist leadership. Finally, the continued search for ways and means to lighten the burden on the Soviet Union's transportation system, and other purely economic factors, caused the Soviet administrators to favor some industrialization of Central Asia. It was judged uneconomic, for example, that in 1925-6 half of the manufactured goods shipped into the region consisted of cotton textiles, manufactured in Russian industrial centers from cotton supplied in large part by Central Asian producers.[1]

One of the main aspects of the Soviet development program was that all of its parts—economic, political, cultural—were quite highly integrated. Even though they will be treated separately in the discussion that follows, it must be kept in mind that they are pieces of a whole. The interrelation of these factors can be most clearly seen in the Soviet cultural program and in the approach to the traditional social structure of Central Asia.

In the opinion of the Soviet leaders, the Moslem hierarchy had to be destroyed. This was necessary to remove a political threat to

1. Warren Wilhelm, "Soviet Central Asia: Development of a Backward Area," *Foreign Policy Reports*, XXV (February 1, 1950), 219.

156

the new Soviet regime, to free women from the veil and the home and release them for more productive work in the region's economy, and to free the mass of peasants from change-inhibiting superstition.[2] This policy was facilitated by the early alignment of the Moslem leaders with the White Russian forces. The land reform of the early and middle 1920's completed the destruction of the economic and political power of the traditional ruling classes, except in parts of the countryside. Collectivization completed the policy of transforming the social structure. There were other aspects of this policy. The nomadic Kazakhs had to be settled if they were to progress economically and socially. It was necessary to build an educational system to wean the youth away from Moslem social attitudes and to train them to operate a modernized economy. Medical facilities had to be developed if the people were to be healthy and thus economically productive. These policies were seen as necessary to build a modern economy and to win the allegiance of the mass of people.

The nationalities policy on culture was also part of the Soviet program, but it will be largely omitted here since it has little relevance for present purposes. Wilhelm has summarized this aspect as follows:

> The Soviet organizers . . . under the leadership of Stalin, a Georgian and the Communist party's expert on nationality policy, showed an overweening interest in native "culture," which was taken to mean folk-dancing, music, art, literature and the native languages. All of these were to be fostered and protected. The region was not Russianized; but it was pitilessly Sovietized, and such elements of culture as religion, family organization, economic arrangements, were fitted on the Procrustean bed of the Soviet State. Those parts of the culture which stood in the way of maximum economic development, or which threatened Soviet control, were destroyed. Certain social and economic groups were marked for "liquidation as a class," a delicate phrase which in application, often meant extermination, by starvation if not by violent death.[3]

2. "Although fiercely suppressed in the inter-war years as confederates of 'feudal reaction' the Moslem priesthood is now tolerated and is reconciled to monogamy and female education." United Nations, Economic Commission for Europe, "Regional Economic Policy in the Soviet Union: The Case of Central Asia," *Economic Bulletin for Europe*, Vol. IX, No. 3 (November, 1957), p. 73. Part of the statistics in this report were obtained directly by the U.N. Secretariat from the All-Union or Central Asian authorities and have not been published elsewhere.

3. Wilhelm, "Soviet Central Asia," p. 220. A sympathetic account of the nationalities policy is found in Corliss Lamont, *The Peoples of the Soviet Union* (New York: Harcourt, Brace & Co., 1946), pp. 93-122, 145-210. For a critical account with emphasis on Russian political control see: Richard E. Pipes, "The Soviet Impact on Central Asia," *Problems of Communism,*

Most likely some of these policies alienated the peoples of Central Asia and, thus, were an inhibiting factor in the over-all development program. But counteracting these undesirable results was the fact that ". . . individual Russians were never granted the superior status which characterized the old European standing in Asian or African society. This remained the single most important positive factor in Russian-Moslem relations."[4]

EDUCATION, CULTURE, AND PUBLIC HEALTH

Investment in physical assets is a key factor in economic development, but possibly as important, or more so, is investment in human capital.[5] And this is probably the most impressive achievement of the Soviet regime in Central Asia. "The picture would . . . remain incomplete without a discussion of the very impressive investments in the bodies and minds of men, that is in health and education. In these fields the standards in central Asia have improved so strikingly in the period of Soviet rule that the relevant comparison is no longer with neighboring Asian countries, but with the countries of western Europe."[6]

A fundamental problem that must be faced in the economic development of a backward country is the typically low educational level of the population. Not only is there usually a lack of technicians, but even of persons able to read any language at all.

The great increase in literacy in Central Asia since the advent of the Soviet regime is due to the strongly developed compulsory school system and to the mass campaigns launched against adult illiteracy.

Vol. VI, No. 2 (March/April, 1957); Frank A. Ecker, "Transition in Asia: Uzbekistan and the Soviets," (Ph.D. dissertation; Dept. of Political Science: University of Michigan, 1952); Michael Rywkin, *Russia in Central Asia*, Russian Civilization Series (New York: Collier Books, 1963), pp. 75-152; and the entire issue of *Problems of Communism*, Vol. XIII, No. 1 (January/February, 1964).

4. Rywkin, *Russia in Central Asia*, p. 99.

5. For theoretical discussions of the importance of human capital, see: T. W. Schultz, "Investment in Human Capital," *American Economic Review*, Vol. LI, No. 1 (March, 1961); and T. W. Schultz, "Capital Formation by Education," *Journal of Political Economy*, Vol. LXVIII (1960). For the role of human capital in the economic development of Germany, see: Thorstein Veblen, *Imperial Germany and the Industrial Revolution* (New York: The Macmillan Company, 1915). And for its role in the United States, see: Edward F. Denison, *The Sources of Economic Growth in the United States and the Alternatives Before Us*, Supplementary Paper No. 13 (New York: Committee for Economic Development, 1962).

6. United Nations, *Economic Bulletin for Europe*, p. 71.

Table VIII-1 shows the changes that have occurred. Since the Soviet statistics cover only up to age 49, the adult literacy rate is probably less than that shown in Table VIII-1. If it is arbitrarily assumed that the literacy rate for those over age 49 is 50 per cent, then the total adult literacy rate for Soviet Central Asia in 1959 works out to 86.9 per cent. This is still a remarkable increase over the 1926 rate of 16.1 per cent. The very large investments in education were the primary reason for the success in eliminating illiteracy.

*TABLE VIII-1*

*Adult Literacy in Soviet Central Asia:*
*Ages, 9-49*

| Republic | 1897 | 1926 | 1939 | 1959 |
|----------|------|------|------|------|
| Uzbekistan | 3.6 | 11.6 | 78.7 | 98.1 |
| Kazakhstan | 8.1 | 25.1 | 83.6 | 96.9 |
| Kirgizia | 3.1 | 16.5 | 79.8 | 98.0 |
| Tadjikstan | 2.3 | 3.8 | 82.8 | 96.2 |
| Turkmenistan | 7.8 | 14.0 | 77.7 | 95.4 |

Source:
TsSU, *Itogi vsyesoyuznoi pyeryepisi nasyelyeniya 1959 goda, SSSR,* p. 89.

During the years of the Soviet regime educational achievements have been impressive. In 1914-15, there were 137,100 students, or 1.1 per cent of the population, in all types of schools. In 1961-62, there were 5,880,000 students, or 22.5 per cent of the population.[7] In 1914-15, there were no schools of higher education. In 1961-62, there were 75 such schools with an enrollment of 255,200.[8] In 1955-56, the number of students in secondary and higher education was 5.46 per cent of the total population which ranked Soviet Central Asia sixth highest in the world.[9] The U.S.S.R. as a whole was ranked twelfth with 4.35 per cent and the United States third with 6.02 per cent of the population attending secondary or higher educational establishments.[10] The number of teachers in primary schools per

7. TsSU, *Narkhoz, 1961*, p. 685.
8. *Ibid.*, p. 691.
9. TsSU, *Kulturnoye stroityelstvo SSSR*, pp. 124, 126, 128, 130, 208, 210, 232, 234; Norton Ginsburg, *Atlas of Economic Development* (Chicago: University of Chicago Press, 1961), p. 44.
10. Ginsburg, *Atlas of Economic Development*, p. 44.

thousand students in 1955 was 43 in Central Asia, 45 in the U.S.S.R., 34 in Iran, 31 in Iraq, 30 in Afganhistan and India, 28 in Pakistan, 27 in France, 39 in Western Germany, and 33 in England and Wales.[11] Table VIII-2 summarizes the basic educational changes that have taken place in Central Asia. The data illustrate that Soviet Central Asia has progressed to the point, in providing for the education of its people, where it is comparable to the more advanced countries.

*TABLE VIII-2*

*Educational Statistics for Soviet Central Asia:*
*Selected Years, 1914 to 1962*

| Item | 1914-15 | 1927-28 | 1940-41 | 1955-56 | 1961-62 |
|---|---|---|---|---|---|
| Total number of students in all levels (thousands) | 137.1 | 523.9 | 3,487.3 | 3,907.1 | 5,880.0 |
| Per cent of population | 1.05 | 3.85 | 20.98 | 18.69 | 22.52 |
| Students in secondary and higher educational establishments | — | 22.1 | 278.1 | 1,140.5 | — |
| Per cent of population | — | .16 | 1.67 | 5.46 | — |
| Students in higher educational establishments | — | 3.9 | 37.8 | 154.9 | 255.2 |
| Per cent of population | — | .03 | .23 | .74 | .98 |

Sources:

Calculated from: TsSU, *Kulternoye stroityelstvo SSSR*, pp. 16-19, 30-33, 36-37, 124-31, 208-11, 232-35; TsSU, *Narkhoz, 1961*, pp. 685, 691.

One of the most formidable problems was the extreme cultural and educational backwardness of the native peoples of Central Asia. Prior to the 1917 Revolution they made up less than 10 per cent of the total student enrollment. By the 1940's, elementary school attendance was more or less the same among European and native males. But among secondary school, college, and university students, natives were underrepresented. "This situation cannot be attributed to a lack of encouragement, but rather to the still existing gap in

11. United Nations, *Economic Bulletin for Europe*, p. 72. Figure for Central Asia does not include Kazakhstan.

cultural levels between Russian and native communities."[12] In 1927, only 2.4 per cent of the students at the Central Asian State University in Tashkent were from local national groups.[13] However, by 1961, national groups of Central Asia, which made up 68 per cent of the population, accounted for over one-third of the students in universities, institutes, and technical schools in the area.[14] "Taking into consideration that no universities existed in Central Asia before the Revolution, the presence of 250,000 students in the institutions of higher learning in Central Asia in 1961 . . . is a remarkable achievement."[15]

The most difficult problem involved in the educational program was to persuade the Moslem women and girls to participate. Before the Revolution they took no part in public life and received no education. They lived for the most part in a state of servitude to their fathers and husbands.[16] "The following figures . . . despite the progress they show, suggest the extent of the difficulties that must have been encountered. In 1927-28, of the 4,930 students in Tadzhikstan schools, only forty-four were women. By 1931-32, of 135,976 students, only 22,317 were women. It is not surprising, however, for during the turbulent years of the Basmachestvo revolt in the mid-twenties the village teachers and the 'emancipated' women were not infrequently assassinated."[17]

In light of women's place in the traditional culture of Central Asia, "Soviet educational statistics are especially impressive in regard

12. Rywkin, *Russia in Central Asia*, p. 96. "In 1955 Central Asian nationals formed 1.16 per cent of all 'scientific workers' in the Soviet Union (against an estimated 5 per cent of total population), but the speed of advance (as recently as 1950 the share was 0.77 per cent) and present matriculation rates are indicative of future progress." United Nations, *Economic Bulletin for Europe*, p. 72. Kazakhstan is excluded from the U.N. report.

13. Walter McKenzie Pintner, "Initial Problems in the Soviet Economic Development of Central Asia," *Royal Central Asian Society Journal*, XL (July/October, 1953), 284.

14. TsSU, *Narkhoz, 1961*, pp. 691, 693, 700.

15. Rywkin, *Russia in Central Asia*, p. 97.

16. "After the change of regime the provision of school education for girls had necessarily to go hand in hand with the elimination of *purdah*, of which the Emir of Bukhara had been among the strictest exponents in Islam. The main law on women's rights dates from 1928—forbidding marriage by purchase or compulsion, polygamy and child marriage—and it was accompanied by forceful propaganda against other aspects of female servitude." United Nations, *Economic Bulletin for Europe*, pp. 72-73.

17. Pintner, "Initial Problems in the Soviet Economic Development of Central Asia," p. 286.

to Moslem women."[18] The per cent of girls in total primary, seven-year, and secondary school enrollment at the beginning of the 1955-56 school year was 43.7 in Uzbekistan, 48.0 in Kazakhstan, 45.9 in Kirgizia, 42.3 in Tadjikstan, and 45.7 in Turkmenistan. In the whole of the U.S.S.R. the figure was 49.6 per cent.[19] However, the per cent of girls in rural eighth to eleventh grade enrollment was only 25.7 in Uzbekistan, 46.1 in Kazakhstan, 36.1 in Kirgizia, 21.8 in Tadjikstan, and 33.7 in Turkmenistan. For the U.S.S.R. the figure was 51.9 per cent.[20] The problem is greater in higher education. Kirgiz women were approximately 3 per cent of the total enrollment in Kirgizia higher education in 1955-56. Uzbek women were approximately 16 per cent of the enrollment in Uzbekistan in 1954-55.[21] Behind the low enrollment figures for women in higher education of Central Asia "lies the problem of the cultural differences between Central Asians and the Soviet regime. In the Central Asiatic conception the place of women is in private and not in public life. Education, and especially higher education, takes women into public life."[22]

One of the best over-all indicators of the progress made in Central Asia is the educational level attained by the population. Table VIII-3 presents data on the number of persons with a secondary education or a higher education in the census years of 1939 and 1959. Central Asia is still behind the all-Union average but is rapidly catching up.

Other cultural indices reflect a similar change in Soviet Central Asia since the 1917 Revolution. Table VIII-4 summarizes some of the more important of these indices. Like education and medical services, many of these indices not only reflect a rise in the cultural level, but since they are components of a people's standard of living, reflect a rise in this also.[23]

"It is a commonplace that investment in education may be largely nullified by the failure to maintain literacy by providing suitable reading matter."[24] Book publishing in the five major national languages

18. Rywkin, *Russia in Central Asia*, p. 97.
19. TsSU, *Kulturnoye stroityelstvo SSSR*, pp. 176-77.
20. *Ibid.*
21. Bureau of Social Science Research, *Handbook of Central Asia*, II, 500-501.
22. *Ibid.*, p. 501.
23. Unless offset by a fall in other components of the standard of living. This problem will be treated later.
24. United Nations, *Economic Bulletin for Europe*, p. 73.

TABLE VIII-3

Educational Attainment Levels in Soviet
Central Asia and the U.S.S.R.:
1939 and 1959

| Number of persons with specified level of education | Place of residence | | | | | |
|---|---|---|---|---|---|---|
| | U.S.S.R. | | | Soviet Central Asia | | |
| | Urban | Rural | Total | Urban | Rural | Total |
| Secondary education: | | | | | | |
| Number of persons | | | | | | |
| (1,000) — 1939 | 9,806 | 4,883 | 14,689 | 467 | 289 | 756 |
| — 1959 | 34,458 | 20,472 | 54,930 | 2,641 | 2,755 | 5,396 |
| Per 1,000 popula- | | | | | | |
| tion      — 1939 | 162 | 37 | 77 | 114 | 23 | 45 |
| — 1959 | 344 | 188 | 263 | 299 | 195 | 235 |
| 1959 as per | | | | | | |
| cent of 1939 | 212 | 508 | 342 | 262 | 848 | 522 |
| Higher education: | | | | | | |
| Number of persons | | | | | | |
| (1,000) — 1939 | 956 | 221 | 1,177 | 40 | 17 | 57 |
| — 1959 | 3,169 | 608 | 3,777 | 214 | 73 | 287 |
| Per 1,000 popula- | | | | | | |
| lation   — 1939 | 16 | 2 | 6 | 10 | 1 | 3 |
| — 1959 | 32 | 6 | 18 | 24 | 5 | 13 |
| 1959 as per | | | | | | |
| cent of 1939 | 200 | 300 | 300 | 249 | 364 | 357 |

Sources:
    TsSU, *Itogi vsyesoyuznoi pyeryespisi nasyelyeniya 1959 goda, SSSR,*
p. 81. TsSU, *Itogi vsyesoyuznoi pyeryespisi nasyelyeniya 1959 goda,
Kazakh SSR,* p. 50. TsSU, *Itogi vsyesoyuznoi pyeryespisi nasyelyeniya
1959 goda, Uzbek SSR,* p. 36. TsSU, *Itogi vsyesoyuznoi pyeryespisi
nasyelyeniya 1959 goda, Tadjik SSR,* p. 32. TsSU, *Itogi vsyesoyuznoi
pyeryespisi nasyelyeniya 1959 goda, Turkmen SSR,* p. 34. TsSU, *Itogi
vsyesoyuznoi pyeryespisi nasyelyeniya 1959 goda, Kirgiz SSR,* p. 32.

of Soviet Central Asia has increased rapidly. In 1913, 77 volumes
were published with a circulation of 247,000 copies. In 1961,
3,138 volumes were published with a circulation of 36,167,000
copies.[25] Of the 5,304,000 daily circulation of newspapers in 1961,
2,704,000 were in the five major national languages.[26] The daily

25. TsSU, *Narkhoz, 1961,* p. 727.
26. *Ibid.,* p. 732.

TABLE VIII-4

*Cultural Statistics for Soviet Central Asia:*
*1914–1961*
*Selected Years*

| Item | 1914 | 1928 | 1940 | 1955 | 1961 |
|---|---|---|---|---|---|
| Number of public libraries | 139 | 495 | 7,407 | 13,311 | 12,917 |
| Their book-stock (thousands) | 98 | 997 | 9,898 | 41,932 | 66,561 |
| Number of museums | 7 | 21 | 53 | 54 | 55 |
| Number of theaters | 3 | 14 | 140 | 66 | 60 |
| Number of film projectors | 52 | 253 | 2,519 | 5,488 | 9,443 |
| Annual circulation of books and magazines (thousand copies) | 104 | 7,100 | 26,800 | 57,500 | 90,413 |
| Daily circulation of newspapers (thousand copies) | 86 | 509 | 2,637 | 2,989 | 5,304 |

Sources:
TsSU, *Kulturnoye stroityelstvo SSSR,* pp. 16-19, 30-33, 36-37; TsSU, *Narkhoz, 1961,* pp. 713, 721, 722, 724, 728-32.

newspaper circulation of 203 copies per thousand population compares with 330 copies in the U.S.S.R. as a whole, 11 in India, 15 in Iran, 45 in Turkey, 278 in the Netherlands, 210 in Israel, 101 in Italy, and 326 in the United States.[27]

Both before World War II and in the postwar years the personnel occupied in medical and educational services in Soviet Central Asia ". . . accounted for no less than 17-20 per cent of the active population outside agriculture. The comparable figure for India is about 3 per cent."[28] In contrast with state investment in physical assets, which has been below the average for the U.S.S.R. as a whole, investment in health and education has tended to be higher. During the Second Five-Year Plan (1932-37) per capita expenditure on health and education in Central Asia was about one-fifth higher than the average for the U.S.S.R. In the Fifth Five-Year Plan (1951-55)

27. *Ibid.,* p. 725; United Nations, *Statistical Yearbook, 1962,* pp. 649-50; U.S. Bureau of the Census, *Statistical Abstract of the United States, 1963,* pp. 932-33.
28. United Nations, *Economic Bulletin for Europe,* p. 71. The data exclude Kazakhstan.

per capita expenditure was about the same in Central Asia as the average for the U.S.S.R. In this period, such expenditure in Soviet Central Asia was 150 per cent of total state investment in physical assets within the region.[29]

The improvement in medical services obtained from expenditures of this magnitude can be seen in Table VIII-5. The number of physicians per thousand population, which before the Revolution had been much lower than it is in the neighboring Asian countries today, now equals that of the Western European countries. The number of hospital beds per thousand population is five to twenty times higher than in Asian countries and almost equal that of the advanced western European countries and the United States. In all of Soviet Central Asia in 1913 there were 408 physicians and 3,240 hospital beds. In 1961, there were 36,294 physicians and 213,400 hospital beds.

This, together with higher food consumption,[30] has contributed to the decline in mortality to levels—even when account is taken of the favorable age-distribution and of some under-registration of deaths—that ". . . must be characterized as highly satisfactory by any standard."[31] In 1940, the crude death rate was 14.6 for all Central Asia. In 1961, it was 6.0 in Uzbekistan, 6.5 in Kazakhstan, 6.7 in Kirgizia, 5.2 in Tadjikstan, and 6.6 in Turkmenistan.[32] This compares with a 1959 crude death rate of 7.5 in Japan, 7.6 in the U.S.S.R., 9.4 in the United States, 11.3 in France, 11.7 in the United Kingdom, 13.5 in Turkey (provincial capitals only), 19.0 in India, and 25.0 in Iran.[33] The estimated infant mortality rate for 1926 in Central Asia was 203 deaths per 1,000 live births. In 1959, the rate was 51.2 for Kazakhstan.[34] This compares with 26.4 in 1959 in the United States, 29.5 in France, 33.7 in Japan, 40.6 for the U.S.S.R., 45.4 in Italy, 145.9 for rural India, and 165.0 in Turkey.[35]

The changes wrought in the social structure of Central Asia

29. *Ibid.*
30. The question of food consumption and the standard of living will be taken up later.
31. United Nations, *Economic Bulletin for Europe*, p. 71.
32. *Ibid.*, p. 53; U.S. Congress, Joint Economic Committee, *Annual Economic Indicators for the U.S.S.R.*, 88th Cong., 2nd Sess., 1964, p. 5.
33. United Nations, *Demographic Yearbook, 1962*, pp. 468-83, 502-31.
34. Frank Lorimer, *The Population of the Soviet Union: History and Prospects*, Series of League of Nations Publications–Economic and Financial (Geneva: League of Nations, 1946), pp. 82, 119, for the 1926 rate. James W. Brackett of the U.S. Census Bureau supplied the 1959 rate for Kazakhstan. It was obtained from a life table for the republic. No data were available for the other Central Asian republics.
35. United Nations, *Demographic Yearbook, 1962*, pp. 502-31.

TABLE VIII-5

### Medical Services in Soviet Central Asia and Selected Other Countries: Per Thousand Population

| Country | Year | Physicians | Hospital beds |
|---|---|---|---|
| Soviet Central Asia | 1913 | .03 | .24 |
| | 1940 | .44 | 3.59 |
| | 1961 | 1.39 | 8.18 |
| Soviet Union | 1913 | .17 | 1.26 |
| | 1940 | .74 | 4.15 |
| | 1961 | 1.97 | 8.54 |
| India | 1956 | .17 | .44 |
| Iran | 1959-60 | .25 | 1.01 |
| Turkey | 1959-60 | .34 | 1.71 |
| Japan | 1959-60 | 1.09 | 9.01 |
| Italy | 1959-60 | 1.60[a] | 9.03 |
| France | 1959 | 1.01 | 14.74 |
| United Kingdom | 1960 | .91 | 10.63 |
| United States | 1961 | 1.28 | 9.26 |

Sources:
   TsSU, *Narkhoz, 1961*, pp. 743, 746; United Nations, *Statistical Yearbook, 1962*, pp. 603-6; U.S. Bureau of the Census, *Statistical Abstract of the United States, 1963*, pp. 936-37; World Health Organization, *Annual Epidemiological and Vital Statistics: 1960* (Geneva: World Health Organization, 1963), pp. 714-25.
   [a] Includes dentists.

during the years of the Soviet regime have been great, as the above analysis has illustrated. The importance of these changes was summed up in the report on Soviet Central Asia by the United Nations Economic Commission for Europe.

Resources devoted to the improvement of education and training as well as health represent a long-term investment in the sense that their fruits, in terms of higher productivity, are reaped only with considerable delay. It may therefore be expected that the impressive achievements in these fields will contribute much to the increase of productivity over the next one or two decades. A higher level of education is not only a source of higher productivity within the given occupational pattern, but it is also apt to exert pressure for further change of that pattern, in the direction of industrialization and urbanization. It is important in this respect, that cultural change has affected the rural, no less than the urban, population. . . . The revolution in cultural patterns already carried out in central Asia therefore contributes to make the long-term economic prospects for the region favorable.[36]

It would seem that the Soviet regime was successful in implementing, in Central Asia, the strategy of the Soviet model of economic development dealing with changing the social structure and culture to make it conducive to development. Most of the Central Asian peoples are now oriented toward change. A relatively educated and healthy people have emerged who are now utilizing their increased energies and talents to further transform and develop their society.

But criticisms of this cultural transformation have been levied by Turkestani nationalists who "see a direct correlation between Soviet socio-economic achievements and the policy of Russification. 'Sovietization, industrialization, Russification' was the sequence of events, they say."[37] This is a misreading of the meaning of cultural change. As Richard Pipes, a Harvard specialist on Central Asian affairs, has argued: ". . . The social and cultural processes occurring in Soviet Central Asia do not differ fundamentally from those taking place in other colonial or ex-colonial areas of the world. In both instances native societies, under the impact of European culture, become secularized, westernized."[38]

36. United Nations, *Economic Bulletin for Europe*, p. 75.
37. Inner quote from B. Nikitin, "Probleme National et Evolution Technique en Asie Sovietique," *L' Afrique et L' Asie*, No. 31 (1955), p. 21. Quoted in Rywkin, *Russia in Central Asia*, p. 98.
38. Pipes, "The Soviet Impact on Central Asia," p. 32.

# IX. AGRICULTURAL DEVELOPMENT

For the most part the 1920's were a period of economic stabilization in agriculture. The first steps taken in the direction of land reform were in 1921, and were directed against Russians with large land holdings. Though of little economic significance, these steps formed an important part of the campaign designed to gain the loyalty of the native peasants. As Central Asia came more firmly under the control of the Soviet regime, more radical steps were taken. "In December, 1922, the land and water were nationalized, and large and absentee holdings confiscated. The proportion of peasants leasing their land was reduced from 45.2 per cent to 5.6 per cent. Work animals and equipment also were confiscated from the more prosperous."[1] The land reform, however, was not considered as anything more than a temporary expedient, and was never ". . . effective in the more remote regions. The Party did not approve of it in the long run because it was an aid to the middle peasant but did little for the poorest class."[2]

COLLECTIVIZATION

This period of economic stabilization was interrupted in 1928-29 by the social and economic revolution caused by the collectivization of agriculture. In Central Asia, as in all of Russia, collectivization served many purposes.

It brought the supply of agricultural produce under state control and weakened, although it did not entirely destroy, the bargaining position of the farmer. It also permitted a shift to large-scale methods of agriculture. While these large-scale methods did not always produce more crops per acre, they usually did produce more crops per man, and permitted a flow of manpower to industry. In Central Asia, especially, col-

1. Walter McKenzie Pintner, "Initial Problems in the Soviet Economic Development of Central Asia," *Royal Central Asian Society Journal,* XL (July/October, 1953), 289.
2. *Ibid.*

168

*TABLE IX-1*

Livestock Numbers in Soviet Central Asia

| | Thousand head | | | Total in live- |
| Year | Horses | Cattle | Hogs | Sheep and goats | stock units: 1928 = 100[a] |
|---|---|---|---|---|---|
| 1928 | 5,138 | 11,273 | 339 | 44,521 | 100 |
| 1933 | 1,382 | 3,643 | 214 | 8,655 | 28 |
| 1953 | 3,200 | 9,971 | 1,046 | 42,344 | 92 |
| 1962 | — | 13,881 | 2,878 | 51,681 | 129 |

Sources:

For 1928 and 1933; Naum Jasny, *The Socialized Agriculture of the U.S.S.R.: Plans and Performance,* Grain Economic Series No. 5 (Stanford: Stanford University Press, 1949), p. 634. For 1953: Central Statistical Board of the U.S.S.R. Council of Ministers, *National Economy of the U.S.S.R.: Statistical Returns* (Moscow: Foreign Languages Publishing House, 1957), pp. 111-13; Bureau of Social Science Research, *Handbook for Central Asia,* III, 925; United Nations, *Economic Bulletin for Europe,* p. 57. For 1962: TsSU, *Narkhoz, 1961,* pp. 384-87. Variations in the census dates render the figures not fully comparable. Data for 1928 and 1933 refer to June; for 1953 to 1 October; and for 1962 to 1 January.

[a] Excludes horses. Livestock numbers are weighted as follows: cattle, 1.0; hogs, 0.4; sheep and goats, 0.12. The weights are taken from Jasny, *The Socialized Agriculture of the U.S.S.R.,* p. 786.

lectivization proved crucial because it gave to the state considerable control over the agricultural process; the strategic dates for cotton planting and harvesting could now be controlled, and available irrigation water could be used more effectively.[3]

In the beginning, "because collectivization was handled with incredible stupidity, it proved a disaster,"[4] especially to livestock raising. In Central Asia, even more than in any other area of the Soviet Union, collectivization resulted in "vast and senseless slaughter of the important livestock herds by the peasants, who were being forced rather than led into collectivization."[5] Table IX-1 dramatically illustrates the impact of collectivization on the livestock herds of Central Asia and their subsequent recovery.

3. Warren Wilhelm, "Soviet Central Asia: Development of a Backward Area," *Foreign Policy Reports,* XXV (February 1, 1950), 219.
4. *Ibid.*
5. *Ibid.*

Wilhelm has stated that "the decline in livestock herds was the single major setback of the Soviet development program in Central Asia. In all other purely economic respects, the progress attained in the decade 1928-37 was impressive."[6]

What were the causes of this depletion of livestock? A large majority of the livestock was possessed by the Kazakhs, who for centuries had been nomads. The collectivization program attempted to settle them *and* to collectivize their herds all at once. The Kazakhs objected and when coercion was applied they slaughtered their livestock before entering the collectives. The basic problems were the tempo of collectivization and the decision to collectivize personal livestock. In 1935, the ban on personal livestock was rescinded. And, in 1942, former nomad cattle breeders were allowed to resume their traditional way of life. The success of Outer Mongolia in collectivizing nomadic tribes illustrates that if the tempo is slow and the policy one of persuasion the Central Asian experience need not be repeated.[7]

It is "impossible to ascertain from the Soviet literature the degree to which coercion was used in forming the Central Asian collectives. It is clear, however, that the resistance to collectivization was strong."[8] Again, the greatest resistance came from the Kazakhs. A number of Kazakhs fled to Sinkiang. Eleanor Lattimore gives the total number of Kazakhs in Sinkiang, about 1940, as 247,000.[9] A large number must also have died because of famine induced causes. "There was an absolute decrease of about 869,000 persons in the number reported as Kazakhs between 1926 and 1939, whereas at the average rate of increase of the whole Soviet population (15.9 per cent) we would have expected an absolute increase of 631,000 persons. The sum of these figures gives a deficit of exactly 1.5 million below the expected number in 1939. . . . It is impossible to escape the conclusion that there must have been heavy losses in this region due to excess deaths."[10]

6. *Ibid.*, p. 220.

7. See Owen Lattimore, *Nomads and Commissars: Mongolia Revisited* (New York: Oxford University Press, 1962).

8. Pintner, "Initial Problems in the Soviet Economic Development of Central Asia," p. 289.

9. Eleanor Lattimore, "Behind the Sinking Incident," *Far Eastern Survey*, Vol. XIII, No. 9 (May 3, 1944), pp. 78-81. Cited in Frank Lorimer, *The Population of the Soviet Union: History and Prospects*, Series of League of Nations Publications–Economic and Financial (Geneva: League of Nations, 1946), p. 140.

10. Lorimer, *The Population of the Soviet Union*, p. 140.

The large depletion of livestock in Central Asia must have led to a sharp reduction in the traditional diet. But the figure of 1.5 million persons does not necessarily reflect that many excess deaths. As mentioned above, a large number of Kazakhs fled into Sinkiang. And there was a "considerable exodus of Kazakhs into other parts of the Soviet Union."[11] Moreover, it is very likely that the average rate of increase was lower for the Kazakhs, because of the normally higher death rates, than it was for the U.S.S.R. as a whole. Nevertheless, there was an unnecessarily large loss of life due to the inept, brutal, and dogmatic implementation of the collectivization program. Undoubtedly wiser policies could have avoided much of this tremendous social cost.

Collectivization went much more smoothly in the other four republics of Central Asia. For the most part the peoples of these republics were sedentary, and thus there was no settlement problem.

In addition to the negative sanctions used to stimulate their development, the collectives offered many positive advantages unavailable to the private peasant. They were given first priority in the allotment of credit, work animals, and other equipment. "Since large numbers of those entering the collectives had no equipment or animals, this was probably a substantial incentive to the poor peasant who had formerly had to lease his tools and animal power."[12]

### THE STRUCTURE OF CENTRAL ASIAN AGRICULTURE

Central Asian agriculture differs considerably from that characteristic of the bulk of Soviet farming, or at least it did until the "New Lands" program began in Kazakhstan in 1954. The most important crop in Kazakhstan is wheat. In the other four republics of Central Asia, cotton is the most important crop. Animal husbandry is important in all of Central Asia, but particularly in Kazakhstan. Cotton has been grown as a main crop on irrigated land for at least seven centuries, together with rice and silk from the mulberry. Animal husbandry, mainly of sheep and goats, is carried on in the steppe regions and between the oases of the desert. Grain is grown on the steepes of Kazakhstan and on the nonirrigated and low-yielding land of the other republics.

11. *Ibid.*
12. Pintner, "Initial Problems in the Soviet Economic Development of Central Asia," p. 289.

*Cotton.* Agricultural yields, per unit of land or of livestock, are not much higher than those obtained under similar natural conditions in neighboring countries.[13] Yields per man, however, are generally higher. The most important exception to the low yields per unit of land is cotton. Through collectivization, tractorization, better agro-technics, improvements in seed, greater use of mineral fertilizer, expansion of sown area, expansion of the irrigation system, and strong financial incentives to the cotton growers, yields have been raised to a level slightly higher than in Egypt, where the climate is more propitious for cotton production than in large parts of the Central Asian cotton areas. Average yields *per hectare* in Central Asia are now among the highest in the world. In 1963, the yield of cotton lint in the United States was 517 lb. per acre and in Central Asia 637 lb. per acre.[14] On the other hand, the labor input per centner of cotton output in 1956-57 was 18.8 man hours in the United States, and 29.8 man hours on state farms and 42.8 man hours on collective farms in Central Asia.[15] Table IX-2 summarizes the changes in cotton production since 1913.

As can be seen from Table IX-2, cotton production in Central Asia is now over six times what it was before the Revolution. Also, the quality has improved, and an ever larger share of production consists of long-fibre cotton. This increase was obtained by almost quadrupling the area under cotton and raising yields per hectare by a little over two-thirds. The increase in area was obtained partly by increasing the irrigated area by 35 per cent, and partly by replacing other crops, primarily grains, by cotton on the original irrigated area. The increase in yields was obtained mainly by the application of very large amounts of fertilizer. While the application of mineral fertilizer is low by United States standards in Soviet agriculture as a whole, it is generous on cotton areas. Fertilizer application in Uzbekistan in 1933 was 15 kilograms per hectare and the cotton yield was 890 kilograms per hectare. In 1939, the amount

13. See United Nations, *Economic Bulletin for Europe*, pp. 55-61.

14. U.S. Congress, Joint Economic Committee, *Current Economic Indicators for the U.S.S.R.*, 89th Cong., 1st Sess., 1965, p. 57. However, all cotton in the U.S.S.R. is grown on irrigated land while only 30 per cent of U.S. cotton is irrigated. In Arizona, California, and New Mexico almost all cotton is grown on irrigated land. The yields per acre are 1,075 lbs. in California, and 713 lbs. in New Mexico. See U.S. Department of Agriculture, *Agricultural Statistics, 1964* (Washington: Government Printing Office, 1964), p. 62.

15. U.S. Congress, Joint Economic Committee, *Comparisons of the United States and Soviet Economies*, 86th Cong., 1st Sess., 1960, p. 125.

*TABLE IX-2*

### Cotton Production in Soviet Central Asia

| Year | Production[a] | | | Index numbers, 1913 = 100 | | |
|------|------|------|------|------|------|------|
| | Area 1,000 hectares | Crop 1,000 tons | Yield 100 kg. per ha. | Area | Crop | Yield |
| 1913 | 543 | 646 | 11.9 | 100 | 100 | 100 |
| 1928 | 793 | 665 | 8.4 | 146 | 103 | 71 |
| 1932 | 1,194 | 998 | 8.4 | 220 | 155 | 71 |
| 1934 | 1,354 | 1,396 | 10.3 | 249 | 216 | 87 |
| 1940 | 1,346 | 1,958 | 14.5 | 249 | 303 | 122 |
| 1961 | 2,082 | 4,247 | 20.4 | 383 | 657 | 171 |

Sources:

TsSU, *Narkhoz, 1961,* pp. 332, 357. Area figures for 1928, 1932, and 1934 are from Henze, "The Economic Development of Soviet Central Asia to the Eve of World War II," p. 290. Crop figures for 1928, 1932, and 1934 are computed from Wilhelm, "Soviet Central Asia," p. 220, and United Nations, *Economic Bulletin for Europe,* p. 56.

[a] Production figures for Kazakhstan are unobtainable for 1928, 1932, and 1934. Since production was negligible it was omitted until 1940.

of fertilizer was increased to 566 kilograms per hectare and yields increased to 1,700 kilograms per hectare.[16] By 1953, about one-third of the total production of mineral fertilizers in the U.S.S.R. was used on cotton fields.[17]

#### AGRICULTURAL PRODUCTION AND PRODUCTIVITY

The preceding pages have stressed cotton cultivation because it is one of Central Asia's two most important agricultural resources. Since the nineteenth century, Central Asia has been a deficit area in grain production. But with the "New Lands" program in Kazakhstan this has changed. The old grain areas are mainly located on poorer soils and only 10 per cent is irrigated. Thus yields have always been low. The extensive type cultivation of the new lands area produced good yields in the beginning, but they have declined since 1958. Increased production of chemical fertilizers and expanded irrigation offer hope that this trend will be reversed. Table

16. Mirko Lamer, *The World Fertilizer Economy* (Stanford: Stanford University Press, 1957), p. 573.
17. United Nations, *Economic Bulletin for Europe,* p. 57.

TABLE IX-3

### Production of Selected Agricultural Crops in Soviet Central Asia

| Crop | Production Area 1,000 hectares | Production Crop 1,000 tons | Production Yield 100 kg. per ha. | Index numbers, 1913 = 100 Area | Index numbers, 1913 = 100 Crop | Index numbers, 1913 = 100 Yield |
|---|---|---|---|---|---|---|
| **Grain:** | | | | | | |
| 1913 | 6,629 | 3,984 | 6.0 | 100 | 100 | 100 |
| 1940 | 8,825 | 3,613[a] | 4.1 | 133 | 91 | 68 |
| 1958 | 25,492 | 23,667 | 9.3 | 385 | 594 | 155 |
| 1961 | 24,371 | 15,999 | 6.6 | 368 | 402 | 110 |
| **Sugar beets:** | | | | | | |
| 1913 | — | — | — | | | |
| 1940 | 30 | 1,013 | 337.6 | | | |
| 1961 | 96 | 2,418 | 251.9 | | | |
| **Sunflowers:** | | | | | | |
| 1913 | 19 | 8 | 4.2 | 100 | 100 | 100 |
| 1940 | 169 | 25 | 1.5 | 889 | 313 | 36 |
| 1961 | 101 | 43 | 4.3 | 532 | 538 | 102 |
| **Potatoes:** | | | | | | |
| 1913 | 54 | 253 | 46.9 | 100 | 100 | 100 |
| 1940 | 150 | 656 | 43.7 | 278 | 259 | 93 |
| 1961 | 217 | 1,606 | 74.0 | 402 | 635 | 158 |
| **Vegetables:** | | | | | | |
| 1913 | 37 | 355[b] | 9.6 | 100 | 100 | 100 |
| 1940 | 63 | 604 | 9.6 | 170 | 170 | 100 |
| 1961 | 104 | 1,079 | 10.4 | 281 | 304 | 108 |
| **Meat:** | | | | | | |
| 1913 | | 674 | | | 100 | |
| 1940 | | 401 | | | 59 | |
| 1961 | | 946 | | | 140 | |
| **Milk:** | | | | | | |
| 1913 | | 1,344 | | | 100 | |
| 1940 | | 1,909 | | | 142 | |
| 1961 | | 4,170 | | | 310 | |
| **Eggs (million pieces):** | | | | | | |
| 1913 | | 377 | | | 100 | |
| 1940 | | 568 | | | 151 | |
| 1961 | | 1,706 | | | 453 | |
| **Clipped wool:** | | | | | | |
| 1913 | | 64.5 | | | 100 | |
| 1940 | | 30.3 | | | 47 | |
| 1961 | | 129.8 | | | 201 | |

Sources:
   TsSU, *Narkhoz, 1961,* pp. 324-25, 332, 334-36, 346-47, 357-59, 362-64, 393-96.
   [a] The official grain output figure was 4,153 thousand tons. But the biological yield method of computing the harvest, which was in use in 1940, overstates the actual crop. The official output figure for the entire U.S.S.R. was 95.5 million tons. Johnson and Kahan estimate the actual output to be 83.0 million tons. The Central Asian grain output was reduced proportionately. See U.S. Congress, Joint Economic Committee, *Comparisons of the United States and Soviet Economies,* p. 231.
   [b] Estimate based on 1940 yield.

IX-3 summarizes the changes in production of grain and other agricultural products since the Revolution.

There are no statistics available on Central Asian agricultural output between 1913 and 1940, except for cotton and the 1928 output for grain. There is no doubt, however, that livestock products such as meat and milk declined markedly during the early 1930's. This would have to be true because of the drastic decline in livestock herds between 1928 and 1933. Also grain output must have fallen in the early 1930's because grain was replaced on the best land by cotton and was demoted to inferior fields. However, between 1928 and 1932, the sown area not devoted to cotton increased by 1,237 thousand hectares.[18] Wilhelm reported that Central Asian (excluding Kazakhstan) grain output in 1928 was 2.0 million tons and about 1.9 million tons in 1937.[19]

Animal husbandry has been a neglected activity until recently. For example, Central Asian milk yields are poor by any standard. Most of the cows in Central Asia are privately owned and their yields are very low. As late as 1955, the average milk yield of cows in Uzbekistan was 816 kilograms, which was lower than that obtained before collectivization.[20] Table IX-4 summarizes the situation in milk production.

As can be seen from Table IX-4, the increased emphasis on livestock improvement in state and collective farms, including breed improvement, building of barns, and use of silage have resulted in

   18. Paul B. Henze, "The Economic Development of Soviet Central Asia to the Eve of World War II: An Examination of Soviet Methods As Applied to a Semi-Colonial Area," *Royal Central Asian Society Journal,* XXXVI (July, 1949), 286, 290.
   19. Wilhelm, "Soviet Central Asia," p. 220. The official output was 2.4 million tons but Wilhelm scaled this down by 25 per cent to allow for over-estimation due to use of the biological yield method.
   20. United Nations, *Economic Bulletin for Europe,* p. 58.

TABLE IX-4

*Milk Yields: Kilograms per Cow*[a]

| Area | 1940 | 1953 | 1961 |
|------|------|------|------|
| Uzbekistan | 438 | 450 | 850 |
| Kazakhstan | 876 | 936 | 1,747 |
| Kirgizia | 799 | 715 | 1,613 |
| Tadjikstan | 296 | 351 | 786 |
| Turkmenistan | 504 | 409 | 1,024 |
| U.S.S.R. | 1,124 | 1,157 | 1,851 |
| United States | 2,171[b] | 2,514 | 3,276 |

Sources:

TsSU, *Narkhoz, 1961*, p. 407. U.S. Department of Agriculture, *Agricultural Statistics, 1961*, p. 388. U.S. Department of Agriculture, *Agricultural Statistics, 1964*, p. 379.

[a] On state and collective farms only.

[b] 1945.

a considerable increase of yields. The spread within farms brought by the gradual introduction of improved breeds is remarkable. "On the Lenin collective farm near Stalinabad in early 1957 there were 170 cows in a modern byre (barn), with an average yield of 3,600 kg., and 720 other cows with an average yield of only 500 kg."[21] The major reason that yields have been so low is that one breed of cow has been used to obtain both milk and meat.

To obtain some idea of the relative efficiency of agriculture in Central Asia, Table IX-5 has been constructed. Here the cost of production on collective farms for selected agricultural products is shown as a per cent of the U.S.S.R. average. As can be seen, the cost of production on Central Asian collective farms was generally higher than the U.S.S.R. average except for livestock products.

It would be worthwhile if some over-all index of the growth of Central Asian agriculture could be constructed. The official index of gross agricultural output by individual republic begins in 1953. Table IX-6 sets forth this index.

Tables IX-7 and IX-8 set forth this writer's attempt to construct an index of gross agricultural output from 1913 to 1961. The official physical output figures are weighted by 1926-27 ruble prices. Fruits and grapes are the only products of consequence omitted. This is

21. *Ibid.*

*TABLE IX-5*

### Cost of Production on Central Asian Collective Farms, 1953-1955: U.S.S.R. Average = 100

| Product | Uzbekistan | Kazakhstan | Kirgizia | Tadjikstan | Turkmenistan |
|---|---|---|---|---|---|
| Grain | 153 | 72 | 105 | 194 | 158 |
| Potatoes | 233 | 230 | 236 | 277 | 879 |
| Vegetables | 93 | 131 | 153 | 109 | 130 |
| Sugar beets | — | 115 | 103 | — | — |
| Sunflower | — | 195 | — | — | — |
| Cotton | 101 | 108 | 121 | 98 | 116 |
| Beef | 90 | 65 | 95 | 88 | 66 |
| Pork | 34 | 84 | 100 | — | — |
| Milk | 97 | 73 | 93 | 90 | 76 |
| Wool | 39 | 68 | 75 | 62 | 30 |
| Eggs | 122 | 160 | 119 | 131 | 103 |

Source:
    U.S. Congress, Joint Economic Committee, *Comparisons of the United States and Soviet Economies,* p. 259.

*TABLE IX-6*

### Official Index of Gross Agricultural Output: 1953-1961

| | Value of output in 1958 rubles: million rubles | | | Index: 1953 = 100 | | |
|---|---|---|---|---|---|---|
| | 1953 | 1958 | 1961 | 1953 | 1958 | 1961 |
| U.S.S.R. | — | — | — | 100 | 151 | 159 |
| Uzbekistan | 1,233 | 1,603 | 1,698 | 100 | 130 | 138 |
| Kazakhstan | 1,440 | 2,952 | 2,943 | 100 | 205 | 205 |
| Kirgizia | 319 | 440 | 450 | 100 | 138 | 141 |
| Tadjikstan | 286 | 338 | 413 | 100 | 118 | 144 |
| Turkmenistan | 229 | 320 | 317 | 100 | 140 | 139 |
| Central Asia | 3,507 | 5,653 | 5,821 | 100 | 161 | 166 |
| w/o Kazakhstan | 2,067 | 2,701 | 2,878 | 100 | 131 | 139 |

Source:
    TsSU, *Narkhoz, 1961,* p. 294. The index numbers and the output figures for 1958 and 1961 were obtained from the above source. The 1953 output was obtained by dividing the 1958 index numbers into the 1958 value of output figures.

*TABLE IX-7*

### Gross Agricultural Output for Soviet
### Central Asia: 1913-1961

| Product | 1926-27 Prices rubles/T | Physical output: 1,000 metric tons | | | | |
|---|---|---|---|---|---|---|
| | | 1913 | 1940 | 1953 | 1958 | 1961 |
| Grain | 55.5 | 3,984 | 3,613 | 6,953 | 23,667 | 15,999 |
| Raw cotton | 282.0 | 661 | 1,958 | 3,427 | 4,032 | 4,247 |
| Sugar beets | 11.6 | — | 1,013 | 1,129 | 2,456 | 2,418 |
| Sunflowers | 66.5 | 8 | 25 | 43 | 52 | 43 |
| Potatoes | 25.0 | 253 | 656 | 900 | 1,269 | 1,606 |
| Vegetables | 60.5 | 355 | 604 | 539 | 817 | 1,079 |
| Meat | 421.2[b] | 674 | 401 | 503 | 707 | 946 |
| | 340.0 | | | | | |
| Milk | 59.8 | 1,344 | 1,909 | 2,282 | 3,730 | 4,170 |
| Eggs[a] | 30.47 | 377 | 568 | 873 | 1,482 | 1,706 |
| Clipped wool | 1,079.0 | 64.5 | 30.3 | 74.2 | 112.0 | 129.8 |
| Total | | | | | | |

Source:

1926-27 Ruble prices from: U.S. Congress, Joint Economic Committee, *Comparisons of the United States and Soviet Economies,* p. 204. Physical output series from: TsSU, *Narkhoz, 1961,* pp. 346-47, 357-59, 362-64, 393-96.

[a] Price in rubles per 1,000 pieces. Physical output in million pieces.
[b] Old concept price, 421.2 rubles, is used for 1913. New concept price, 340.0 rubles, is used for later years.

because physical output figures before 1953 are not available. Table IX-8 summarizes the index of gross agricultural output.

As can be observed from Table IX-8, gross agricultural output in Central Asia grew at a faster rate than for the U.S.S.R. as a whole from 1928 to 1940, and at a much faster rate from 1940 to 1961. In 1940 and 1953, the value of raw cotton made up about one-half of the total value of agricultural output. And, from 1940 to 1953, the output of raw cotton almost doubled. This explains the rapid growth for this period. In the 1953-58 period, the New Lands were opened in Kazakhstan. The total output of grain tripled in this period. The fall of gross agricultural output from 1958 to 1961 is explained by the large fall of output in the New Lands. Two factors caused the decline in grain production in the New Lands. First, the natural fertility of the virgin soil declined as it was used year after

| Value of gross agricultural output in 1926-27 rubles | | | | |
|---|---|---|---|---|
| 1913 | 1940 | 1953 | 1958 | 1961 |
| 221,112,000 | 200,521,500 | 385,891,500 | 1,313,518,500 | 887,944,500 |
| 186,402,000 | 552,156,000 | 966,414,000 | 1,137,024,000 | 1,197,654,000 |
| — | 11,750,800 | 13,096,400 | 28,489,600 | 28,048,000 |
| 532,000 | 1,662,500 | 2,859,500 | 3,458,000 | 2,859,500 |
| 6,325,000 | 16,400,000 | 22,500,000 | 31,725,000 | 40,150,000 |
| 21,477,500 | 36,542,000 | 32,609,500 | 49,428,500 | 65,279,950 |
| 283,888,800 | 136,340,000 | 171,020,000 | 240,380,000 | 321,640,000 |
| 80,371,200 | 114,158,200 | 136,463,600 | 223,054,000 | 249,366,000 |
| 11,487,190 | 17,306,960 | 26,600,310 | 45,156,540 | 51,981,820 |
| 69,595,500 | 32,693,700 | 80,061,800 | 120,848,000 | 140,054,200 |
| 881,191,190 | 1,119,531,660 | 1,837,516,610 | 3,193,182,140 | 2,984,977,970 |

year. Second, the area receives just enough precipitation to grow grain. When the weather is bad, the harvest is bad. Official grain output figures for Kazakhstan were 21.9 million metric tons in 1958, 19.0 million in 1959, 18.7 million in 1960, 14.6 million in 1961, 15.9 million in 1962, 10.6 million in 1963, and 23.9 million in 1964.[22]

Since some writers believe that the New Lands program is not properly a part of Central Asian development, Table IX-8 includes separate agricultural output indices for the rest of Central Asia and for Kazakhstan. The performance of Central Asia is better without than with Kazakhstan for the period 1913-61. This is so because the slaughter of livestock in Kazakhstan caused a sharp fall in animal products during the 1930's.

The computed index shown in Table IX-8 is not precise and should be used with caution. However, it should be accurate enough to give an approximate idea of the growth of Central Asian agriculture. Johnson and Kahan[23] compute a similar index for the U.S.S.R. They also compute two other indices using 1925-29 and 1958 price weights. All three indices come out practically the same

22. TsSU, *Narkhoz, 1961*, pp. 346-47. TsSU, *Narkhoz, 1964*, p. 296.
23. U.S. Congress, Joint Economic Committee, *Comparisons of the United States and Soviet Economies*, pp. 203-5.

TABLE IX-8

**Computed Index of Gross Agricultural Output: 1913-1961**

|  | 1913 | 1928 | 1940 | 1953 | 1958 | 1961 |
|---|---|---|---|---|---|---|
| Soviet Central Asia |  |  |  |  |  |  |
| 1913 = 100 | 100.0 | 100.0 | 127.0 | 208.5 | 362.4 | 338.7 |
| 1928 = 100 |  | 100.0 | 127.0 | 208.5 | 362.4 | 338.7 |
| 1940 = 100 |  |  | 100.0 | 164.1 | 285.2 | 275.6 |
| 1953 = 100 |  |  |  | 100.1 | 173.8 | 162.4 |
| Soviet Central Asia (excluding Kazakhstan) |  |  |  |  |  |  |
| 1913 = 100 | 100.0 | 100.0 | 166.6 | 260.9 | 329.7 | 339.8 |
| 1928 = 100 |  | 100.0 | 166.6 | 260.9 | 329.7 | 339.8 |
| 1940 = 100 |  |  | 100.0 | 156.6 | 197.9 | 204.0 |
| 1953 = 100 |  |  |  | 100.0 | 126.4 | 130.2 |
| Kazakhstan |  |  |  |  |  |  |
| 1913 = 100 | 100.0 | 100.0 | 84.5 | 152.3 | 395.1 | 335.0 |
| 1928 = 100 |  | 100.0 | 84.5 | 152.3 | 395.1 | 335.0 |
| 1940 = 100 |  |  | 100.0 | 180.2 | 467.6 | 396.4 |
| 1953 = 100 |  |  |  | 100.0 | 259.4 | 220.0 |
| U.S.S.R. |  |  |  |  |  |  |
| 1928 = 100 |  | 100.0 | 120.3 | 128.6 | 192.0 | 203.0 |
| 1940 = 100 |  |  | 100.0 | 106.9 | 159.6 | 168.7 |
| 1953 = 100 |  |  |  | 100.0 | 149.3 | 157.9 |

Sources:

Table IX-7 for Central Asia. U.S.S.R. index from U.S. Congress, Joint Economic Committee, *Comparisons of the United States and Soviet Economies*, p. 204; U.S. Congress, Joint Economic Committee, *Annual Economic Indicators for the U.S.S.R.*, p. 32.

in the final year—1957. Thus, 1926-27 ruble prices are probably acceptable weights.

In Table IX-8, the year 1928 is included despite its omission from Table IX-7. Physical output figures for 1928 are not available for many of the crops. It is this writer's estimate that gross agricultural output was either the same as in 1913 or a little less. Thus, in Table IX-8, 1928 output is taken to be the same as 1913 output. There is good evidence that this may not be far wrong. And since 1928 marks the beginning of the Soviet industrialization period, and the prior years a period of reconstruction, it would be very valuable to have 1928 output. The first piece of evidence is cotton production.

TABLE IX-9

### Growth Rates of Gross Agricultural Output in Central Asia

|  | 1913-1961 | 1928-1961 | 1928-1940 | 1940-1961 | 1953-1961 |
|---|---|---|---|---|---|
| Annual growth rate | 2.6 | 3.8 | 2.0 | 4.9 | 6.3 |
| Per capita | 1.2 | 2.2 | 1.0 | 2.6 | 3.4 |

Source:
   Table IX-8.

In 1913, it was 646 thousand tons and in 1928, 665 thousand tons.[24] The livestock herds in 1916 amounted to 55 million head and in 1928, 61 million head.[25] Between 1913 and 1916, large numbers of horses were drafted into the army and, hence, were not counted in 1916. And, finally, the area sown to all crops other than cotton in 1913 amounted to 7,249 thousand hectares and in 1928 to 6,956 hectares.[26] Therefore, if used with due caution, the growth rates of gross agricultural output presented in Table IX-9, can be informative.

These growth rates compare favorably with those achieved by other countries. Table IX-10 compares average annual agricultural growth rates in Soviet Central Asia with the Soviet Union, the United States, Japan, Mexico, and selected underdeveloped countries. Wherever possible, time periods were chosen to correspond to the initial development period for each country.

The computed index yields an annual growth rate of 6.3 per cent between 1953 and 1961. The official index shown in Table IX-6 yields a rate of 6.5 per cent. This provides some collaboration for the accuracy of the computed index.

As another way of checking the validity of the Central Asian agricultural index, it can be compared to one computed by Wilhelm. Taking 1928 as a base of 100.0, he calculates that gross agricultural output in 1937, for all of Central Asia except Kazakhstan, was

24. TsSU, *Narkhoz, 1961*, p. 357; United Nations, *Economic Bulletin for Europe*, p. 56; and Wilhelm, "Soviet Central Asia," p. 220.

25. Naum Jasny, *The Socialized Agriculture of the U.S.S.R.: Plans and Performance*, Grain Economic Series No. 5 (Stanford: Stanford University Press, 1949), p. 634; United Nations, *Economic Bulletin for Europe*, p. 57; Bureau of Social Science Research, *Handbook of Central Asia*, III, 925.

26. TsSU, *Narkhoz, 1961*, p. 324; Henze, "The Economic Development of Soviet Central Asia to the Eve of World War II," p. 286.

*TABLE IX-10*
### Agricultural Growth Rates in Soviet Central Asia and Selected Other Countries

| Countries and time periods | % Total | % Per capita |
|---|---|---|
| Soviet Central Asia, 1928-1961 | 3.8 | 2.2 |
| U.S.S.R., 1928-1961 | 2.2 | 1.1 |
| U.S.A., 1870-1900 | 3.3 | 1.2 |
| Japan, 1861/65-1891/95 | 2.0 | 0.8 |
| Mexico, 1940-1960 | 5.1 | 2.2 |
| Afghanistan, 1952/55-1964/65 | 1.7 | −0.2 |
| Colombia, 1952/55-1964/65 | 2.7 | −0.1 |
| India, 1952/55-1964/65 | 2.8 | 0.6 |
| Iran, 1952/55-1964/65 | 2.0 | −0.4 |
| Malaya, States of, 1952/55-1964/65 | 3.6 | 0.4 |
| Taiwan, 1952/55-1964/65 | 3.8 | 0.5 |
| Turkey, 1952/55-1964/65 | 2.8 | −0.1 |
| United Arab Republic, 1952/55-1964/65 | 2.9 | 0.4 |

Sources:
Tables III-3, IX-8, and IX-9; U.S. Department of Agriculture, *The 1965 World Agricultural Situation* (Washington: Government Printing Office, 1964), pp. 27, 34, 38.

165.5.[27] This yields an annual growth rate of 5.8 per cent, while according to this writer's calculation from Table IX-8, it was 4.3 per cent between 1928 and 1940 for all of Central Asia excluding Kazakhstan.

Joseph Willet believes that Soviet output figures for grain in 1958 and 1961 are overstated.[28] Part of the overstatement is due to counting corn silage as grain and part to excess moisture content. He estimates the grain crop was 125 million tons in 1958 and 115 million in 1961, instead of the official figure of 141 million in 1958 and 137 million in 1961. If his contention is correct, and Central Asian grain production is overstated on a proportionate basis, then the annual growth rate between 1928 and 1961 would be 3.6 per cent instead of 3.8 per cent, and between 1953 and 1961, it would be 5.5 per cent instead of 6.3 per cent.

27. Wilhelm, "Soviet Central Asia," p. 222.
28. U.S. Congress, Joint Economic Committee, *Hearings, on Sec. 5 (a) of P. L. 304, Dimensions of Soviet Economic Power*, 87th Cong., 2nd. Sess., 1962, p. 99.

AGRICULTURAL INVESTMENT

Heavy investment in agriculture has been the major reason that Central Asian agriculture has been relatively successful. During 1928-32, 51.8 per cent of all state and kolkhoz investment was allocated to agriculture, 34.7 per cent during 1933-37, 37.6 per cent during 1938-41, 34.7 per cent during 1946-50, 33.7 per cent during 1951-55, and 31.8 per cent during 1956-61.[29] The above figures do not include Kazakhstan, for which no data are available. The proportion of investment allocated to agriculture has been higher in Central Asia than in the Soviet Union as a whole, which probably explains the different agricultural growth rates shown in Table IX-10.

This agricultural investment made it possible to provide large numbers of agricultural machines and to expand the irrigated area. On January 1, 1962, in Central Asian agriculture there was a motive power of 33,087,000 h.p. Of this, mechanical power supplied 32,556,000 h.p. or 98 per cent, and animal power 531,000 h.p. or 2 per cent of the total.[30] In terms of 15 h.p. units, the number of tractors in Central Asia increased from 2,000 in 1928 to 79,700 in 1940 and 498,700 in 1961. This provided per 10,000 hectares of sown area, 2.5 tractors in 1928, 65.8 in 1940, and 146.5 in 1961.[31] The number of grain combines increased from 14,800 in 1940 to 105,000 in 1963. This provided per 10,000 hectares sown to grain, 16.8 combines in 1940 and 43.1 in 1961.[32]

The total number of agricultural specialists with a higher technical education in Central Asia in 1961 was 15,114, and with a secondary technical education, 38,580.[33]

The Central Asian modification of the Soviet model's minimization of investment in agriculture seems to have paid off in considerably higher growth rates of agricultural production.

29. Sredneaziatskoye statisticheskoye upravleniye, *Narodnoye khozyaystvo Sredney Azii v 1963 godu: statisticheskiy sbornik* (Tashkent: Izdatyelatvo Uzbekistan, 1964), pp. 242, 251.

30. TsSU, *Narkhoz, 1961,* p. 413.

31. *Ibid.,* pp. 322-23, 414. Henze, "The Economic Development of Soviet Central Asia to the Eve of World War II," pp. 286-88.

32. TsSU, *Narkhoz, 1961,* pp. 324-25, 415.

33. *Ibid.,* p. 464.

# X. INDUSTRIAL DEVELOPMENT

The industrial development of Central Asia is of relatively recent origin. Prior to 1917, it was "a purely agrarian and cattle-breeding area, with a few cotton-ginning and silk-spinning mills."[1] The five-year plans, however, have brought about great changes. It is these changes that must be examined in this chapter.

## TRANSPORTATION

A basic and essential factor in the economic development of any area is construction of transport facilities. A modern industrial economy requires rapid, efficient, and low-cost transportation. Rail and water are usually the most important types of transport, followed by motor and air transport. "The Soviet Government since the middle 20's has pursued a vigorous programme of railroad construction,"[2] in Central Asia. Central Asia is on the whole a very arid region and has few rivers capable of extensive development as transportation arteries. They are too few and too shallow to be of great importance. Therefore, the improvement of transportation facilities in Soviet Central Asia has meant almost exclusively the construction and improvement of railroads. Table X-1 summarizes the development of railroad mileage in Central Asia.

Most railroad construction has taken place in the two largest republics of Uzbekistan and Kazakhstan. However, the intensity of use has increased greatly in all of the Central Asian republics. The amount of railway freight originations and terminations is shown in

1. Michael Rywkin, *Russia in Central Asia*, Russian Civilization Series (New York: Collier Books, 1963), p. 67. Also, see Geoffrey Wheeler, *The Modern History of Soviet Central Asia* (New York: Frederick A. Praeger, Inc., 1964).

2. Paul B. Henze, "The Economic Development of Soviet Central Asia to the Eve of World War II: An Examination of Soviet Methods As Applied to a Semi-Colonial Area," *Royal Central Asian Society Journal*, XXXVI (July, 1949), 292-93. For a detailed study of Soviet railroad transportation policy, see Holland Hunter, *Soviet Transportation Policy* (Cambridge: Harvard University Press, 1957).

TABLE X-1

Operating Length of Rail Lines in Central Asia

| Republic | Kilometers | | | | |
|---|---|---|---|---|---|
| | 1913 | 1933 | 1940 | 1950 | 1961 |
| Uzbekistan | 1,100 | 1,890 | 1,910 | 2,070 | 2,330 |
| Kazakhstan | 2,042 | 5,186[a] | 6,580 | 8,410 | 11,640 |
| Kirgizia | — | 180 | 220 | 370 | 370 |
| Tadjikstan | 110 | 190 | 250 | 260 | 260 |
| Turkmenistan | 1,490 | 1,700 | 1,750 | 1,740 | 2,100 |
| Total | 4,742 | 9,146 | 10,710 | 12,850 | 16,700 |

Sources:

TsSU, *Transport i svyaz SSSR*, p. 30; TsSU, *Narkhoz, 1961*, p. 477; SsU, *Narkhoz Sredney Azii, 1963*, p. 219; Statisticheskoye upravleniye *Kazakhstan SSR, Narodnoye khozyaystvo Kazakhstan SSR: statisticheskiy sbornik* (Alma-Ata: Kazakhstan Gosudarstvyennoye Izdatyelstvo, 1957), p. 241; Robert N. Taaffe, *Rail Transportation and the Economic Development of Soviet Central Asia*, Department of Geography Research Paper No. 64 (Chicago: Chicago University Press, 1960), p. 52; Henze, "The Economic Development of Soviet Central Asia to the Eve of World War II," p. 293.

[a] 1932.

Table X-2. As can be seen, the volume of freight traffic has increased much more rapidly than the length of rail lines. Here is an important example of the Soviet strategy of conserving the scarce factor, capital, by intensifying its use.

To put the growth of railway freight turnover (originations plus terminations) in Central Asia in perspective, it is noteworthy that the 1961 freight turnover of 287,300 thousand tons was more than twice as large as the freight turnover for the entire U.S.S.R. in 1913, which was 140,200 thousand tons. In 1913, Central Asia accounted for 3.6 per cent of total freight turnover in the U.S.S.R. and in 1961 for 12.2 per cent. Thus, freight turnover has grown more rapidly in Central Asia than in the Soviet Union as a whole.

Motor freight transportation in millions of ton-kilometers was 875 in 1940 and 15,789 in 1961 for Soviet Central Asia. As late as 1950 in all of the Soviet Union, motor freight transportation was 20,121 million freight-ton-kilometers. In 1940, Central Asia accounted for 9.8 per cent and in 1961 for 15.0 per cent of the total.[3]

3. TsSU, *Narkhoz, 1961*, p. 504.

TABLE X-2

The Growth of Central Asian Rail Freight, 1913-1961

| Republic | Thousands of metric tons | | | | | | | |
| --- | --- | --- | --- | --- | --- | --- | --- | --- |
| | 1913 | | 1928 | | 1940 | | 1961 | |
| | Orig. | Term. | Orig. | Term. | Orig. | Term. | Orig. | Term. |
| Uzbekistan | 1,100 | 1,700 | 1,600 | 2,400 | 5,400 | 8,700 | 21,000 | 31,200 |
| Kazakhstan | 600 | 500 | 1,400 | 1,500 | 15,500 | 12,200 | 102,000 | 92,500 |
| Kirgizia | — | — | 100 | 100 | 2,000 | 1,300 | 4,900 | 6,900 |
| Tadjikstan | 100 | 40 | 100 | 100 | 1,800 | 900 | 4,000 | 5,200 |
| Turkmenistan | 500 | 500 | 1,300 | 1,000 | 3,700 | 2,900 | 9,500 | 10,100 |
| Total | 2,300 | 2,740 | 4,500 | 5,100 | 28,400 | 26,000 | 141,400 | 145,900 |

Sources:
TsSU, *Transport i svyaz SSSR*, p. 67; TsSU, *Narkhoz, 1961*, p. 484.

INDUSTRY

Table X-3 sets forth factory production of selected industrial goods in Soviet Central Asia. As can be seen from the index numbers, the growth of production of each product has been very rapid, the most rapid being in producers' goods. However, this is parly explained by the fact that capital goods industries were completely underdeveloped prior to 1928. Thus, small increases in output, starting from a very small base, will yield very high rates of growth. This does not obviate the fact that substantial industrial growth has taken place. With one-seventh the population, Central Asian output in 1961 for many products was greater than the 1928 production in the entire U.S.S.R. Coal production was larger, oil production a little less, electricity generation four times larger, cement production over twice as large, output of bricks larger, and production of machine tools almost three times as large.

The last section of Table X-3 illustrates that the output of most products was a lower percentage of total U.S.S.R. output than the proportion of Central Asian population. However, the percentage of Central Asian output to total U.S.S.R. output has steadily increased for most products. Thus, the average annual growth of all these industrial products has been faster in Soviet Central Asia than in the Soviet Union as a whole.

Another way of checking the relative growth of industrial production in Central Asia to the U.S.S.R. is to compare their indices of gross industrial production. This is done in Table X-4.

While these gross indices should not be used to measure the absolute magnitude of growth, they should be adequate to measure relative growth in Central Asia and the U.S.S.R. If anything, they may understate Central Asia's relative growth. Three major factors affect the gross industrial output index and, thus, the comparability of the indices. First, it is probably safe to assume that the amount of integration of industrial enterprises was not significantly different in Central Asia from the U.S.S.R. as a whole. Second, the inflationary bias in the index was probably less for Central Asia. The assigned 1926-27 ruble prices for new products, which give the inflationary bias to the index, are most important in the electrical products and machinery industries, and these industries are relatively small in Central Asia. Third, cotton ginning bulks large in Central Asian industrial production and its growth was slower than most products in the index. Since it has a very low value added (6.2 per cent for 1946-48 in the United States), it understates the growth of the index relative to the U.S.S.R. From Table X-4 and the above discussion it seems probable that gross industrial production grew faster in Central Asia between 1928 and 1961 (and the subperiods 1928-40 and 1940-61) than in the U.S.S.R. as a whole.

While the above discussion answers the problem of ascertaining relative industrial growth as between the U.S.S.R. as a whole and Central Asia, it casts no light on the absolute magnitude of industrial growth in Central Asia. The only available indicator of the increase in aggregate output of the region's industry is the official index of gross industrial production. As was noted in Chapter IV, there are three main deficiencies in the way the index is computed. First, since it is a gross output index, changes in the integration of industrial enterprises will affect the index. Second, Soviet statisticians have not fully corrected for price level changes when entering new products into the index. As was seen above, this is less important for Central Asia. Third is the unavoidable "index number problem." Because of these deficiencies, Western experts have made independent calculations of the rate of industrial growth in the Soviet Union. However, since 1950, most of these deficiencies have been corrected.[4] In Table X-5, two of these estimates of U.S.S.R. industrial

4. Robert W. Campbell, *Soviet Economic Power* (Cambridge: Houghton Mifflin Company, 1960), p. 49.

*TABLE X-3*

### Factory Production of Selected Industrial Goods in Soviet Central Asia

| Product | Unit | Quantity | | | |
|---|---|---|---|---|---|
| | | 1913 | 1928 | 1940 | 1953 |
| **Central Asian population** (estimated) | 1,000's | 13,000 | 15,000 | 17,000 | 21,000 |
| **Energy** | | | | | |
| Coal | 1,000 tons | 248 | 268 | 8,657 | 26,204 |
| Oil | 1,000 tons | 270 | 275 | 1,457 | 5,270 |
| Natural gas | million m³ | 0 | 2 | 16 | 178 |
| Electricity | million kwh | 7 | 53 | 1,310 | 8,316 |
| **Building materials** | | | | | |
| Sawn timber | 1,000 m³ | — | — | 429 | 1,758 |
| Cement | 1,000 tons | 0 | 19 | 267 | 549 |
| Bricks (baked) | million pieces | — | — | 715 | 1,391 |
| Roofing slate | million pieces | 0 | 0 | 0 | 0 |
| Window glass | 1,000 m² | 0 | 2,000 | 2,237 | 5,617[a] |
| **Other producer goods** | | | | | |
| Pig iron | 1,000 tons | 0 | 0 | 0 | 0 |
| Steel | 1,000 tons | 0 | 0 | 11 | 391 |
| Rolled ferrous metals | 1,000 tons | 0 | 0 | 0 | 330 |
| Mineral fertilizers | 1,000 tons | 0 | 0 | 2 | 828 |
| Machine tools | Number | 0 | 0 | 139 | 1,385 |
| Power shovels | Number | 0 | 0 | 0 | 204 |
| Spinning machinery | Number | 0 | 0 | 0 | 1,296 |
| Tractor-drawn seed drills | Number | 0 | 0 | 500 | 3,000 |
| Tractor-drawn cultivators | Number | 0 | 0 | 1,900 | 6,700 |
| Tractor rakes | Number | 0 | 0 | 0 | 11,243 |
| Cotton pickers | Number | 0 | 0 | 0 | 3,346 |
| **Food products** | | | | | |
| Granulated sugar | 1,000 tons | 0 | 0 | 136 | 147 |
| Confectionery | 1,000 tons | 0 | 0 | 27 | 74 |
| Vegetable oils | 1,000 tons | 40 | 75 | 165 | 318 |
| Tinned food | million tins | 0 | — | 92 | 274 |
| Wine | million litres | — | — | 27 | — |
| **Other consumers' goods** | | | | | |
| Paper | tons | 0 | 0 | 1,900 | — |
| Cotton cloth | million m | 0 | 0 | 117 | 271 |
| Woolen cloth | 1,000 m | 139 | 129 | 660 | 3,669 |
| Silk cloth | 1,000 m | 0 | 0 | 6,305 | 30,050 |
| Knitted underwear | 1,000 units | 0 | 0 | 3,700 | 20,520 |
| Knitted outerwear | 1,000 units | 0 | 0 | 1,500 | 3,166 |
| Leather footwear | 1,000 pairs | 0 | 0 | 6,400 | 13,291 |

Sources:
　　TsSU, *Narkhoz, 1961,* pp. 197, 206, 209, 211, 220, 224, 237-38, 240, 245-46, 251-55, 259, 261, 265, 267-73; TsSU, *Promyshlyennost SSSR: statisticheskiy sbornik* (Moscow: Gosudarstvyennoye Statisticheskoye Izdatyelatvo, 1957), pp. 77, 79, 91-93,

| | Index numbers: various years = 100 | | | | | Percentage of total U.S.S.R. output | | | | |
|---|---|---|---|---|---|---|---|---|---|---|
| 1961 | 1913 | 1928 | 1940 | 1953 | 1961 | 1913 | 1928 | 1940 | 1953 | 1961 |
| 25,000 | 100 | 115 | 131 | 162 | 192 | 9.7 | 9.4 | 8.7 | 10.4 | 11.9 |
| 43,169 | 3 | 3 | 100 | 303 | 499 | .9 | .7 | 5.2 | 8.2 | 8.5 |
| 9,956 | 19 | 19 | 100 | 362 | 683 | 2.6 | 2.4 | 4.7 | 10.0 | 6.0 |
| 1,451 | 0 | 10 | 100 | 1,112 | 9,068 | .0 | .5 | .4 | — | 2.5 |
| 21,313 | 1 | 4 | 100 | 635 | 1,626 | .3 | 1.1 | 2.7 | 6.2 | 6.5 |
| 3,797 | — | — | 100 | 410 | 835 | — | — | 1.2 | 2.7 | 3.6 |
| 4,441 | 0 | 7 | 100 | 205 | 1,661 | .0 | 1.0 | 4.7 | 3.4 | 8.7 |
| 3,597 | — | — | 100 | 194 | 503 | — | — | 9.6 | 8.3 | 9.8 |
| 278 | 0 | 0 | 0 | 0 | 100 | .0 | .0 | .0 | .0 | 8.2 |
| — | 0 | 89 | 100 | 251 | — | .0 | 1.0 | 5.0 | 6.0 | — |
| 956 | 0 | 0 | 0 | 0 | 100 | .0 | .0 | .0 | .0 | 1.9 |
| 631 | 0 | 0 | 100 | 3,427 | 5,533 | .0 | .0 | .1 | 1.0 | .9 |
| 528 | 0 | 0 | 0 | 100 | 160 | .0 | .0 | .0 | 1.1 | 1.0 |
| 1,777 | 0 | 0 | 100 | 51,781 | 111,094 | .0 | .0 | .1 | 11.9 | 11.6 |
| 5,010 | 0 | 0 | 100 | 1,000 | 3,604 | .0 | .0 | .2 | 1.5 | 3.0 |
| 917 | 0 | 0 | 0 | 100 | 458 | .0 | .0 | .0 | 4.9 | 5.7 |
| — | 0 | 0 | 0 | 100 | — | .0 | .0 | .0 | 75.0 | — |
| 7,900[b] | 0 | 0 | 100 | 600 | 1,580 | .0 | .0 | 2.3 | 3.2 | 6.4 |
| 8,000[b] | 0 | 0 | 100 | 353 | 421 | — | — | 5.8 | 7.7 | 7.1 |
| 23,100[b] | 0 | 0 | 0 | 100 | 205 | — | — | .0 | 52.8 | 90.2 |
| — | 0 | 0 | 0 | 100 | — | — | — | .0 | 93.0 | — |
| 363 | 0 | 0 | 100 | 108 | 266 | .0 | .0 | 6.3 | 4.3 | 4.3 |
| 154 | 0 | 0 | 100 | 276 | 203 | .0 | .0 | 3.4 | 5.2 | 8.6 |
| 392 | 24 | 45 | 100 | 192 | 237 | 8.5 | 16.7 | 20.7 | 27.5 | 21.6 |
| 501 | 0 | — | 100 | 300 | 545 | — | — | 8.3 | 8.5 | 9.0 |
| 91 | — | — | 100 | — | 332 | — | — | .1 | — | .1 |
| 9,900 | 0 | — | 100 | — | 521 | .0 | .0 | .2 | — | .4 |
| 341 | 0 | — | 100 | 231 | 291 | .0 | .0 | 3.0 | 5.1 | 5.3 |
| 5,963 | 21 | 19 | 100 | 556 | 903 | .1 | .1 | .6 | 1.7 | 1.7 |
| 57,118 | 0 | 0 | 100 | 477 | 906 | .0 | .0 | 8.2 | 7.5 | 7.0 |
| 38,600 | 0 | 0 | 100 | 555 | 1,043 | .0 | .0 | 3.0 | 7.1 | 7.9 |
| 8,200 | 0 | 0 | 100 | 211 | 547 | .0 | .0 | 2.5 | 4.8 | 6.9 |
| 33,300 | 0 | 0 | 100 | 208 | 520 | .0 | .0 | 3.0 | 5.6 | 7.5 |

97, 396; TsSU, *Promyshlyennost SSSR, 1964,* pp. 256-57, 273, 299, 370-71, 388-89, 444, 448, 452; TsSU, *Forty Years of Soviet Power,* pp. 117-18, 125-26, 128; United Nations, *Economic Bulletin for Europe,* p. 62.

[a] 1955         [b] 1956

*TABLE X-4*
### Official Index of Gross Industrial Production
### for Soviet Central Asia
### and the U.S.S.R.

|                        | 1928 | 1940  | 1961  |
|------------------------|------|-------|-------|
| Uzbekistan             | 100  | 522   | 2,350 |
| Kazakhstan             | 100  | 790   | 6,478 |
| Kirgizia               | 100  | 1,100 | 7,480 |
| Tadjikstan             | 100  | 880   | 4,136 |
| Turkmenistan           | 100  | 609   | 2,193 |
| All Central Asia[a]    | 100  | 723   | 4,892 |
|                        |      | 100   | 677   |
| U.S.S.R.               | 100  | 645   | 3,712 |
|                        |      | 100   | 576   |

Sources:

TsSU, *Narkhoz, 1961,* pp. 169, 175, 182; TsSU, *Forty Years of Soviet Power,* pp. 117-18, 125-26, 128.

[a] The All Central Asian index was obtained by weighting the individual republic index numbers for 1940 and 1961 by the relative number of industrial workers in each republic. In 1940 and 1961 respectively, these weights were .31 and .32 for Uzbekistan, .50 and .48 for Kazakhstan, .07 and .09 for Kirgizia, .06 and .06 for Tadjikstan, and .06 and .05 for Turkmenistan.

growth have been used to correct the Central Asian index. Also included is Wilhelm's calculation for the period 1928-37 for Central Asia excluding Kazakhstan.

The Hodgman index was chosen because it was one of the higher Western estimates and the Nutter index because it was one of the lower estimates. The Hodgman index was 67 per cent of the official index in 1940. The Nutter index was 40 per cent of the official index in 1940 and 24 per cent in 1955. The official index for Central Asia was corrected downward in 1940 and 1955 to these extents. The Hodgman index was extended to 1955 to 1961, and the Nutter index to 1961, by the Joint Economic Committee index.

Wilhelm made an independent calculation from 1928 and 1937 industrial output figures (in 1926-27 rubles) for Central Asia. He adjusted cotton ginning downward to 6.2 per cent of its official value and all other production to 50 per cent for both 1928 and 1937. This adjustment was made in order to obtain a value-added index.

TABLE X-5

### Computed Index of Industrial Production in Soviet Central Asia

|  | 1928 | 1940 | 1955 | 1961 |
|---|---|---|---|---|
| Official index | 100 | 723 | 2693 | 4892 |
| Hodgman type index | 100 | 484 | 1481 | 2299 |
| Nutter type index | 100 | 289 | 727 | 1174 |
| Wilhelm calculation | 100 | 953[a] |  |  |

Sources:
Tables IV-3 and X-4; Wilhelm, "Soviet Central Asia," pp. 221-22; Campbell, *Soviet Economic Power,* p. 48; U.S. Congress, *Dimensions of Soviet Economic Power,* p. 120.
[a] 1937.

TABLE X-6

### Average Annual Growth Rates of Industrial Production in Soviet Central Asia

|  | 1928-1940 | 1928-1961 | 1940-1961 | 1955-1961 |
|---|---|---|---|---|
| SOVIET CENTRAL ASIA: |  |  |  |  |
| Official index | 17.9 | 12.5 | 9.5 | 10.5 |
| Hodgman type index | 14.1 | 11.0 | 7.7 | 7.6 |
| Nutter type index | 9.2 | 7.7 | 6.9 | 8.3 |
| Wilhelm calculation | 28.5[a] |  |  |  |

Sources:
Table X-5. If Kazakhstan is excluded the official growth rates for the rest of Central Asia are 17.0 per cent for 1928-40, 11.6 per cent for 1928-61, and 8.6 per cent for 1940-61.
[a] 1928-37.

All of these indices yield very high annual growth rates. And, as was noted in the discussion of relative industrial growth rates, the Central Asian index was less overstated than the index of the U.S.S.R. Thus, the Hodgman and Nutter indices may actually understate the magnitude of industrial growth in Central Asia. Table X-6 sets forth the average annual growth rates of industrial production for Central Asia derived from the above indices.

Table X-7 presents a comparison of growth rates of industrial

TABLE X-7

*Average Annual Growth Rates of Industrial Production
in Soviet Central Asia and Selected Countries*

| Countries and Years | % Growth Rates |
|---|---|
| Soviet Central Asia: | |
| 1928-1940: | |
| Hodgman type index | 14.1 |
| Nutter type index | 9.2 |
| 1928-1961: | |
| Hodgman type index | 11.0 |
| Nutter type index | 7.7 |
| U.S.S.R.: | |
| 1928-1940: | |
| Seton index | 13.6 |
| Nutter index | 8.3 |
| 1928-1963: | |
| Seton index | 9.3 |
| Nutter index | 6.9 |
| U.S.A., 1839-1869 | 5.6 |
| Japan, 1905/9-1930/34[a] | 6.9 |
| Mexico, 1940-1960 | 6.2 |
| India, 1953-1962 | 7.2 |
| Pakistan, 1953-1962 | 13.0 |
| Philippines, 1953-1962 | 3.8 |
| Taiwan, 1953-1962 | 10.7 |

Sources:

Tables IV-3, IV-4, and X-6. United Nations, *Statistical Yearbook,
1963* (New York: United Nations, 1964), pp. 95-97.

[a] A gross industrial production index.

production in Soviet Central Asia with selected other countries.
While Soviet Central Asia may not yet be highly industrialized compared to the Soviet Union as a whole, great progress has been made.

DEVELOPMENT POLICIES

Since Soviet Central Asia is a *region*, not a sovereign country, there
have been a number of deviations from the Soviet model presented
in the first part of this study. For example, "international trade"
(interregional) has been more extensively utilized, since no attempt
has been made to construct the whole spectrum of industries. The

major policies followed are analyzed below. Since there are large data gaps for regions in the Soviet Union, the following analysis is incomplete and is forced to rely upon indirect evidence in a number of cases.

*Investment.* One of the major factors enabling Soviet Central Asia to develop at a rapid rate has been the large amount of investment made every year. Since 1928, in Central Asia as elsewhere in the U.S.S.R., a large share of national income has been devoted to investment. This investment can be classed into three categories: (1) state investment in physical assets; (2) investment by collective farms; and (3) investment in human capital.

The figures given in Table X-8 show that state investment in physical assets per capita has generally been close to 70-80 per cent of the all-Union average.

*TABLE X-8*

*State Investment in Central Asia*

| Annual average during | Rubles per capita in constant prices | As percentage of all-Union average |
|---|---|---|
| 1928-32 | 63 | 70 |
| 1933-37 | 141 | 72 |
| 1938-40 | 187 | 82 |
| 1946-50 | 271 | 70 |
| 1951-55 | 560 | 82 |
| 1956-61 | 1,121 | 93 |

Source:
TsSU, *Narkhoz, 1961,* pp. 548-49.

The information which is available on investments made by collective farms in Central Asia (Kazakhstan is excluded since no information is available before 1950; since then it has been about 15 per cent), indicates that these are on much higher levels than elsewhere in the U.S.S.R. They amounted to 26 per cent of state investments over the period 1928 to 1961, while they averaged 10 per cent for the U.S.S.R. as a whole.[5] They were 42 per cent of state investments in Uzbekistan in 1955.[6] Thus, it may well be that total

5. TsSU, *Narkhoz, 1961,* pp. 548-49, 553. SsU, *Narkhoz Sredney Azii, 1963,* pp. 240, 250.
6. United Nations, *Economic Bulletin for Europe,* p. 69.

*TABLE X-9*

### Allocation of State and Kolkhoz Investment
### in Soviet Central Asia
### (w/o Kazakhstan)

| Sector | Percentage allocation by period | | | | | |
|--------|------|------|------|------|------|------|
|  | 1928-1932 | 1933-1937 | 1938-1940 | 1946-1950 | 1951-1955 | 1956-1961 |
| Industry | 15.2 | 22.5 | 23.9 | 32.1 | 36.0 | 34.2 |
| Transport and communication | 17.4 | 14.7 | 8.7 | 6.2 | 6.9 | 6.2 |
| Housing construction | 6.1 | 6.0 | 10.3 | 7.7 | 9.8 | 11.5 |
|  | 38.7 | 43.2 | 42.9 | 46.0 | 52.7 | 51.9 |
| Agriculture | 51.8 | 34.7 | 37.6 | 34.7 | 33.7 | 31.8 |
| Construction of trade and communal enterprises, and scientific, cultural, educational, and public health establishments | 9.5 | 22.1 | 19.5 | 19.3 | 13.6 | 16.3 |

Source:
Ssu, *Narkhoz Sredney Azii, 1963*, pp. 242, 251.

investment per capita in Central Asia is about 90-95 per cent of the U.S.S.R. average.

In contrast with state investment in physical assets, which has been below the U.S.S.R. average, expenditures on education, health, and other social services, which comprise investment in human capital, have tended to be higher in Central Asia. During the second Five-Year Plan (1932-37), per capita expenditures on human capital were one-fifth higher than the U.S.S.R. average. During the fifth Five-Year Plan (1951-55) they were about equal and amounted to 150 per cent of state investment in physical assets within Central Asia.[7] These large investments in physical and human capital have contributed greatly to the rapid economic development of the region.

The allocation of investment in Central Asia has deviated from the extreme emphasis on industry that characterized the Soviet Union as a whole. Table X-9 sets out the sectoral allocation of investment

7. *Ibid.*

in physical assets for Soviet Central Asia, excluding Kazakhstan for which no data are available.

Between 1928 and 1961, Kazakhstan accounted for 50 per cent of state investment in Central Asia. Investment in agriculture in Kazakhstan before 1953 was similar to the all-Union average. If data on investment allocation in Kazakhstan were available, the percentage share received by agriculture in Central Asia would decline markedly. This would be particularly true of 1928-32, if net investment were used, because of the large negative net investment due to the slaughter of livestock. The large share of investment allocated to agriculture during 1928-32 was primarily to expand cotton production. This in turn was designed to make the Soviet Union independent of cotton imports. Even with these qualifications, the fact remains that agriculture consistently received a larger share of investment than the all-Union average.

There are no data on the allocation of investment among the various branches of industry. Table X-3 indicates, however, that heavy industry must have received a somewhat smaller share of investment than the all-Union average. In 1962, ferrous metals, fuels, electricity and power, chemicals and rubber, and metal working accounted for 64.1 per cent of total industrial production in the Soviet Union, 49.2 per cent in Kazakhstan, and 55.7 per cent in the rest of Central Asia.[8] Labor force statistics also indicate a smaller allocation of investment to industry and within the industrial sector a smaller share to heavy industry than the U.S.S.R. average. Table X-10 presents the relevant statistics for the U.S.S.R. and Central Asia.

A number of policies pursued in Soviet Central Asia have deviated from the Soviet model. This is to be expected, of course, since Central Asia is a region, not a sovereign country. While the policy of a high rate of investment has been followed, the allocation of that investment has differed. The share of investment allocated to agriculture has been larger and the share to industry somewhat smaller in Soviet Central Asia. The share allocated to heavy industry has been smaller and the share to human capital formation has been larger. In addition, the same policies of labor force construction, such as on-the-job training, have been followed.[9] The strategy of a dual technology in the Soviet model has been followed and increasing

8. TsSU, *Narkhoz, 1961,* p. 187. Ssu, *Narkhoz Sredney Azii, 1963,* p. 62.
9. See A. Mots, "Industrialization and Technical Training in the Kazakh S.S.R.," *International Labour Review,* Vol. XC, No. 6 (December, 1964), pp. 521-43.

*TABLE X-10*    Labor Force Statistics for the U.S.S.R.
and Soviet Central Asia, 1939-1959

| | Percentage of work force employed by sector | | | | | | 1959 Industry only = 100.0 | |
| | Industry, construction, transport | | | Agriculture | | | Heavy industry[a] | Light industry[b] |
| | 1939 | 1959 | Increase | 1939 | 1959 | Decrease | | |
|---|---|---|---|---|---|---|---|---|
| U.S.S.R. | 30.1 | 36.9 | 6.8 | 50.1 | 38.8 | 11.3 | 79.4 | 20.6 |
| Soviet Central Asia: | | | | | | | | |
| Uzbekistan | 14.3 | 21.1 | 6.8 | 70.8 | 58.9 | 11.9 | 66.4 | 33.6 |
| Kazakhstan | 21.7 | 33.8 | 12.1 | 54.0 | 39.1 | 14.9 | 80.6 | 19.4 |
| Kirgizia | 13.9 | 24.9 | 11.0 | 70.9 | 52.2 | 18.7 | 72.6 | 27.4 |
| Tadjikstan | 10.9 | 18.9 | 8.0 | 75.3 | 62.0 | 13.3 | 63.5 | 36.5 |
| Turkmenistan | 20.3 | 26.7 | 6.4 | 59.1 | 48.6 | 10.5 | 69.7 | 30.3 |

Source:

Alec Nove and J. A. Newth, *The Soviet Middle East: A Communist Model for Development?* (London: George Allen and Unwin Ltd., 1967), pp. 41, 101.

[a] Mining, metallurgy, chemicals, building materials, ceramics, glass, timber, wood, paper, and engineering.
[b] Textiles, clothing, leather, footwear, food.

output per unit of capital, such as in transportation, has been emphasized. The main deviations from the industrial strategy of the Soviet model in Central Asia, therefore, have been in the allocation of investment and in the greater use of "international" (interregional) trade.

## XI. THE RESULTS OF THE SOVIET MODEL IN
## CENTRAL ASIA

This final chapter in the case study of Soviet Central Asia attempts to sum up the changes that have occurred since the 1917 Revolution. The first section of the chapter analyzes the changes that have occurred in living standards since 1913. The second section attempts to analyze the over-all development of Central Asia since 1928, and to compare this development with selected developed and under-developed countries using the nonmonetary index constructed in Chapter VII. The chapter will conclude with some final observations on the significance of Central Asia as an example of the Soviet development model.

### LIVING STANDARDS IN SOVIET CENTRAL ASIA

Two questions arise when considering the economic development of Soviet Central Asia, or, for that matter, any developing economy. First, what happened to living standards during the early years of industrialization? Was the necessary investment obtained by squeezing living standards or was some improvement in living standards achieved along with the development of other aspects of the economy? Second, what are living standards now, after a relatively long period of industrialization has occurred?

Unfortunately, no data exist which would measure the movement of living standards during the crucial years of 1928-1934. It is difficult to believe that living standards did not fall during this period as a result of the destruction of livestock and the general fall in grain output. However, while there is no conclusive evidence for the period 1928-1934, there are data available for 1928 and 1937. These data indicate "that the capital used in the region's development was not to any significant extent obtained by squeezing living

198

standards in the region."[1] Wilhelm concludes from an examination of the data:

> . . . it appears virtually certain that around 1925-30 the commodity intake per capita in the region was considerably, perhaps one quarter, below the all-Russian average. And this impression is buttressed by accounts of travelers in the region in the late Tzarist and early Soviet days. But by the end of the period in question, that is around 1935-37, it appears that industrial workers in the region were faring approximately as well as industrial workers in the rest of Russia, while the *kolkhozniks* (collective farmers) there appear to have had a commodity intake actually greatly in excess of the all-Union average for *kolkhozniks*. Since during the same period, late 1920's to late 1930's, the commodity intake averages for all of Russia were probably standing about still—the decline in some commodities (especially animal products) being approximately offset by increases in other items—and this region was gaining on the all-Russian averages, it appears probable that the living standards of the region were not being forced down but, on the contrary were slowly improving.[2]

In the period 1925-30, agricultural output per capita of farm population was about 80 per cent of the all-Soviet average.[3] In Uzbekistan, the most industrially advanced of the Central Asian republics, industrial wages averaged 78.71 rubles per month in 1930, as against an average of 83.59 rubles per month for the U.S.S.R. as a whole.[4] And prices in Uzbekistan were considerably higher in 1930 than the average for the Soviet Union as a whole. Wheat bread was 19 per cent higher, buckwheat 38 per cent, potatoes 28 per cent, rye bread 33 per cent, salt 47 per cent, eggs 38 per cent, kerosene 20 per cent, and so on.

When rationing was abolished in 1935, new prices were established for important consumer goods, especially essential foods, according to a system of price zones. Central Asia was the zone with the lowest food prices, apparently to encourage farmers to concentrate on cotton production. In 1935, the average wage of workers in large-scale industry was 163, 167, 178, and 204 rubles per month in Uzbekistan, Kirgizia, Tadjikstan, and Turkmenistan respectively. It averaged 185 rubles per month in the U.S.S.R. as a whole. In 1937,

1. Warren Wilhelm, "Soviet Central Asia: Development of a Backward Area," *Foreign Policy Reports*, XXV (February 1, 1950), 223.

2. *Ibid.*, pp. 223-24.

3. Frank Lorimer, *The Population of the Soviet Union: History and Prospects* (Geneva: League of Nations, 1946), p. 77.

4. These and the following statistics are all taken from Wilhelm, "Soviet Central Asia," pp. 223-24.

the industrial wage level in Central Asia was approximately 258 rubles per month, which was equal to the all-Union average. In 1937, average gross income per household on collective farms in Tadjikstan, Turkmenistan, and Uzbekistan was 1,909, 2,369, and 3,069 rubles respectively, while a comparable U.S.S.R. average was only 786 rubles. Moreover the average Soviet collective farm was able to distribute only 47.7 per cent of its gross income to farm households in 1937, while the Central Asian collectives, with their much larger gross income, distributed 65.1 per cent in Tadjikstan, 61.2 per cent in Turkmenistan, and 66.2 per cent in Uzbekistan. Thus, the average money income distributed to collective farm households in 1937 amounted to 375 rubles in the Soviet Union as a whole, 1,243 rubles in Tadjikstan, 1,447 rubles in Turkmenistan, and 2,032 rubles in Uzbekistan. A part of this large differential is due to the cash crop nature of Central Asian agriculture, and to the fact that in most of the U.S.S.R. a large percentage of the collective farm household's real income consisted of distribution in kind, primarily grain and potatoes, while such distributions were very small in Central Asia. However, the average collective farm household in Uzbekistan spent only 39.5 per cent of its money income on agricultural produce, which still left it with a considerably larger balance of money income than the average Soviet collective farm family. Furthermore, the average collective farm household in a sample of 29 regions of the Soviet Union spent only 42 per cent as much on manufactured goods in 1937, as did the average collective farm household in Uzbekistan. In Wilhelm's opinion the sharp contrast between collective farm incomes in Central Asia and the U.S.S.R. as a whole "reflects the very low living standard of the average Soviet *kolkhoznik* rather than inflation of the data concerning Central Asia."[5] Thus, what evidence there is seems to indicate that living standards did not fall (or if they did, they recovered by 1937) during the early years of industrialization. This conclusion is strengthened if the noncommodity portion of living standards is included. As was noted in Chapters VIII and X, medical, educational, and cultural services increased dramatically during the period 1928-37.

The second question about living standards in Soviet Central Asia remains to be discussed. What are living standards now, after a relatively long period of economic development? Probably the only

5. *Ibid.*, p. 224.

feasible way of measurement is comparison of consumption spending in Central Asia to the U.S.S.R. average.

Statistics of retail sales show that the value of turnover per capita in state and co-operative shops was 50 per cent of the U.S.S.R. average in 1928, 64 per cent in 1940, and 80 per cent in 1961.[6] Central Asia has been gaining rapidly on the U.S.S.R. average. So aggregate a statistic, however, is of limited significance. First, it does not include farm market sales for which no republican breakdown is available. Second, farmers, who produce part of their own food, are a larger percentage of the population in Central Asia than in the U.S.S.R. as a whole. And, finally, information is lacking on the extent to which Central Asian farmers obtain their imported grain supplies through the retail stores.

It is more revealing, therefore, to disaggregate and compare Central Asian and average U.S.S.R. purchases of those consumers' goods which are not produced on farms and sold on farm markets and which are not direct substitutes for such products.[7] Such a comparison is made in Table XI-1. Unfortunately, the last breakdown of republican trade statistics was for the year 1955. The figures show that the ruble value of per capita consumption of manufactured consumers' goods in Central Asia is about 15 per cent below the U.S.S.R. average. The difference is the greatest in manufactured clothing and food not directly produced on farms.[8] There is no way of telling what the difference would be in the former if home produced clothing was included. In evaluating the ruble figures shown in Table XI-1, the inclusion of turnover tax should be remembered. The real difference in textile consumption per capita is somewhat larger than that shown, because a larger portion of retail sales in Central Asia are in rural stores, where there is a 10 per cent surcharge on textile prices. Most important, the larger proportion of children in the Central Asian population—30 per cent under nine years of age in Central Asia and 22 per cent in the U.S.S.R. as a

6. TsSU, *Narkhoz, 1961*, p. 636.

7. The following analysis is modeled on a study prepared by the United Nations. See United Nations, *Economic Bulletin for Europe*, pp. 63-68.

8. Since there is no breakdown of collective farm market sales by republic, no information on food consumption from private plots, and no statistics on consumption of imported grains in Central Asia, comparison of consumption standards with regard to food is impossible. However, travelers in the Central Asian region, such as Professor Norton Dodge of the University of Maryland, report that there is a greater abundance of fresh vegetables, fruits, and similar food products on sale in the farm markets than elsewhere in the U.S.S.R.

*TABLE XI-1*

### Retail Sales of Selected Industrial Products in Soviet Central Asia in 1955

| Product | In rubles per capita | As percentage of per capita sales in U.S.S.R. |
|---|---|---|
| Food not directly produced on farms: | | |
| Sugar | 71 | 70 |
| Confectionery | 72 | 69 |
| Tea | 48 | 400 |
| Other foodstuffs | 364 | 70 |
| | 555 | 74 |
| Clothing and footwear: | | |
| Cloth | 284 | 125 |
| Manufactured clothing | 186 | 65 |
| Footwear | 102 | 85 |
| Haberdashery | 40 | 77 |
| | 612 | 89 |
| Durable consumers' goods: | | |
| Bicycles and motorcycles | 12 | 100 |
| Radios | 10 | 71 |
| Sewing machines | 5 | 100 |
| Clocks | 14 | 82 |
| Furniture | 25 | 74 |
| | 66 | 80 |
| Other goods: | | |
| Tobacco | 50 | 83 |
| Soap and perfumes | 29 | 91 |
| Cutlery, glassware, china | 36 | 103 |
| Toys, sporting goods, musical instruments | 15 | 79 |
| Books, other printed matter and stationery | 31 | 82 |
| Other and unspecified (nonfood) | 135 | 129 |
| | 296 | 102 |
| Building materials | 54 | 120 |
| Total of products listed | 1,583 | 85 |

Source:

TsSU, *Sovetskaya torgovlya: statisticheskiy sbornik* (Moscow: Gosudarstvyennoye statisticheskoye Izdatyelstvo, 1956), pp. 40-43, 69, 240-47, 268-75, 280-83.

whole in 1959—tends to overstate the difference in consumption levels, particularly with regard to those products such as tobacco, not used by children. If persons over nine years of age are given a weight of one and persons under nine a weight of one-half, the per capita consumption level in Central Asia increases to 89 per cent of the U.S.S.R. average.

Since Central Asia is less industrialized than the U.S.S.R. as a whole, it is to be expected that consumption standards are below the average for the entire country. Throughout the U.S.S.R., industrial incomes are greater than agricultural incomes. And since Central Asia has a smaller proportion of salary and wage earners, income and thus consumption, tend to be less than the U.S.S.R. average. However, Central Asian income and consumption levels are higher than other regions in the U.S.S.R. with a similar level of industrialization.[9] The explanation is that agricultural incomes, due to cotton, are much higher in Central Asia than elsewhere in the U.S.S.R.

Statistics of money earnings and retail sales do not account for some important elements of consumption. One of the most important items is housing. The housing standard in Central Asia is limited not by the ability of the population to pay the cheap subsidized rents but by the quantity and quality of housing available. At the same time that quality of housing has improved in Central Asia, dwelling space per urban inhabitant has increased from 6.1 square meters in 1926 to 6.7 in 1940, and 8.0 in 1962.[10] In comparison with the dwelling space per inhabitant in all republican capitals, including Moscow, these figures yielded 76 per cent as much space in Central Asia in 1926, 94 per cent in 1940, and 85 per cent in 1962. Total urban housing space in Central Asia in 1962 was 8.0 square meters per urban inhabitant, which was 88 per cent of the all U.S.S.R. average. The small improvement in the Central Asian housing situation in the towns is a result primarily of the very rapid increase in the urban population. Between 1926 and 1962, while total housing space in the five Central Asian capitals increased 650 per cent, the population of these cities increased 500 per cent. Due to the much lower rate of increase in the rural population, the annual additions to the rural housing supply, even though smaller per capita than additions to the urban housing supply, are many times larger per additional rural inhabitant.

9. United Nations, *Economic Bulletin for Europe*, pp. 64-65.
10. TsSU, *Narkhoz, 1961*, pp. 20-21, 616; Lorimer, *The Population of the Soviet Union*, pp. 250-52.

As was seen in Chapter VIII, the consumption of most public services, such as medical care and education, in Central Asia is on a par or slightly below the all U.S.S.R. average.

It can be concluded from the foregoing analysis, that even though average collective farm household income is probably higher than elsewhere in the U.S.S.R., average living standards in Central Asia as a whole are possibly some 10 to 15 per cent below the Soviet average. This is so partly because there are more children per family, partly because urban incomes are lower than those in the rest of the U.S.S.R., and partly because the urban population is a smaller proportion of total population. However, "this regional disparity in living standards cannot be regarded as large compared with those found in other countries. There is hardly any European country without regions where per capita income or consumption is one-fifth or more below the national average."[11] And, in most countries, including the United States, there are regions with one-third to one-half the average income of the country. While Soviet Central Asia still lags behind the U.S.S.R. average in standards of living, the differential has been reduced considerably since 1928.

The conclusion that average living standards in Soviet Central Asia are only some 10 to 15 per cent less than those of the U.S.S.R. as a whole is tantamount to saying: ". . . they are on much higher levels than those in neighboring Asian countries, and that they have improved very considerably in the three decades since the end of the civil war. This statement remains true even though there are certain fields, such as dwelling space per head in towns and per capita consumption of animal food, where there has been very little change in quantity, although some improvement in quality, during the period of Soviet rule.[12]

It should be remembered that living standards in Central Asia on the eve of the Soviet regime were as low as in the neighboring Asian countries. And beyond private consumption standards, the improvement in the health and education of the population has been so great that the "relevant comparison is no longer with neighboring Asian countries, but with the countries of Western Europe."[13]

If the above discussion is accurate, if Central Asian commodity intake increased from 75 per cent to 85 per cent of the all-Soviet average between 1928 and 1955, if communal consumption

11. United Nations, *Economic Bulletin for Europe*, p. 68.
12. *Ibid.*
13. *Ibid.*, p. 71.

(health and education) increased in the same proportion, and if relative consumption of Central Asia and the Soviet Union was the same in 1958 as in 1955, then the average annual growth of per capita consumption can be computed. Using 1937 adjusted market prices, the annual increase for the Soviet Union was 2.4 per cent, and for Central Asia it was 2.8 per cent.[14]

COMPARISONS AND CONCLUSIONS

At the beginning of this study of the Central Asian economy, an index was constructed and presented in Tables VII-1 and VII-2 which attempted to measure the level of economic development in Soviet Central Asia in 1926-28, relative to that of selected underdeveloped countries in 1960-62. This same index can be utilized to measure the level of economic development in Soviet Central Asia in 1960-62, relative to that of selected developed and underdeveloped countries in 1960-62. This index is presented in Tables XI-2 and XI-3.

Again, it should be emphasized, due caution must be used in evaluating the results of this index. However, rankings probably carry enough significance to be useful for present purposes. As can be seen from Table XI-3, Soviet Central Asia in 1926-28 ranked last with a total score of 118.7 out of a possible 1,400, and Soviet Central Asia in 1960-62 ranked third, just above Italy, with a score of 846.7. Since Soviet Central Asia and Italy are so close together, little reliance should be placed on their rankings. This is particularly true since indicator (8), million freight-ton-kilometers, alone accounts for a 96 point differential between the two countries. The most significant and conclusive finding from the index is the fact that Soviet Central Asia in 1926-28, Colombia, India, Iran, Pakistan, and Turkey are all grouped together at the bottom of the index with an average score of 215, and Soviet Central Asia in 1960-62, France, Italy, and Japan are grouped at the top of the index with an average score of 964. The conclusion would seem to be that Soviet Central Asia in 1926-28 was definitely an underdeveloped area, but by 1960-62 had moved up to the level of countries generally classified as more or less developed.

As in Table VII-3, weights can be assigned to the various indicators. Two alternative weighting systems have been used, along with the unweighted index, in Table XI-4. The "welfare" weighted

14. See Table VI-1 for sources of the all-Union Rate.

*TABLE XI-2*

### Nonmonetary Indicators of Economic Development for Soviet Central Asia and Selected Other Countries: Absolute Data

| Country | (1) Wheat yields, 100 kg. per ha. | (2) Tractors per 1000 ha. of cultivated land | (3) Prod. of cotton and woolen fabrics m per capita | (4) Electricity generation, kwh. per capita | (5) Prod. of steel MT per 1,000 pop. | (6) Cons. of oil, MT per 1,000 pop. |
|---|---|---|---|---|---|---|
| Soviet Central Asia (1926-28) | 8.7 | .25[a] | .01 | 4 | .0 | 27.7 |
| Colombia (1960-62) | 9.1 | 4.56 | 17.52[e] | 259 | 12.2 | 223.8 |
| India (1960-62) | 8.5 | .23 | 10.64 | 51 | 9.2 | 19.5 |
| Iran (1960-62) | 7.8 | .73[b] | 7.11 | 44[i] | .0 | 317.9 |
| Pakistan (1960-62) | 8.2 | .18[c] | 6.82 | 15 | .1 | 15.8[j] |
| Turkey (1960-62) | 9.1 | 2.68 | 18.88 | 99 | 9.9 | 57.0 |
| Soviet Central Asia (1960-62) | 6.6 | 14.65 | 13.35 | 820 | 24.3 | 479.5 |
| France (1960-62) | 25.2 | 39.18 | 35.52[f] | 1,317 | 381.9 | 695.1 |
| Italy (1960-62) | 14.9 | 17.48 | 19.96[g] | 1,512 | 180.5 | 539.7 |
| Japan (1960-62) | 25.4 | 1.74[d] | 34.96[h] | 1,404 | 300.7 | 519.4 |

Sources:

(1) Food and Agricultural Organization, *Production Yearbook, 1962,* Vol. 16 (Rome: Food and Agricultural Organization, 1963), pp. 35-36; Vladimir P. Timoshenko, *Agricultural Russia and the Wheat Problem*, Grain Economic Series No. 1 (Stanford: Food Research Institute and the Committee on Russian Research of the Hoover War Library, 1932), pp. 534, 538, 540, 542. TsSU, *Narkhoz, 1961*, pp. 326-27.

(2) Food and Agricultural Organization, *Production Yearbook, 1962*, pp. 3, 266-69; A. E. Steinberg (ed.), *The Stateman's Yearbook, 1961-1962* (New York: St. Martin's Press, 1961), pp. 210, 911, 1004, 1128, 1187, 1449; TsSU, *Narkhoz, 1961*, p. 414; Paul B. Henze, "The Economic Development of Soviet Central Asia to the Eve of World War II: An Examination of Soviet Methods As Applied to a Semi-Colonial Area," *Royal Central Asian Society*

| (7) | (8) | (9) | (10) | (11) | (12) | (13) | (14) |
|---|---|---|---|---|---|---|---|
| Cons. of coal MT per 1,000 pop. | Million freight-ton-km. per 100,000 pop. | Per cent of pop. in cities of 20,000 and more | Per cent of pop. in secondary and higher education | Per cent of adults (over 9) literate | Daily newspaper circ. per 1,000 pop. | Physicians per 100,000 pop. | Reciprocal of infant mortality rates |
| 35.4 | 55.5[l] | 9.3 | .16 | 16 | 35 | 17.4 | 4.3[q] |
| 186.9 | 5.3 | 22.4 | 1.88 | 62 | 56 | 41.3 | 11.2 |
| 125.0 | 16.4 | 11.9 | 2.34 | 24 | 11 | 17.4 | 6.8[r] |
| 12.2 | 9.8 | 15.0[n] | 1.53 | 15 | 15 | 25.4 | 5.0 |
| 28.1[k] | 8.8 | 8.0 | 1.77 | 16 | 7 | 11.4 | 15.9[s] |
| 188.4 | 13.0 | 14.5 | 2.00 | 30 | 45 | 34.4 | 6.1 |
| 1,699.3 | 771.0[m] | 27.8 | 5.46[o] | 87[p] | 203 | 139.1 | 24.4 |
| 1,450.1 | 127.9 | 29.8 | 5.73 | 97 | 257 | 106.9 | 39.1 |
| 206.3 | 30.7 | 30.3 | 5.13 | 85 | 101 | 160.3 | 24.6 |
| 698.3 | 60.3 | 43.1 | 8.55 | 95 | 416 | 106.2 | 35.0 |

*Journal,* XXXVI (July, 1949); XXXVII (Jan., 1950); XXXVI (July, 1949), 279.

(3) United Nations, Department of Economic and Social Affairs, *Statistical Yearbook, 1962* (New York: United Nations, 1963), pp. 222, 226; Steinberg (ed.), *The Stateman's Yearbook, 1961-1962,* p. 1129; TsSU, *Forty Years of Soviet Power,* pp. 117-18, 125-26, 128; TsSU, *Narkhoz, 1961,* pp. 252-53.

(4) United Nations, *Statistical Yearbook, 1962,* pp. 310-18; United Nations, *Statistical Yearbook, 1963,* pp. 332, 334; TsSU, *Forty Years of Soviet Power,* pp. 117-18, 125-26, 128; TsSU, *Narkhoz, 1961,* p. 215.

(5) United Nations, *Statistical Yearbook, 1962,* p. 257; United Nations, *Statistical Yearbook, 1963,* p. 283; TsSU, *Forty Years of Soviet Power,* pp. 117-18, 125-26, 128; TsSU, *Narkhoz, 1961,* p. 197

(6) United Nations, *Statistical Yearbook, 1962,* pp. 147-48; United Nations, *Statistical Yearbook, 1963,* pp. 172-73; United Nations, *Yearbook of Inter-*

*national Trade Statistics, 1961,* pp. 158-60, 317, 320, 331-32, 476, 493, 639; United Nations, *Yearbook of International Trade Statistics, 1962,* pp. 238, 240, 354, 356, 377, 379; TsSU, *Forty Years of Soviet Power,* pp. 117-18, 125-26, 128; TsSU, *Transport i svyaz SSSR,* p. 71; Robert N. Taaffe, *Rail Transportation and the Economic Development of Soviet Central Asia,* Department of Geography Research Paper No. 64 (Chicago: The University of Chicago Press, 1960), pp. 120-24; TsSU, *Narkhoz, 1961,* pp. 209, 486.

(7) United Nations, *Statistical Yearbook, 1962,* pp. 143-46; United Nations, *Statistical Yearbook, 1963,* p. 168; United Nations, *Yearbook of International Trade Statistics, 1961,* pp. 158-60, 317, 320, 331-32, 476, 493, 639; TsSU, *Forty Years of Soviet Power,* pp. 117-18, 125-26, 128; TsSU, *Transport i svyaz SSSR,* p. 70; TsSU, *Narkhoz, 1961,* pp. 206, 485; Taaffe, *Rail Transportation and the Economic Development of Soviet Central Asia,* p. 118.

(8) United Nations, *Statistical Yearbook, 1962,* pp. 143-46; United Nations, *Statistical Yearbook, 1963,* pp. 376-77; TsSU, *Transport i svyaz SSSR,* p. 67; TsSU, *Narkhoz, 1961,* p. 484; Taaffe, *Rail Transportation and the Economic Development of Soviet Central Asia,* pp. 139, 164.

(9) Figures are for 1955. Norton Ginsburg, *Atlas of Economic Development* (Chicago: The University of Chicago Press, 1961), p. 34; TsSU, *Itogi vsyesoyuznoi pyeryepisi nasyelyeniya 1959 goda, Kazakh SSR* (Moscow: Gosstatizdat, 1962), p. 18; TsSU, *Itogi vsyesoyuznoi pyeryepisi nasyelyeniya 1959 goda, Uzbek SSR,* p. 16; TsSU, *Itogi vsyesoyuznoi pyeryepisi nasyelyeniya 1959 goda, Tadjik SSR,* p. 14; TsSU, *Itogi vsyesoyuznoi pyeryepisi nasyelyeniya 1959 goda, Turkmen SSR,* p. 14.

(10) United Nations, *Statistical Yearbook, 1962,* pp. 623-40; United Nations, *Statistical Yearbook, 1963,* pp. 654, 657, 658; TsSU, *Kulturnoye stroityelstvo SSSR,* pp. 124, 126, 128, 130, 208, 210, 232, 234.

(11) United States, Agency for International Development and Department of Defense, *Proposed Mutual Defense and Assistance Programs, FY 1964: Summary Presentation to the Congress* (Washington: U.S. Government Printing Office, 1963), pp. 181-84; Frank Lorimer, *The Population of the Soviet Union: History and Prospects* (Geneva: League of Nations, 1946), p. 70; TsSU, *Itogi vsyesoyuznoi pyeryepisi nasyelyeniya 1959 goda, SSSR,* p. 89; The figures for France, Italy, and Japan are for 1955. Ginsburg, *Atlas of Economic Development,* p. 38.

(12) United Nations, *Statistical Yearbook, 1962,* pp. 649-50; United Nations, *Statistical Yearbook, 1963,* pp. 676-77; TsSU, *Forty Years of Soviet Power,* pp. 273, 275, 281, 283, 287; TsSU, *Narkhoz, 1961,* p. 732.

(13) United Nations, *Statistical Yearbook, 1962,* pp. 603-6; United Nations, *Statistical Yearbook, 1963,* pp. 626-27; TsSU, *Forty Years of Soviet Power,* pp. 273, 275, 281, 287; TsSU, *Narkhoz, 1961,* p. 743.

(14) United Nations, *Statistical Yearbook, 1963,* p. 53; United Nations, *Demographic Yearbook, 1962,* pp. 502-15; Ginsburg, *Atlas of Economic Development,* p. 24; Lorimer, *The Population of the Soviet Union,* pp. 82, 119; *Iran Almanac,* 3rd ed. (Tehran, 1963).

Notes:

a The number of tractors, 2,000, was estimated from Henze, "The Economic Development of Soviet Central Asia to the Eve of World War II, p. 288, and TsSU, *Narkhoz, 1961,* p. 414.

b 1959          c 1956          d 1959          e 1959

f France reports production of cotton and woolen fabrics in metric tons. For cottons, a conversion factor of 6.23 linear meters per kilogram was used. U.S. Bureau of the Census, "Cotton Broad-Woven Fabrics: Average Weight and Width of Fabrics," *Current Industrial Reports* (March 26, 1964), p. 3. For woolens, a conversion factor of 0.43 kilograms per linear meter was used. U.S. Bureau of the Census, "Wool Broad-Woven Goods: Average Weight and Width of Fabrics," *Current Industrial Reports* (April 14, 1964), p. 3.

g *Ibid.*

h Japan reports production of cotton and woolen fabrics in square meters. For cottons, a conversion factor of 1.07 square meters per linear meter, and, for woolens, a factor of 1.55 square meters per linear meter was used. Sources were same as in note f.

i 1959.          j 1959.          k 1959.

l This figure is only a rough estimate. Total freight originations and terminations in 1928 were obtained from TsSU, *Transport i svyaz SSSR*, p. 67. These had to be corrected for double counting of interregional traffic statistics which were obtained from Taaffe, *Rail Transportation and the Economic Development of Soviet Central Asia*, p. 139. To convert from a freight-ton basis to freight-ton-kilometers, average length of haul statistics for 1952 were used. These were obtained from *ibid.*, p. 164.

m Computed same way as in note 1.

n Estimated from Ginsburg, p. 34.

o 1956.          p 1959.

q The infant mortality rate of 230 per 1,000 live births was estimated from Lorimer, *The Population of the Soviet Union*, pp. 82, 119.

r 1958-59.          s 1954.

index includes double weights for indicators (3), (10), (11), (13), and (14). All others have single weights. The "industrial" weighted index includes double weights for indicators (4), (5), (6), (7), and (8). All others have single weights.

Neither of these alternative weighting systems gives rise to any significant changes from the unweighted index. The only change in rankings occurs in the "welfare" weighted index, where India and Iran exchange positions. Thus, the original unweighted index, if due precaution is taken, can serve as a rough measure of relative levels of economic development.[15] As indicated in Table XI-4, Soviet Central Asia in 1926-28 ranked last in all three indices, and in 1960-62 ranked third, just above Italy in all three. Here again, however, the relative rankings of Soviet Central Asia and Italy are probably not reliable since their scores are so close together.

It is also possible to compute the average annual rate of "eco-

15. It is worthwhile noting that the coefficient of rank correlation between the unweighted index and Gross National Product per capita, in dollars for 1962, omitting Soviet Central Asia for which no GNP data exist, is 0.976. There would be a perfect rank correlation except for the relatively low, $459, per capita GNP for Japan. It is an open question whether GNP or the nonmonetary index more correctly measures the level of economic development in Japan. Taking the underdeveloped countries only, the Pearsonian coefficient of correlation $(r)$ is 0.9735, and the coefficient of determination $(r^2)$ is 0.9477 between per capita GNP and the unweighted index.

TABLE XI-3

Nonmonetary Indicators of Economic Development
for Soviet Central Asia and Selected
Other Countries: Relative Data[a]

| | (1)[b] | (2) | (3) | (4) | (5) | (6) | (7) |
|---|---|---|---|---|---|---|---|
| Soviet Central Asia | | | | | | | |
| (1926-28) | 34.2 | .6 | .0 | .3 | .0 | 4.0 | 2.1 |
| Colombia | | | | | | | |
| (1960-62) | 35.8 | 11.6 | 49.3 | 17.1 | 3.2 | 32.2 | 11.0 |
| India | | | | | | | |
| (1960-62) | 33.5 | .6 | 30.0 | 3.4 | 2.4 | 2.8 | 7.4 |
| Iran | | | | | | | |
| (1960-62) | 30.7 | 1.9 | 20.0 | 2.9 | .0 | 45.7 | .7 |
| Pakistan | | | | | | | |
| (1960-62) | 32.3 | .5 | 19.2 | 1.0 | .1 | 2.3 | 1.6 |
| Turkey | | | | | | | |
| (1960-62) | 35.8 | 6.8 | 53.1 | 6.5 | 2.6 | 8.2 | 11.1 |
| Soviet Central Asia | | | | | | | |
| (1960-62) | 26.0 | 37.4 | 37.6 | 54.2 | 6.4 | 69.0 | 100.0 |
| France | | | | | | | |
| (1960-62) | 99.2 | 100.0 | 100.0 | 87.1 | 100.0 | 100.0 | 85.3 |
| Italy | | | | | | | |
| (1960-62) | 58.7 | 44.6 | 56.2 | 100.0 | 47.3 | 77.6 | 12.1 |
| Japan | | | | | | | |
| (1960-62) | 100.0 | 4.4 | 98.4 | 92.9 | 78.7 | 74.7 | 41.1 |

Notes:
 [a] Highest-ranking country = 100.0, each indicator.
 [b] For sources and definitions of indicators, see Table XI-2.

nomic development" using the nonmonetary index. Instead of using different countries at one point in time to construct the index, the same country at different points in time is substituted. This is done in Table XI-5 for Soviet Central Asia for the period 1926-28 to 1960-62.

These growth rates do not seem to be out of line with the results obtained from this case study of economic development in Soviet Central Asia. For example, the average annual growth rate of gross agricultural output was calculated at 3.8 per cent over the period 1928-61. The rate was 2.2 per cent on a per capita basis. The average annual growth rate of gross industrial output was estimated to be between 7.7 and 11.0 per cent over the same period. Neither of these growth rates includes educational or medical services, which were among the fastest growing items in Central Asia. Thus,

| (8) | (9) | (10) | (11) | (12) | (13) | (14) | Total |
|---|---|---|---|---|---|---|---|
| 7.2 | 21.6 | 1.9 | 16.5 | 8.4 | 10.9 | 11.0 | 118.7 |
| .7 | 52.0 | 22.0 | 63.9 | 13.5 | 25.8 | 28.6 | 366.7 |
| 2.1 | 27.6 | 27.4 | 24.7 | 2.6 | 10.9 | 17.4 | 192.8 |
| 1.3 | 34.8 | 17.9 | 15.5 | 3.6 | 15.8 | 12.8 | 203.6 |
| 1.1 | 18.6 | 20.7 | 16.5 | 1.7 | 7.1 | 26.6 | 149.3 |
| 1.7 | 33.6 | 23.4 | 30.9 | 10.8 | 21.5 | 15.6 | 261.6 |
| 100.0 | 64.5 | 63.9 | 89.7 | 48.8 | 86.8 | 62.4 | 846.7 |
| 16.6 | 69.1 | 67.0 | 100.0 | 61.8 | 66.7 | 100.0 | 1,152.8 |
| 4.0 | 70.3 | 60.0 | 87.6 | 24.3 | 100.0 | 62.9 | 805.6 |
| 7.8 | 100.0 | 100.0 | 97.9 | 100.0 | 66.3 | 89.5 | 1,051.7 |

the growth rates of "economic development" obtained from the non-monetary indices seem reasonable.

CONCLUSION

A few strictures are necessary before concluding this study of the application of Soviet development methods in Central Asia. Central Asia has certainly been successful in initiating and sustaining economic development, but has this been due to the use of Soviet development methods? Given existing data limitations, and, of course, the very nature of the question, no conclusive answer can be given. However, a number of important questions need to be considered.

First, how closely does the development of Central Asia adhere to the Soviet model outlined in Part I of this study. In Central Asia, as in the Soviet model, industry was nationalized, agriculture was collectivized, and comprehensive central planning with centralized distribution of essential resources was utilized. The strategy of col-

*TABLE XI-4*

Nonmonetary Indices of Relative Economic
Development: 1960-1962

| | Unweighted index | | "Welfare" index | | "Industrial" index | |
|---|---|---|---|---|---|---|
| | Score | % Rank | Score | % Rank | Score | % Rank |
| France | 1,152.8 | 100 | 1,586.5 | 100 | 1,641.8 | 100 |
| Japan | 1,051.7 | 91 | 1,503.8 | 95 | 1,445.3 | 88 |
| Soviet Central Asia | | | | | | |
| (1960-62) | 846.7 | 73 | 1,174.6 | 74 | 1,213.9 | 74 |
| Italy | 805.6 | 70 | 1,172.3 | 74 | 1,102.8 | 67 |
| Colombia | 366.7 | 32 | 556.3 | 35 | 480.2 | 29 |
| Turkey | 261.6 | 22 | 406.1 | 26 | 344.8 | 21 |
| Iran | 203.6 | 18 | 285.6 | 18 | 274.2 | 17 |
| India | 192.8 | 16 | 303.2 | 19 | 240.9 | 14 |
| Pakistan | 149.3 | 13 | 239.4 | 15 | 174.6 | 10 |
| Soviet Central Asia | | | | | | |
| (1926-28) | 118.7 | 10 | 159.0 | 10 | 132.3 | 8 |

Sources:
See Table XI-3.

lectivizing agriculture to release labor for industry and to collect the surplus output was followed. The strategy of using modern, capital-intensive technologies in key processes combined with labor-intensive techniques in auxiliary operations, and heavy investment in human capital was also followed. Central Asia diverged from the Soviet model in allocating a larger share of investment to agriculture and within industry a larger share to light industry. Also, because it is a region, Central Asia made greater use of international (inter-regional) trade. In sum, the divergencies in Central Asia do not seem to violate the basic model but rather are modifications of particular strategies of the model necessary to account for the specific conditions of the area.

Second, did Central Asia receive "foreign aid" in the form of net capital imports from the rest of the Soviet Union? While data limitations make it impossible to give a conclusive answer, Wilhelm, on the basis of scattered data and a number of assumptions, concludes that between 1928 and 1937, net imports of capital were very small

TABLE XI-5

Average Annual Rate of "Economic Development":
Soviet Central Asia

| Index | 1926-28 | 1960-62 | % Growth rate 1926-28 to 1960-62 |
|---|---|---|---|
| Unweighted | 118.7 | 846.7 | 6.1 |
| "Welfare" | 159.0 | 1,174.6 | 6.3 |
| "Industrial" | 132.3 | 1,213.9 | 6.9 |

Sources:
    See Table XI-4.

and that the bulk of investment was generated locally.[16] However, "foreign aid" from the rest of the Soviet Union to Central Asia may have been significant if immigration of Russians is counted as an inflow of human capital or technical assistance. The number of Russians in Kazakhstan increased from 20.0 per cent of the total population in 1926 to 43.1 per cent in 1959, from 6.0 per cent to 13.6 in Uzbekistan, from 12.0 per cent to 30.2 per cent in Kirgizia, from 8.0 per cent to 17.3 per cent in Turkmenistan, and from less than 1.0 per cent to 13.3 per cent in Tadjikistan.[17] In addition, a United Nations report points out that before 1940, "the new industries which were set up in the region were manned overwhelmingly by the numerous immigrants from other parts of the Soviet Union."[18] While this is no longer true, this immigration probably played a vital role during the 1930's. How much this altered what would have been the impact of the unmodified Soviet model in Central Asia is difficult to say, just as it is difficult to say how much immigration influenced nineteenth-century capitalist development in the United States. It is possible, of course, that equivalent technical assistance could be made available to underdeveloped countries from Soviet and Western sources.

Another question is whether Central Asia would have developed simply from the "spread" effects of development in the rest of the Soviet Union. This is probably another unanswerable question.

16. See Wilhelm, "Soviet Central Asia," pp. 227-228.
17. J. P. Cole and F. C. German, *A Geography of the U.S.S.R.: The Background to a Planned Economy* (London: Butterworths, 1961), p. 58.
18. United Nations, *Economic Bulletin for Europe*, p. 75.

However, in this writer's opinion, it is very possible that "backwash" effects would have cancelled any "spread" effects because of geographic separation, inadequacy of transportation, and racial, cultural, and linguistic differences. This has been a common historical phenomenon. Without the consciously planned program of economic development followed in Central Asia, it seems probable that the rate of development would have been much less.

A final question to be considered is whether economic development would have been as great in Central Asia, if it had been an independent country instead of a region of the Soviet Union. Undoubtedly, the inflow of a labor supply with a higher skill level than the domestic, would have been less if Central Asia had been independent. How much difference this would have made, and what substitutes would have been found, is, of course, impossible to say. Given reasonable assumptions about the international flow of technical assistance and skilled labor, development would probably have been less.

The above, or similar, strictures on Central Asian development, while interesting, could be applied to most historical examples of successful economic development. While it is important to remember these strictures, the general conclusion that emerges from this case study of Soviet Central Asia is still valid.

In spite of inumerable blunders and hardships, Central Asia has been transformed from a stagnant, illiterate, disease-ridden, simifeudal society into a modern, dynamic, progress-oriented society,[19] which goes far to prove that "the Soviet planning system is a workable method for achieving impressive economic advances in underdeveloped areas."[20] The challenge posed by the example of economic development in Soviet Central Asia has been ably stated by Maurice Hindus, who is generally critical of the Soviet regime and its policies, in his latest book on the Soviet Union.

. . . Uzbekistan is an example of an underdeveloped Asian country which within a brief space of time—as time is reckoned in history— Moscow has lifted to an advanced stage of industrial development, of science and technology. . . . The Asian, the African, the visitor from

19. This is not to deny that parts of Central Asia, particularly the rural areas, are still backward and stagnant. There are large urban-rural differences, but they are narrowing as the development program proceeds. And, of course, these urban-rural differences are not unique to Central Asia; they are found in most countries, including the United States.

20. Henze, "The Economic Development of Soviet Central Asia to the Eve of World War II," p. 43.

any underdeveloped country, who comes to Tashkent can only compare the miseries of his homeland with the achievements of Uzbekistan: the health of the people, the rise in living standards, the upsurge of education, technology, industry, and science.

. . . Uzbekistan is a non-Slavic Asian land, and at the beginning of the Soviet revolution it was one of the most backward in Asia. This is what lends the Kremlin formula of development its global significance.[21]

21. Maurice Hindus, *House Without a Roof: Russia After Forty-three Years of Revolution* (New York: Doubleday & Company, Inc., 1961), pp. 481, 531.

*Part Three*

*CONCLUSION*

# XII. SUMMARY AND CONCLUSIONS

The present study has attempted to construct the model of economic development implicit in the historical experience of the Soviet Union, modified where appropriate by the later experience of the other socialist countries. No attempt has been made to prove that alternative models are inadequate or that the Soviet model is a sufficient and necessary condition of rapid economic growth. Rather, the less ambitious attempt has been made to demonstrate that the Soviet model contains relevant lessons for underdeveloped countries.

As the word has been used here, "Soviet" has meant primarily the Soviet Union. The experience of the other Soviet type economies has been used only to provide modifications of the basic model. The term "model" has not meant a detailing of every strategy, correct and incorrect, used by the Soviet Union. Rather, it has been an abstraction of the essentials from the Soviet historical experience.

The Soviet model, as historically derived from socialist development experience, can be subdivided into three aspects: the preconditions of the model, the institutions characteristic of the model, and the strategy of development in the model.

The preconditions of the Soviet model include severance of any existing colonial bond with capitalist countries, elimination of economic domination by foreign capitalists, and redistribution of political and economic power. This is carried out by expropriating private property in landed estates and industrial enterprises.

After destruction of the old political and economic institutions and mechanisms, new socialist forms are substituted. Collectivized agriculture replaces landed estates and peasant proprietorship. Public ownership and operation replace private in industry and trade. Central planning, centralized distribution of essential materials and capital goods, and a system of administrative controls and pressures on enterprises partially supplant the market mechanism and the profit motive.

219

The strategy of development in the Soviet model encompasses a number of interrelated policies. Agricultural investment is held to the minimum necessary to allow agriculture to provide industry with a growing marketed surplus of agricultural products and an expanding source of labor supply. In addition, the collective farm system is used as a convenient organizational framework for the utilization of surplus agricultural labor on social overhead projects such as roads, canals, and irrigation works.

The strategy of development in the model encompasses a high rate of capital formation, with the bulk allocated to industry as the leading sector. Industrial investment is allocated on an unbalanced growth pattern. Soviet planning concentrates on certain key branches in each plan period to overcome particular bottlenecks. Scarce resources and talent are concentrated on these key targets. In the successive campaigns, investment is allocated to those industries that yield the largest external economies.

Choice of technique in the Soviet model encompasses a number of policies designed to utilize the most advanced technology while accounting for existing factor proportions. Soviet strategy consists of developing a "dual technology." On the one hand, in key processes, the most advanced technology is used. On the other hand, differences in factor proportions (between a developed and an underdeveloped economy) are accounted for by utilizing labor-intensive technology in auxiliary operations, by aiming at high performance rates per unit of capital instead of per man, and by utilizing plants of greatly differing vintages and technological levels in the same industries and sectors.

A major aspect of Soviet development strategy is an emphasis on human capital formation. Large amounts of investment are allocated to education and health services. Besides formal education and after-work vocational training, factories are overstaffed to provide on-the-job training. Propaganda, monetary incentives, and nonmonetary rewards are all used as incentives.

The international trade policy in the Soviet model is primarily one of import-substitution. Capital goods, prototypes, blueprints, and technicians are imported in exchange for traditional exports until this imported capital can be used to construct industries that will replace the imports.

Development strategy in Central Asia differed somewhat from the Soviet model. This was due primarily to Central Asia's being a region of the Soviet Union. In Central Asia, a larger share of investment was allocated to agriculture, and within industry, a larger share to light industry than in the Soviet Union as a whole.

The results of the Soviet model of development, as presented in previous chapters, have been impressive. Growth in gross national product and industrial production has been very great. Growth in agricultural production has been respectable. Large increases have been made in living standards, particularly health and education.

In the Soviet model of development, the economy is a war economy harnessed to the attainment of one overriding objective—economic development. All physical and human resources are concentrated on the one basic objective of promoting economic development. Resources are centrally allocated to prevent leakages to production that does not promote economic development. The production of consumer goods is restricted to the minimum necessary to maintain morale. Propaganda and nonmaterial incentives are used. Civil liberties are restricted and conscription is utilized. These are common practices in war time. If leaders of underdeveloped countries are willing to view economic development as a war against poverty, the Soviet model offers an alternative to the capitalist methods offered by the West.

Our discussion of the Soviet industrial model has shown that it is not an irrational construct of Marxist theorists but possesses a definite economic rationale. This rationale is founded on the presence in the Soviet economy during the 1920's and 1930's of certain circumstances characteristic of underdeveloped economies—a shortage of capital and skilled labor, obstacles in the form of inertia or traditional ways of doing things, and so forth. Where similar circumstances and obstacles to development exist, the Soviet model of development should provide some useful suggestions for an effective development program.

In appraising the value of the Soviet model as a guide to underdeveloped countries, the reader should keep in mind the remark at the close of Seton's article that "the dispassionate search for valid ideas admits no guilt (or merit) by association."[1] On the one hand, the greatly exaggerated claims of the Soviets for the universal applicability of their political and economic system to underdeveloped countries must be dismissed as exaggeration and propaganda. But most Western writers, on the other hand, seem to have erred in the opposite direction by rejecting the Soviet model too hastily and too

1. Francis Seton, "Planning and Economic Growth: Asia, Africa and the Soviet Model," *Soviet Survey*, XXXI (January-March, 1960), 38-40.

completely. Their error was in failing to differentiate between the essential and accidental aspects of Soviet experience. This writer agrees wholeheartedly with their rejection of the totalitarian aspects of the Soviet system, but this study has shown that there are valuable lessons to be learned from Soviet development experience. These lessons, if followed, do not necessarily lead to a Soviet-type political system since the characteristics of the Soviet development model that have been stressed here are compatible with varying degrees of governmental intervention and control. Indeed, the presence of certain of these characteristics arising from the circumstances of backwardness, such as a dual technology, can be observed in other developing countries such as Japan. Therefore, it should not be alarming that underdeveloped countries look to the Soviets for economic guidance in their development programs. They should, of course, exercise discrimination in their choice of the aspects of the model that will be useful in their own circumstances.

A final point on the relevance of the Soviet model of development needs to be made. No model is transferable complete and in detail. Each country must take into account its own resource base, factor proportions, and historical and cultural traditions when evaluating development strategies and how to adapt them. In some cases this will mean only minor modifications of the basic model. More often it will mean a major overhauling of the model to adapt it to local conditions. For instance, Poland has not collectivized agriculture and Cuba does not stress heavy industry.

The basic concern of this study has been to develop the model that emerges from Soviet experience and to evaluate it in that context. To determine the exact degree to which the model is relevant for Brazil, Turkey, or any other country would require a separate analysis of each one.

QUESTIONS FOR FURTHER INVESTIGATION

A number of questions arise from this study of the Soviet model of development that cannot be answered without further investigation. The first, and possibly most important, question is whether it has to be a Communist party that operates the Soviet model. This writer believes further research would show that there is no inherent reason why the Soviet model must be operated by a dogmatic, totalitarian Communist party. A halfway democratic socialist regime could probably supply whatever compulsion was necessary to implement the model. In fact, a regime not bound by the dogmatism of communism could probably do a better job of implementing the model. However, Brzezinski believes: "At the moment . . . there appear to be no viable institutions or alternative programs of sufficient appeal and scope to match the Communist Party organization, with its Soviet support, and its ideological explanation of the past and 'scientific' assessment of the future, once the disintegrative consequences of rapid industrialization begin to make themselves felt in largely backward and traditional societies."[2] Even if Brzezinski's assessment is correct, however, it does not imply the impossibility of another regime managing the Soviet model, only that an alternative to the Communist party does not at present exist.

Another question that arises is whether the oppressiveness of past Communist regimes was historically conditioned or inherent in the ideology of communism. That is, what role have war and threat of war played in creating the climate for oppression? Heilbroner has posed a related question: "What will happen to the harsh disciplining forces of the communist system once the great transition has been made we do not know. But surely the hope of the future rests in the possibility that with communism, as with capitalism, the completion of the industrial transformation may soften and mellow the rigors of the transitional phase."[3]

Another question concerns the necessity of public ownership in the Soviet model. Is some degree of private ownership compatible with the model? Would public ownership of utilities and the "commanding heights" of industry be sufficient to reap the benefits of central planning?[4] Would a large private sector in agriculture, as in Poland and Yugoslavia, be feasible and desirable?

A final question that emerges from this study concerns the role of United States foreign economic policy. Should the United States be alarmed by the development of a Soviet type economy in an underdeveloped country if it is not politically aligned to the U.S.S.R. or China? Would a better policy be that voiced by Heilbroner when he wrote that the governments of underdeveloped countries must be given "the strongest possible encouragement—and not merely a

2. Zbigniew Brzezinski, "The Politics of Underdevelopment," *World Politics,* Vol. IX, No. 1 (October, 1956), p. 69.

3. Robert L. Heilbroner, *The Future As History* (New York: Harper & Bros., 1959), p. 101.

4. For a pioneering attempt to evaluate this question, see V. N. Bandera, "The New Economic Policy (NEP) As an Economic System," *Journal of Political Economy,* Vol. LXXI, No. 3 (June, 1963), pp. 265-79.

grudging acquiescence—in finding independent solutions along indigenous socialist lines."[5]

Is it possible for U.S. aid to help create a true "third force" in the underdeveloped world—a force ultimately characterized by the political structure of the West and the economic structure of the East? To achieve a moderation of the inevitable social costs of rapid capital accumulation and an easing of the need for political repression, the United States may have to be willing to supply extraordinary amounts of aid over a long period of time to countries pursuing some variant of the Soviet model of development. If this is a desirable policy, what other policies are necessary to implement it? Would this mean that the United States should accept social revolution in the underdeveloped world? Or is the Alliance for Progress approach of evolutionary reform and capitalist development more in the long-run interest of the United States and the peoples of the world?

Although the present study provokes these and a host of other interesting and challenging questions, they fall largely outside the area upon which this study focuses. The study has shown, nevertheless, that the Soviet model provides an alternative which is not only feasible for underdeveloped countries, but also possibly attractive to their leaders. It is, therefore, an alternative which deserves further investigation and consideration by both scholars and the political and economic leaders of the underdeveloped world.

5. Robert Heilbroner, *The Great Ascent* (New York: Harper & Row, 1963), p. 175.

*SELECTED BIBLIOGRAPHY*

*INDEX*

# SELECTED BIBLIOGRAPHY

OFFICIAL SOURCES

Alampiev, P. *Where Economic Inequality Is No More: Progress of the Soviet Eastern Republics As Exemplified by Kazakhstan.* Moscow: Foreign Languages Publishing House, 1959.

Alimov, Arif. *Uzbekistan.* The Fifteen Soviet Socialist Republics Today and Tomorrow. London: Soviet Booklets, 1960.

Dikambayev, Kazy. *Kirghizia.* The Fifteen Soviet Socialist Republics Today and Tomorrow. London: Soviet Booklets, 1960.

Dodkhudoyev, Nazarsho. *Tajikistan.* The Fifteen Soviet Socialist Republics Today and Tomorrow. London: Soviet Booklets, 1960.

Food and Agriculture Organization. *Production Yearbook, 1962.* Vol. 16. Rome: Food and Agricultural Organization, 1963.

Goncharov, N. "Trends in the Economic Development of the North Kazakhstan Economic Region," *Problems of Economics,* Vol. II, No. 1 (May, 1959), pp. 53-54.

Kakharov, A. "The Outlook for the Economic Development of Tadzhikistan," *Problems of Economics,* Vol. II, No. 1 (May, 1959), pp. 49-51.

Lagovskaya, E. I. *Soyuznye Respubliki Sredney Azii.* Moscow: Gosudarstvyennoye, Uchyebno-Pyedagogichyeskoye Izdatyelbstvo, Ministyerstva Prosvyeshchyeniya RSFSR, 1959.

Ovezov, Balysh. *Turkmenia.* The Fifteen Soviet Socialist Republics Today and Tomorrow. London: Soviet Booklets, 1960.

Sredneaziatskoye statisticheskoye upravleniye. *Narodnoye Khozyaystvo Sredney Azii v 1963 godu: statisticheskiy sbornik.* Tashkent: Izdatyelatvo Uzbekistan, 1964.

Tsentralnoye statisticheskoye upravleniye pri Sovete Ministrov SSSR. *Forty Years of Soviet Power: In Facts and Figures.* Moscow: Foreign Languages Publishing House, 1958.

————. *Itogi vsyesoyuznoi pyeryepisi nasyelyeniya 1959 goda, Kazkh SSR.* Moscow: Gosstatizdat, 1962.

————. *Itogi vsyesoyuznoi pyeryepisi nasyelyeniya 1959 goda, Kirgiz SSR.* Moscow: Gosstatizdat, 1962.

————. *Itogi vsyesoyuznoi pyeryepisi nasyelyeniya 1959 goda, SSSR.* Moscow: Gosstatizdat, 1962.

————. *Itogi vsyesoyuznoi pyeryepisi nasyelyeniya 1959 goda, Tadjik SSR.* Moscow: Gosstatizdat, 1962.

————. Itogi vsyesoyuznoi pyerpeyisi nasyelyeniya 1959 goda, Turkmen SSR. Moscow: Gosstatizdat, 1962.

————. Itogi vsyesoyuznoi pyeryepisi nasyelyeniya 1959 goda, Uzbek SSR. Moscow: Gosstatizdat, 1962.

————. Kulturnoye stroityelstvo SSSR: statisticheskiy sbornik. Moscow: Gosudarstvyennoye Statisticheskoye Izdatyelstvo, 1956.

————. Narodnoye khozyaystvo SSSR v 1959 godu: statisticheskiy yezhegodnik. Moscow: Gosstatizdat, 1960.

————. Narodnoye khozyaystvo SSSR v 1961 godu: statisticheskiy yezhegodnik. Moscow: Gosstatizdat, 1962.

————. Narodnoye Khozyaystvo SSSR v 1963 godu: statisticheskiy yezhegodnik. Moscow: Gosstatizdat, 1965.

————. Narodnoye khozyaystvo SSSR v 1964: statisticheskiy yezhegodnik. Moscow: Gosstatizdat, 1965.

————. Promyshlyennost SSSR: statisticheskiy sbornik. Moscow: Gosudarstvyennoye Statisticheskoye Izdatyelstvo, 1957.

————. Promyshlyennost SSSR: statisticheskiy sbornik, 1964. Moscow: Gosudarstvyennoye Statisticheskoye Izdatyelstvo, 1964.

————. Sovetskaya torgovlya: statisticheskiy sbornik. Moscow: Gosudarstvyennoye Statisticheskoye Izdatyelstvo, 1956.

————. Transport i svyaz SSSR: statisticheskiy sbornik. Moscow: Gosudarstvyennoye Statisticheskoye Izdatyelstvo, 1957.

United Nations. Demographic Yearbook, 1962. New York: United Nations, 1962.

————. The Economic Development of Latin America in the Post-War Period. New York: United Nations, 1964.

————. Economic Survey of Latin America, 1963. New York: United Nations, 1965.

————. Measures for the Economic Development of Under-Developed Countries. New York: United Nations, 1951.

————. Statistical Yearbook, 1963. New York: United Nations, 1964.

————. Yearbook of International Trade Statistics, 1961. New York: United Nations, 1963.

United Nations, Economic Commission for Europe. "Regional Economic Policy in the Soviet Union: The Case of Central Asia," Economic Bulletin for Europe, Vol. IX, No. 3 (November, 1957).

U.S. Bureau of the Census. Historical Statistics of the United States: Colonial Times to 1957. Washington: Government Printing Office, 1960.

————. Historical Statistics of the United States: Continuation to 1962 and Revisions. Washington: Government Printing Office, 1965.

————. Statistical Abstract of the United States, 1963. Washington: Government Printing Office, 1963.

U.S. Congress, Joint Economic Committee. Annual Economic Indicators for the U.S.S.R. 88th Cong., 2nd Sess., 1964.

————. Comparisons of the United States and Soviet Economies. 86th Cong., 1st Sess., 1960.

———. *Current Economic Indicators for the U.S.S.R.* 89th Cong., 1st Sess., 1965.

———. *Soviet Economic Growth: A Comparison with the United States.* 85th Cong., 1st Sess., 1957.

U.S. Department of Agriculture. *Agricultural Statistics: 1964.* Washington: Government Printing Office, 1964.

———. *The 1965 World Agricultural Situation.* Washington: Government Printing Office, 1964.

———. *Soviet Agriculture Today: Report of 1963 Agriculture Exchange Delegation.* Foreign Agricultural Report No. 13. Washington: Government Printing Office, December, 1963.

———. *The U.S.S.R. and Eastern Europe Agricultural Situation.* Washington: Government Printing Office, 1966.

World Health Organization. *Annual Epidemiological and Vital Statistics.* Geneva: World Health Organization, 1963.


BOOKS

Agarwala, A. N., and S. P. Singh. (eds.). *The Economics of Underdevelopment.* Oxford: Oxford University Press, 1958.

Baran, Paul A. *The Political Economy of Growth.* New York: Monthly Review Press, 1957.

Baykov, Alexander. *The Development of the Soviet Economic System.* New York: The Macmillan Company, 1947.

Bergson, Abram. *The Economics of Soviet Planning.* New Haven: Yale University Press, 1964.

———. *The Real National Income of Soviet Russia Since 1928.* Cambridge: Harvard University Press, 1961.

Berliner, Joseph S. *Factory and Manager in the U.S.S.R.* Cambridge: Harvard University Press, 1957.

Bruchey, Stuart. *The Roots of American Economic Growth, 1607-1861: An Essay in Social Causation.* New York: Harper & Row, 1965.

Bruton, Henry J. *Principles of Development Economics.* Englewood Cliffs: Prentice-Hall, Inc., 1965.

Bureau of Social Science Research, American University. *Handbook of Central Asia.* 3 vols. Subcontractors Monograph HRAF-49. New Haven: Human Relations Area Files, Inc., 1956.

Campbell, Robert W. *Soviet Economic Power.* Boston: Houghton Mifflin Co., 1960.

Caroe, Olaf. *Soviet Empire: The Turks of Central Asia and Stalinism.* London: Macmillan & Co., Ltd., 1954.

Carr, E. H. *What Is History?* New York: Alfred A. Knopf, 1962.

Castro, Josué de. *The Geography of Hunger.* Boston: Little, Brown & Co., 1952.

Clark, M. Gardner. *The Economics of Soviet Steel.* Cambridge: Harvard University Press, 1956.

Cline, Howard F. *Mexico: Revolution to Evolution, 1940-1960.* New York: Oxford University Press, 1963.

Cole, J. P., and F. C. German. *A Geography of the U.S.S.R.: The Background to a Planned Economy*. London: Butterworths, 1961.

Conolly, Violet. *Beyond the Urals: Economic Developments in Soviet Asia*. London: Oxford University Press, 1967.

Davies, R. W. *The Development of the Soviet Budgetary System*. Cambridge: Cambridge University Press, 1958.

Deane, Phyllis, and W. A. Cole. *British Economic Growth: 1688-1959*. Cambridge: Cambridge University Press, 1964.

Dobb, Maurice. *An Essay on Economic Growth and Planning*. London: Routledge and Kegan Paul, 1960.

————. *Some Aspects of Economic Development*. Occasional Paper No. 3. Delhi: Delhi School of Economics, 1951.

————. *Soviet Economic Development Since 1917*. London: Routledge and Kegan Paul, 1960.

————. *Studies in the Development of Capitalism*. London: Routledge and Kegan Paul, 1951.

Dowd, Douglas. *Thorstein Veblen*. New York: Washington Square Press, Inc. 1964.

Dumont, Rene. *Lands Alive*. London: The Merlin Press, 1965.

————. *Types of Rural Economy: Studies in World Agriculture*. New York: Frederick A. Praeger, Inc., 1957.

Eicher, Carl, and Laurence Witt. (eds.). *Agriculture in Economic Development*. New York: McGraw-Hill Book Co., 1964.

Fainsod, M. *Smolensk under Soviet Rule*. Cambridge: Harvard University Press, 1958.

Furtado, Celso. *Development and Underdevelopment*. Berkeley: University of California Press, 1964.

————. *Diagnosis of the Brazilian Crisis*. Berkeley: University of California Press, 1965.

Gerschenkron, Alexander. *Economic Backwardness in Historical Perspective*. New York: Frederick A. Praeger, Inc., 1965.

Ginsburg, Norton. *Atlas of Economic Development*. Chicago: University of Chicago Press, 1961.

Granick, David. *Soviet Metal-Fabricating and Economic Development*. Madison: University of Wisconsin Press, 1967.

Harrod, Roy. *Towards a Dynamic Economics*. London: Macmillan & Co., Ltd. 1948.

Heilbroner, Robert L. *The Future As History*. New York: Harper & Bros., 1959.

————. *The Great Ascent*. New York: Harper and Row, 1963.

Higgins, Benjamin. *Economic Development*. New York: W. W. Norton & Co., Inc., 1959.

————. *United Nations and U.S. Foreign Economic Policy*. Homewood, Illinois: Richard D. Irwin, Inc., 1962.

Hindus, Maurice. *The Great Offensive*. New York: Harrison Smith and Robert Haas, 1933.

————. *Red Bread*. New York: Jonathan Cape & Harrison Smith, 1931.

Hirschman, Albert O. *The Strategy of Economic Development.* New Haven: Yale University Press, 1958.

Hughes, T. J., and D. E. T. Luard. *The Economic Development of Communist China: 1949-1960.* 2nd ed.; London: Oxford University Press, 1961.

International Conference of Economic History, First. *Contributions-Communications.* Paris: Moulton & Co., 1960.

Jasny, Naum. *The Socialized Agriculture of the U.S.S.R.: Plans and Performance.* Grain Economic Series No. 5. Stanford: Stanford University Press, 1949.

Jesus, Carolina Maria de. *Child of the Dark.* New York: E. P. Dutton & Co., 1962.

Johnson, D. Gale. *Climatic and Crop Analogies for the Soviet Union: A Study of the Possibilities of Increasing Grain Yields.* Research Paper No. 5716. University of Chicago Office of Agricultural Economics, December 16, 1957.

Kautsky, John H. (ed.). *Political Change in Underdeveloped Countries: Nationalism and Communism.* New York: John Wiley & Sons, 1962.

Kolarz, Walter. *Russia and her Colonies.* London: George Phillip & Son, 1952.

Kuznets, Simon. *Economic Growth and Structure.* New York: W. W. Norton & Co., Inc., 1965.

Laird, Roy D. *Soviet Agriculture and Peasant Affairs.* Lawrence: University of Kansas Press, 1963.

Lamont, Corliss. *The Peoples of the Soviet Union.* New York: Harcourt, Brace and Co., 1946.

Lange, Oskar. *Economic Development, Planning, and International Cooperation.* New York: Monthly Review Press, 1963.

———. (ed.). *Problems of Political Economy of Socialism.* New Delhi: People's Publishing House, 1962.

Lattimore, Owen. *Nomads and Commissars.* New York: Oxford University Press, 1962.

Lewis, Oscar. *The Children of Sanchez.* New York: Random House, 1961.

Lockwood, W. W. *The Economic Development of Japan: Growth and Structural Change, 1868-1938.* Princeton: Princeton University Press, 1954.

Lorimer, Frank. *The Population of the Soviet Union: History and Prospects.* Geneva: League of Nations, 1946.

Mandel, William. *Russia Re-Examined: The Land, the People and How They Live.* New York: Hill and Wang, 1964.

———. *The Soviet Far East and Central Asia.* Institute of Pacific Relations Inquiry Series. New York: The Dial Press, 1944.

Mandelbaum, K. *The Industrialization of Backward Areas.* Oxford: Basil Blackwell, 1945.

Mason, Edward. *Economic Planning in Underdeveloped Areas.* New York: Fordham University Press, 1958.

Maynard, Sir John. *Russia in Flux: Before October.* New York: Collier Books, 1962.

———. *The Russian Peasant, and Other Studies.* New York: Collier Books, 1962.

Mitchell, B. R., and Phyllis Deane. *Abstract of British Historical Statistics.* Cambridge: Cambridge University Press, 1962.

Moore, Barrington, Jr. *Terror and Progress U.S.S.R.* Cambridge: Harvard University Press, 1954.

Moorsteen, Richard, and Raymond P. Powell. *The Soviet Capital Stock, 1928-1962.* Homewood, Illinois: Richard D. Irwin, Inc., 1966.

Myint, Hla. *The Economics of the Developing Countries.* New York: Frederick A. Praeger, Inc., 1964.

Myrdal, Gunnar. *Economic Theory and Underdeveloped Regions.* London: Gerald Duckworth & Co., Ltd., 1957.

———. *An International Economy.* New York: Harper & Brothers, 1956.

Nehru, Jawaharlal. *The Discovery of India.* New York: Doubleday & Co., 1956.

North, Douglass. *The Economic Growth of the United States: 1790 to 1860.* Englewood Cliffs: Prentice-Hall, Inc., 1961.

Nove, Alec. *The Soviet Economy.* New York: Frederick A. Praeger, Inc., 1961.

Nurkse, Ragnar. *Problems of Capital Formation in Underdeveloped Countries.* Oxford: Basil Blackwell, 1958.

Park, Alexander G. *Bolshevism in Turkestan, 1917-1927.* New York: Columbia University Press, 1957.

Parsons, K. H., R. J. Penn, and P. M. Raup. *Land Tenure.* Proceedings of the Conference on Land Tenure and Related Problems in World Agriculture. Madison: University of Wisconsin Press, 1956.

Pierce, Richard A. *Russian Central Asia: 1867-1917.* Berkeley: University of California Press, 1960.

Polanyi, Karl. *The Great Transformation.* Boston: Beacon Press, 1957.

Randall, Laura (ed.). *Economic Development: Evolution or Revolution?* Boston: D. C. Heath & Co., 1964.

Robinson, E. A. G. (ed.). *Problems in Economic Development.* (Proceedings of a conference held by the International Economic Association) London: Macmillan & Co., Ltd., 1965.

Rogin, Leo. *The Meaning and Validity of Economic Theory: A Historical Approach.* New York: Harper & Bros., 1956.

Rosovsky, Henry (ed.). *Industrialization in Two Systems: Essays in Honor of Alexander Gerschenkron.* New York: John Wiley & Sons, Inc., 1966.

Rostow, W. W. (ed.). *The Economics of Take-Off into Sustained Growth.* (Proceedings of a Conference held by the International Economic Association) New York: St. Martin's Press, Inc., 1963.

———. *The Stages of Economic Growth.* New York: Cambridge University Press, 1960.

Rywkin, Michael. *Russia in Central Asia.* Russian Civilization Series. New York: Collier Books, 1963.

Shackle, G. L. S. *Time in Economics.* Amsterdam: North-Holland Publishing Co., 1958.

Spulber, Nicolas. *Foundations of Soviet Strategy for Economic Growth: Selected Soviet Essays, 1924-1930.* Bloomington: Indiana University Press, 1964.

————. *The Soviet Economy.* New York: W. W. Norton & Co., Inc., 1962.

————. *Soviet Strategy for Economic Growth.* Bloomington: Indiana University Press, 1964.

————. (ed.). *Study of the Soviet Economy.* Bloomington: Russian and East European Series, Vol. 25, Indiana University, 1961.

Staley, Eugene. *The Future of Underdeveloped Countries: Political Implications of Economic Development.* New York: Harper & Bros., 1954.

Steinberg, A. H. (ed.). *The Statesman's Yearbook, 1961-1962.* New York: St. Martin's Press, 1961.

Supple, Barry E. *The Experience of Economic Growth: Case Studies in Economic History.* New York: Random House, 1963.

Swianiewicz, S. *Forced Labour and Economic Development: An Enquiry into the Experience of Soviet Industrialization.* London: Oxford University Press, 1965.

Taaffe, Robert N. *Rail Transportation and the Economic Development of Soviet Central Asia.* Department of Geography Research Paper No. 64. Chicago: University of Chicago Press, 1960.

Thornton, Thomas Perry (ed.). *The Third World in Soviet Perspective: Studies by Soviet Writers on the Developing Areas.* Princeton: Princeton University Press, 1964.

Timoshenko, Vladimir P. *Agricultural Russia and the Wheat Problem.* Grain Economic Series No. 1. Stanford; Food Research Institute and the Committee on Russian Research of the Hoover War Library, 1932.

Tinbergen, Jan. *The Design of Development.* Baltimore: The Johns Hopkins Press, 1958.

Viner, Jacob. *International Trade and Economic Development.* Oxford: Oxford University Press, 1957.

Wheeler, Geoffrey. *The Modern History of Soviet Central Asia.* New York: Frederick A. Praeger, Inc., 1964.

Williams, Eric. *Capitalism and Slavery.* Chapel Hill: The University of North Carolina Press, 1944.

Woodham-Smith, Cecil. *The Great Hunger.* New York: Harper & Row, 1963.

ARTICLES

Alexander, Robert J. "Nature and Progress of Agrarian Reform in Latin America," *Journal of Economic History,* Vol. XXIII, No. 4 (December, 1963), pp. 559-73.

Baran, Paul A. "Economic Progress and Economic Surplus," *Science and Society*, Vol. XVII, No. 4 (Fall, 1953), pp. 289-317.
————. "National Economic Planning: The Soviet Experience," in *The Soviet Economy: A Book of Readings*, eds. Morris Bornstein and Daniel Fusfeld. Homewood: Richard D. Irwin, Inc., 1962, pp. 69-83.
————. "On the Political Economy of Backwardness," *The Manchester School*, XX (January, 1952), 66-84.
Bennett, M. K. "International Disparities in Consumption Levels," *American Economic Review*, Vol. LI, No. 4 (September, 1951), pp. 632-49.
Boulding, Kenneth E., and Pritam Singh. "The Role of the Price Structure in Economic Development," *American Economic Review*, Vol. LII, No. 2 (May, 1962), pp. 28-38.
Bowles, W. Donald. "Soviet Russia As a Model for Underdeveloped Areas," *World Politics*, Vol. XIV, No. 3 (April, 1962), pp. 483-504.
Bronfenbrenner, M. "The Appeal of Confiscation in Economic Development," *Economic Development and Cultural Change*, Vol. III, No. 3 (April, 1955), pp. 201-18.
Brzezinski, Zbigniew. "The Politics of Underdevelopment," *World Politics*, Vol. IX, No. 1 (October, 1956), pp. 55-75.
Chenery, Hollis B. "The Application of Investment Criteria," *Quarterly Journal of Economics*, LXVII (February, 1953), 76-96.
————. "Comparative Advantage and Development Policy," *American Economic Review*, Vol. LI, No. 1 (March, 1961), pp. 18-51.
Clairmonte, Frederick F. "The Chinese and Indian Land Problem— Divergent Approaches," *Malayan Economic Review*, Vol. V, No. 1 (April, 1960), pp. 52-65.
————. "Foreign Investments and Economic Growth," *The Indian Journal of Economics*, Vol. XL, No. 156 (July, 1959), pp. 1-14.
Dalrymple, Dana G. "The Soviet Famine of 1932-1934," *Soviet Studies*, Vol. XV, No. 3 (January, 1964), pp. 250-84.
Dalton, George. "History, Politics and Economic Development in Liberia," *Journal of Economic History*, Vol. XXV, No. 4 (December, 1965) pp. 569-91.
Dillard, Dudley. "Capitalism," *Encyclopedia Britannica*. Reprint from 1963 edition.
————. "The Status of the Labor Theory of Value," *Southern Economic Journal*, II (April, 1945), 345-52.
Dubey, Vinod. "The Marketed Agricultural Surplus and Economic Growth in Underdeveloped Areas," *The Economic Journal*, Vol. LXXIII, No. 292 (December, 1963), pp. 689-702.
Eckaus, R. S. "Factor Proportions in Underdeveloped Areas," *American Economic Review*, Vol. LI, No. 1 (March, 1961), pp. 18-51.
Eckstein, Alexander. "The Role of the State in Economic Growth," in *Capitalism, Market Socialism, and Central Planning*, ed. Jesse W. Markham. Boston: Houghton Mifflin Co., 1963.
Erlich, Alexander. "Development Strategy and Planning: the Soviet

Experience," in *National Economic Planning,* ed. Max F. Millikan. New York: Columbia University Press, 1967.

Fallenbuchl, Z. M. "Investment Policy for Economic Development: Some Lessons of the Communist Experience," *The Canadian Journal of Economics and Political Science,* Vol. XXIX, No. 1 (February, 1963), pp. 26-39.

Galbraith, J. K. "Conditions for Economic Change in Under-Developed Countries," *Journal of Farm Economics,* Vol. 33 (November, 1951), pp. 689-96.

Georgescu-Roegen, Nicolas. "Economic Theory and Agrarian Economics," *Oxford Economic Papers,* Vol. 12 (February, 1960), pp. 1-40.

Gerschenkron, Alexander. "Agrarian Policies and Industrialization: Russia 1861-1917," in *The Cambridge Economic History of Europe,* eds. M. M. Postan and H. J. Habakkuk. Vol. VI. Cambridge: Cambridge University Press, 1965.

————. "The Early Phases of Industrialization in Russia and Their Relationship to the Historical Study of Economic Growth," in *The Experiences of Economic Growth: Case Studies in Economic History,* ed. Barry E. Supple. New York: Random House, 1963.

Glass, D. V., and E. Grebenik. "World Population, 1800-1950," in *The Cambridge Economic History of Europe,* eds. M. M. Postan and H. J. Habakkuk. Vol. VI. Cambridge: Cambridge University Press, 1965.

Grossman, Gregory. "Scarce Capital and Soviet Doctrine," *Quarterly Journal of Economics,* LXVII (August, 1953), 311-43.

————. "Soviet Growth: Routine, Inertia and Pressure," *American Economic Review,* Vol. L, No. 2 (May, 1960), pp. 62-72.

Henze, Paul B. "The Economic Development of Soviet Central Asia to the Eve of World War II: An Examination of Soviet Methods As Applied to a Semi-colonial Area," *Royal Central Asian Society Journal,* XXXVI (July, 1949) and XXXVII (January, 1950).

Hoeffding, Oleg. "The Soviet Union: Model for Asia?—State Planning and Forced Industrialization," *Problems of Communism,* Vol. VIII, No. 6 (November-December, 1959), pp. 38-46.

Holzman, Franklyn D. "Consumer Sovereignty and the Rate of Economic Development," *Economia Internazionale,* Vol. XI, No. 2 (1958), pp. 3-17.

————. "Financing Soviet Economic Development," in *The Soviet Economy: A Book of Readings,* eds. Morris Bornstein and Daniel Fusfeld. Homewood, Illinois: Richard D. Irwin, Inc., 1962, pp. 145-60.

Horvat, Branko. "The Optimum Rate of Investment," *The Economic Journal,* Vol. LXVIII, No. 272, (December, 1958), pp. 747-67.

Hunter, Holland. "Transport in Soviet and Chinese Development," *Economic Development and Cultural Change,* Vol. XIV, No. 1 (October, 1965), pp. 71-84.

Inkeles, Alex. "The Soviet Union: Model for Asia?—the Social System,"

*Problems of Communism,* Vol. VIII, No. 6 (November-December, 1959), pp. 30-38.

Johnston, Bruce F., and John W. Mellor. "The Role of Agriculture in Economic Development," *American Economic Review,* Vol. LI, No. 4 (September, 1961), pp. 566-93.

————., and Soren T. Neilson. "Agricultural and Structural Transformation in a Developing Economy," *Economic Development and Cultural Change,* Vol. XIV, No. 3 (April, 1966), pp. 279-301.

Kahan, Arcadius. "The Collective Farm System in Russia: Some Aspects of Its Contribution to Soviet Economic Development," in *Agriculture in Economic Development,* eds. Carl Eicher and Lawrence Witt. New York: McGraw-Hill Book Co., 1964, pp. 251-71.

————. "The Economics of Vocational Training in the U.S.S.R." *Comparative Education Review,* Vol. 4, No. 2 (October, 1961), pp. 75-83.

Kahn, Alfred E. "Investment Criteria in Development Programs," *Quarterly Journal of Economics,* LXV (February, 1951), 38-61.

Kaplan, Norman M. "Capital Formation and Allocation," in *Soviet Economic Growth,* ed. Abram Bergson. Evanston: Row & Peterson Co., 1953, pp. 37-91.

————., and R. H. Moorsteen. "An Index of Soviet Industrial Output," *American Economic Review,* Vol. L, No. 3 (June, 1960), pp. 295-318.

Klatt, W. "Soviet Agriculture As a Model for Asian Countries," *China Quarterly,* No. 5 (January-March, 1961), pp. 116-30.

Kurihara, Kenneth K. "Theoretical Objections to Agriculture-Biased Economic Development," *Indian Journal of Economics,* Vol. XXXIX, No. 153, Part II (October, 1958), pp. 163-70.

Kuznets, Simon. "Quantitative Aspects of the Economic Growth of Nations: Distribution of Income by Size," *Economic Development and Cultural Change,* Vol. XI, No. 2, Part II (January, 1963), pp. 1-80.

Lebergott, Stanley. "Wage Trends, 1800-1900," *Trends in the American Economy in the Nineteenth Century.* A Report of the National Bureau of Economic Research, Vol. 24 of Studies in Income and Wealth. Princeton: Princeton University Press, 1960.

Lewis, W. Arthur. "Economic Development with Unlimited Supplies of Labour," *The Manchester School of Economic and Social Studies,* XXII (May, 1954), 139-91.

McAuley, Alastair N. D. "Rationality and Central Planning," *Soviet Studies,* Vol. 18, No. 3 (January, 1967), pp. 340-55.

Malenbaum, Wilfred. "India and China: Contrasts in Development Performance," *American Economic Review,* Vol. XLIX, No. 3 (June, 1959), pp. 284-309.

Marglin, Stephen A. "The Social Rate of Discount and the Optimal Rate of Investment," *Quarterly Journal of Economics,* Vol. LXXXVII, No. 1 (September, 1963), pp. 95-111.

Montias, John M. "Planning with Material Balances in Soviet Type

Economies," *American Economic Review,* Vol. XLIX, No. 5 (December, 1959), pp. 963-85.

————. "The Soviet Economic Model and the Underdeveloped Countries," in *Study of the Soviet Economy,* ed. Nicolas Spulber. Russian and East European Series, Vol. 25. Bloomington: Indiana University, 1961, pp. 57-82.

Moravcik, I. "The Marxian Model of Growth and the 'General Plan' of Soviet Economic Development," *Kyklos,* Vol. XIV, No. 4 (1961).

Myint, Hla. "The Classical Theory of International Trade and the Underdeveloped Countries," *Economic Journal,* Vol. 68 (June, 1958), pp. 317-37.

Nash, Manning. "Social Prerequisites to Economic Growth in Latin America and Southeast Asia," *Economic Development and Cultural Change,* Vol. XII, No. 3 (April, 1964), pp. 225-42.

Neale, Walter C. "Must Agriculture Come First?" *Co-Existence,* No. 3 (May, 1965), pp. 40-48.

Nicholls, William H. "An Agricultural Surplus As a Factor in Economic Development," *Journal of Political Economy,* Vol. LXXI, No. 1 (February, 1963), pp. 1-29.

Nove, Alec. "Collectivization of Agriculture in Russia and China," in *Symposium on Economic and Social Problems of the Far East,* ed. E. F. Szczpanik. Hong Kong: Hong Kong University Press, 1962, pp. 16-24.

————. "The Problem of 'Success Indicators' in Soviet Industry," *Economica,* Vol. XXV, No. 97 (February, 1958), pp. 1-13.

————. "The Soviet Model and Underdeveloped Countries," *International Affairs,* Vol. XXXVII, No. 1 (January, 1961), pp. 29-38.

Pintner, Walter McKenzie. "Initial Problems in the Soviet Economic Development of Central Asia," *Royal Central Asian Society Journal,* XL (July/October, 1953), 284-97.

Pipes, Richard E. "The Soviet Impact on Central Asia," *Problems of Communism,* Vol. XI, No. 2 (March/April, 1957).

Pollard, Sidney. "Economic History—a Science of Society?" *Past and Present,* No. 30 (April, 1965), pp. 3-22

Prebisch, Raul. "The Role of Commercial Policy in Underdeveloped Countries," *American Economic Review,* Vol. XLIX, No. 2 (May, 1959), pp. 251-73.

Pryor, Frederic L. "Foreign Trade Theory in the Communist Bloc," *Soviet Studies,* Vol. XIV, No. 1 (July, 1962), pp. 41-61.

Rollins, C. E. "Mineral Development and Economic Growth," *Social Research,* XXIII (October, 1956), 253-80.

Rosenstein-Rodan, P. N. "The Flaw in the Mechanism of Market Forces," in *Leading Issues in Development Economics,* ed. Gerald M. Meier. New York: Oxford University Press, 1964, pp. 416-18.

————. "Problems of Industrialization of Eastern and South-Eastern Europe," in *The Economics of Underdevelopment,* eds. A. N. Agarwala and S. P. Singh. Oxford: Oxford University Press, 1958, pp. 245-56.

Schweinitz, Karl de, Jr. "Economic Growth, Coercion, and Freedom, *World Politics,* Vol. IX, No. 2 (January, 1957), pp. 166-92.

Scitovsky, Tibor. "Two Concepts of External Economies," in *The Economics of Underdevelopment,* eds. A. N. Agarwala and S. P. Singh. Oxford: Oxford University Press, 1958, pp. 295-308.

Sen, A. K. "On Optimising the Rate of Saving," *The Economic Journal,* Vol. LXXI, No. 283 (September, 1961), pp. 479-96.

Seton, Francis. "Planning and Economic Growth: Asia, Africa and the Soviet Model," *Soviet Survey,* XXXI (January-March, 1960), 38-40.

Singer, H. W. "The Distribution of Gains between Investing and Borrowing Countries," *American Economic Review,* Vol. XL, No. 2 (May, 1950), pp. 473-85.

Sombart, Werner. "Economic Theory and Economic History," *Economic History Review,* II (January, 1929), 1-19.

Spencer, D. R., and V. Katkoff. "China's Land Transformation and the U.S.S.R. Model," *Land Economics,* Vol. 33 (August, 1957), pp. 241-56.

Spulber, Nicolas. "Contrasting Economic Patterns: Chinese and Soviet Development Strategies," *Soviet Studies,* Vol. XV, No. 1 (July, 1963), pp. 1-16.

Taylor, A. J. "Progress and Poverty in Britain, 1780-1850: A Reappraisal," in *Essays in Economic History,* ed. E. M. Carus-Wilson. Vol. III. London: Edward Arnold Ltd., 1962.

Wilber, Charles K. "A Nonmonetary Index of Economic Development," *Soviet Studies,* Vol. XVII, No. 4 (April, 1966), pp. 408-16.

Wiles, P. J. D. "Growth versus Choice," *The Economic Journal,* LXVI (June, 1956), 244-55.

Wilhelm, Warren. "Soviet Central Asia: Development of a Backward Area," *Foreign Policy Reports,* XXV (February 1, 1950), 218-28.

Zauberman, Alfred. "Soviet and Chinese Strategy for Economic Growth," *International Affairs,* Vol. XXXVIII, No. 3 (July, 1962), pp. 339-52.

UNPUBLISHED MATERIALS

Dodge, Norton T. "Trends in Labor Productivity in the Soviet Tractor Industry: A Case Study in Industrial Development." Unpublished Ph.D. dissertation; Department of Economics, Harvard University, 1960.

Ecker, Frank A. "Transition in Asia: Uzbekistan and the Soviets," Unpublished Ph.D. dissertation; Department of Political Science, University of Michigan, 1952.